whitman
as editor of
the brooklyn
daily eagle

whitman
as editor of
the brooklyn
daily eagle

Thomas L. Brasher

SOUTHWEST TEXAS STATE UNIVERSITY

Detroit

Wayne State University Press

1970

Library of Congress Catalog Card Number 70-91872
Standard Book Number 8143-1408-2

for Chris and Mark

We really feel a desire to talk on many subjects, to *all* the people of Brooklyn; and it
ain't their ninepences we want so much
either. There is a curious kind of sympathy
(haven't you ever thought of it before?) that
arises in the mind of a newspaper conductor
with the public he serves. . . . Daily commu-
nion creates a sort of brotherhood and sister-
hood between the two parties.

Walter Whitman,
"Ourselves and the 'Eagle,' "
Brooklyn Daily Eagle, 1 June 1846

CONTENTS

four

LITERATURE AND THE ARTS   188

five

APOLOGIA   217

ACKNOWLEDGMENTS

THIS STUDY had its unnoticed conception more than thirty years ago with my purchase, from a secondhand book shop on Royal street in New Orleans, of a two-volume collection of Walt Whitman's editorials, paragraphs, essays, dramatic reviews, and book reviews from the *Brooklyn Daily Eagle*—Cleveland Rodgers and John Black's *Gathering of the Forces.* The two volumes were read, retired to a bookshelf, and totally forgotten until after World War II. Then the late Professor William D. Bond of the Hardin-Simmons University English department, through his reasonable and perceptive interest and pleasure in Whitman (an interest and pleasure I had never experienced), communicated to me, and to many other ex-GIs, a sense of the real Whitman, as solid in flesh as he was solid in soul. As a result I remembered my volumes of Rodgers and Black, and I discovered Emory Holloway's *Uncollected Poetry and Prose of Walt Whitman.* Then began my research into what clearly was a highly germinal but fragmentarily treated period of Whitman's life.

I am indebted to Professor F. Allen Briggs, now of the University of South Florida, and to Professor Lewis P. Simpson, Louisiana State University, for their allowing me, quite a few years ago, to engage in the studies that led to this book. Especially am I under obligation to Miss Edna Huntington, who was librarian of the Long Island Historical Society when, nearly twenty years ago, I asked permission to have microfilmed the society's file of the *Eagle* for the period of Whitman's editorship. Through Miss Huntington's good offices, the Executive Committee of the Long Island Historical Society gave this permission, for which I certainly am obliged.

9

But I still would be struggling with a rough manuscript had not the Faculty Senate, the Policy Committee, the Administration, and the Board of Regents of Southwest Texas State University agreed to give me the leisure of a faculty developmental leave.

PREFACE

UNTIL NOW there has been no complete portrait of the Walter Whitman who edited the *Brooklyn Daily Eagle* for two years in the decade preceding his self-apotheosis as "Walt Whitman, a kosmos." Selected material from the *Eagle* has been reprinted in two collections of Whitman's early journalistic writings, and in a third solely of those in the *Eagle*.[1] These collections, along with a few scholarly articles that have cited some of Whitman's comments in the *Eagle*, have been—rather than the files of the *Eagle* itself—the ordinary sources for reference, scholarly or otherwise, to the period in his life from March 1846 to mid-January 1848. The work of the scholars who compiled these selected collections has been invaluable in calling attention to a period in Whitman's career in which the seeds of *Leaves of Grass* were planted, if not already sprouting.[2]

Yet the tendency to depend largely upon these sources for interpretations of the Whitman of the *Eagle* has led to inadequately supported or erroneous conclusions. For example, his latest and best biographer says he "had nothing to say about male labor except to condemn Negro slavery as unfair competition."[3] On the contrary, an examination of the *Eagle* shows that in covering a strike at the Atlantic dock and basin in the spring of 1846, he had a good deal to say about labor and unions. The same biographer correctly observes that the *Eagle* writings reveal a religious impulse in Whitman's reformist attitude, and he quotes as evidence passages from *The Gathering of the Forces* that identify Christianity with reform and condemn luxurious churches as leading to spiritual complacence.[4]

11

Of perhaps greater importance are some remarks in the *Eagle* that suggest Whitman had some predilection for the liberal doctrines of the Universalists and Unitarians, and show his dislike of sectarian controversy, "hell and damnation" preaching, and what he called the "prostitution of the religious sentiment."[5] Similarly, references to Whitman's literary nationalism in this period have been limited to his editorials on the subject as reprinted in the collections cited above. No one has analyzed his numerous book reviews to determine the extent to which his desire for a native literature revealed itself in them. That has been done here.

The purpose, then, of this study is to present a comprehensive picture of the Whitman who edited the *Brooklyn Daily Eagle* during the two years in which the "roaring forties" reached their climax. These were the years of manifest destiny when most Americans saw the design of Providence in the Oregon Affair and in the Mexican War—though some wished to use the Wilmot Proviso as an instrument to modify the plans of Providence. These were the years, too, when the Jacksonian principles of a low tariff and an independent treasury belatedly triumphed over a chorus of manufacturers and bankers who prophesied ruin. And they were the years when the first flood of Irish immigrants arrived and when Brooklyn turned Whig and doubled in population. Reformers grappled vigorously with the problems of prisons, slavery, the insane, tobacco, capital punishment, education, liquor, the rights of women, and universal peace. Books and periodicals were plentifully published while the question of a national literature was hotly debated. Infectious and dyspeptic ailments were treated by orthodox and unorthodox physicians of warring schools, and doctrinal points were disputed by orthodox and unorthodox religious sectarians. The Nativists damned the Catholic Irish while the Whigs and the Democrats wooed them. The theatres in New York and the lecture rooms in Brooklyn were sometimes well and sometimes poorly attended by citizens seeking amusement or instruction or both. The magnetic telegraph was revolutionizing news coverage at a propitious time when the people of New York and Brooklyn were anxious for the latest report on Old Hickory's doings in the Southwest. Long-

12

fellow's "Excelsior" was a popular concert number and gave its name to omnibusses and steamboats while drunkenness and petty crime flourished in Brooklyn and major felonies were every-day occurrences in New York. The *Eagle's* young editor was engrossed with all the political and social phenomena of the late 1840s—and he wrote about them. And he wrote sincerely.

A second purpose of this study is to vindicate the Whit-man of the *Eagle* as a professional man. There has been a tend-ency—perhaps because Whitman himself depreciated his early journalistic writings and because there seems to be a disparity between the youthful newspaperman and the old poet—to speak of the *Eagle* Whitman as a half-hearted journalist, not really devoted to his profession. An early and influential suggestion of this judgment was made in 1919 by Arthur M. Howe, then editor of the *Eagle*, at the Brooklyn Institute's celebration of the Whit-man Centenary. Speaking of Whitman's editorials and com-mentary in the *Eagle*, Howe said, "He conveys the impression of one who regarded his occupation in journalism as something to which he was compelled by circumstances rather than as a vocation for which he had any positive affection."[6] I believe the contrary to be true. Whitman had a number of things to say in the *Eagle* about the duties of a newspaper editor and he retorted to Captain Marryat's complaints about the labors of newspaper editing by saying, "we *like them*." He plainly showed a journal-istic zest and expansiveness for anything from manifest destiny to swill milk. Though Whitman was capable of quibbling, espe-cially on matters relating to local politics, his remarks in the *Eagle* ordinarily represented his honest reaction to the things said and done in his world of the late 1840s.

But it is not only in his attitude toward his work that Whit-man's professional reputation as editor of the *Eagle* needs defend-ing from prevailing assumptions. It has long been commonplace to speak of the newspaper Whitman as a second-rate or worse journalist whose writings shared the mediocrity of his contem-porary run-of-the-mill editors. Certainly Whitman's articles in the *Eagle* are not "distinguished," a fact that appears to disap-point some persons devoted to the poet Whitman and to delight others contemptuous of his poetical reputation. It seems scarcely to matter, so far as *Leaves of Grass* is concerned, that Whitman was not exceptional as a newspaper writer, since it has never been suggested that his prosody is much indebted to the journalistic tradition. But one wonders if Whitman, for all his syntactical and grammatical blunders in the *Eagle* (and they were not excessive), has not been classified unfairly as an inferior journalist. Such New York editors as Greeley, Bryant, and Godwin certainly were better journalists than their colleague at the *Eagle*. His generally relaxed style was often rough and uneven, and occasionally affected, but at no time did Whitman write anything like the solemn nonsense of the *Norfolk Beacon's* report (as quoted in the *Eagle* on 7 March 1846) that several women and children had been trapped on the local beach and drowned, "the tide being so high as to effectually interdict their egress." On the whole, Whitman's style in the *Eagle* is readable and his matter adequate. Perhaps it would be juster to describe Whitman the editor as being fairly representative of the average competent journalist of his day. As Arthur Howe told his Brooklyn audience in 1919, speaking of Whitman's writings in the *Eagle*, "If the quality was not above the average of his time, if it has added nothing to his reputation, it represents nothing for which apology need be made."[7]

A final though lesser purpose of my examination of the *Eagle* during Whitman's editorship is to see if these journalistic writings in any way foreshadow the later *Leaves of Grass*. According to a late critic and scholar, the fact that Whitman's writings in the *Eagle* are not "distinguished" (hence "desultory or impromptu") "proves the inadvisability of taking the *Eagle* editorials as evidence in any account of the development of Whitman's genius."[8] He admits that there exist "certain superficial relationships of theme and attitude between the editorials and the poetry," but these relationships are not significant because of "the almost total impossibility of predicting the poetry, in any exact literary sense, from the editorials." It is true enough that the prosody of the *Leaves* was not foreshadowed in the *Eagle*; but that is scarcely sufficient reason for dismissing the ideas formulated in that paper as irrelevant to the ideas later expressed in the poetry. The child was father of the man just as surely for Whitman as for any other person.

Another scholar, though he sees "little that is distinctive in manner or matter" in the *Eagle* pieces, points out that the experience of writing for the newspapers was of value to Whitman

> in enlarging his vocabulary and in training him to write directly from life—the varied kind of life which reporters are likely to know. Furthermore, books for review and free passes to the theatres and musical events, especially the opera in New York, aided his self-education in the arts; and the necessity of commenting upon national as well as local affairs kept him in touch with the chief issues of his day.[9]

Surely without this experience it is doubtful that a mystic revelation would have been enough to translate Walter Whitman into "Walt Whitman, a kosmos."

MOST, perhaps four-fifths, of the material I quote from the *Eagle* has not been reprinted elsewhere (though some very few of the "unreprinted" pieces have appeared in several articles of mine over the past ten or twelve years in the *Walt Whitman Review*). I have taken no liberties with Whitman's text except to correct obvious typographical errors, which are remarkably few, and some clearly careless slips such as his use of "principal" when he meant "principle," which happened only once. In trying to avoid *sic*, I have let stand without comment his inconsistencies and his occasional weakness in grammar, punctuation, and spelling. For example, he spelled "champagne" in several ways. I have regularized Whitman's use of quotation marks. Ordinarily he used double quotes but occasionally, for no apparent reason, lapsed into single quotes. A stylistic idiosyncrasy he sometimes affected was to use a series of periods, usually seven or more, without alternating spaces, to denote either a change in thought or topic, or emphasis; I have regularized this device to five periods. All conventional ellipses are my own. Finally, to avoid meaningless ellipses at the beginning and end of citations, I have frequently changed capitalization and punctuation to fit my context, and I have also eliminated the distracting commas Whitman was prone to use with dashes and parentheses.[10]

The reader soon will become accustomed to Whitman's eccentricities in spelling and punctuation and will recognize them as characteristic.

San Marcos, Texas　　　　　　　　　　　　　　　　T. L. B.
May 3, 1968

one

THE BACKGROUND

History of the "Sit"

WILLIAM B. MARSH, editor of the *Brooklyn Daily Eagle* for its first five years, died from a congested liver on 26 February 1846, "brought on [according to the *Eagle* of 2 March 1846] by unflagging attention to his duties of editor and reporter for the Brooklyn Eagle." His successor was Walter Whitman, who assumed the editorial and reportorial duties of the paper by the beginning of March and retained them until sometime near the middle of January 1848.[1] Brooklyn was a thriving city of 40,000 (nearly 70,000 by the beginning of 1848), and it was an achievement for a young man not yet twenty-seven to be chosen to edit "this chief of Long Island journals."[2] His writings in the *Eagle*, facile in language despite grammatical and syntactical blunders, show that Whitman took a healthy pleasure in his daily routine. Though in later years he seldom referred to his tenure as editor of the *Eagle*, on at least one occasion he expressed a generally pleasant memory of the period.[3]

Whitman was an experienced newspaperman. Around the age of thirteen he had become an apprentice printer on the *Long Island Patriot*. From then on, except for a few brief stints as a country schoolmaster, he devoted himself to newspaper work, either as a compositor or as a journalist. In 1838 he founded, and edited for a year, the *Long-Islander*, still flourishing at Huntington. By 1840, when he campaigned for Van Buren around Jamaica, Whitman had become actively interested in politics, and by 1841 he was speaking at Democratic rallies in Kings County.

From 1841 until he joined the *Eagle* in 1846, Whitman worked, sometimes as editor, on a number of New York newspapers such as the *Aurora* and the *Evening Tattler*, and free-lanced for others. Immediately before joining the *Eagle* he was with Colonel Alden Spooner's *Brooklyn Daily Evening Star* and weekly *Long Island Star*. Whitman remarks in "Starting Newspapers," *Specimen Days*, that "with these and a little outside work I was occupied off and on, until I went to edit the 'Brooklyn Eagle,' where for two years I had one of the pleasantest sits of my life—a good owner, good pay, and easy work and hours."

The Brooklyn Eagle and Kings County Democrat (becoming *The Brooklyn Daily Eagle and Kings County Democrat* on 1 June 1846) was published daily except Sunday. It was a typical four-page paper with all but the second page allotted to advertisements and public notices until, beginning 1 June 1846, Whitman devoted one to two or more columns (of the six columns) of the first page to literary matter: poems, tales, sketches, and excerpts from books and periodicals. The *Eagle* was both a liberal and influential paper. Isaac Van Anden, its publisher, was a prominent Democrat, and it may be that Whitman partially owed his new position to his political concurrence with Van Anden. One function of the newspaper of the time was to serve as an organ of the party.[4] During the greater part of Whitman's editorship, the *Eagle* admirably fulfilled this function.

The pieces written by Whitman during his two years on the *Eagle* show him as a conformist and man-about-town. Even when attacking conventions of the day, Whitman usually followed the line of popular reforms. He was active in Kings County politics, sponsored patriotic celebrations, and wrote a completely conventional ode which was sung to the tune of "The Star Spangled Banner" at a Fourth of July ceremony.[5] He attended clambakes, Sunday school picnics, circuses, occasional church services, the theatre, the opera, lectures, ferry-boat christenings, and art exhibits. Whitman records in *Specimen Days* ("Death of William Cullen Bryant") that he and Bryant, editor of the *New York Evening Post*, several times took midafternoon rambles together in the countryside around Brooklyn. This friendly association with Bryant is testimony of Whitman's social conformity during his editorship of the *Eagle*.

Tradition has pictured Whitman as the archetypal lounger during this period in Brooklyn.[6] But probably a truer portrayal of Whitman, the *Eagle* editor, is that given in 1920 by William Henry Sutton, who was a printer's devil at the *Eagle* during Whitman's stay there.

> According to Mr Sutton, Whitman was a good man, a "nice, kind man." He wore a short beard, dressed conventionally, and carried himself with dignity. . . . Most of the editorial work was done at the office, and Mr Sutton is quite sure that Whitman always came down to work early and went at it energetically. He was always either reading or writing while in his room in the office. He had comparatively few visitors, and they were "mostly politicians." Mr Sutton does not recall ever seeing Mr Whitman and Isaac Van Anden together, the latter spending most of his time in the business office of the paper, while Whitman was upstairs in his editorial sanctum.
> Whitman wrote his editorials during the morning and sent them to the composing room, after which he would take a short walk. . . . After his walk Whitman would return to the office to read proof on the material for the day's paper. That ended his work for the day.[7]

Sutton added that then Whitman, taking him along, would customarily go "to Gray's Swimming Bath at the foot of Fulton Street, where he would stay in the water exactly twenty minutes." After his swim Whitman ordinarily took the Fulton ferry to New York. Sutton often saw him later in the day riding along Broadway seated beside the omnibus driver. Whitman, loafing and at his ease, was not "observing a spear of summer grass." Instead, he was observing his favorite phenomenon, man. Regardless of what he observed when he lazily invited his soul, he loafed on his own time, not the time of Mr Van Anden and the *Eagle*.

Whitman left the *Eagle* sometime shortly before 21 January 1848.[8] Again tradition insists that excessive lounging on the part of the young editor led to his dismissal. Some part of this tradition, or myth, doubtlessly is a result of Whitman's self-portrait in *Leaves of Grass*. But the so-called factual basis of the legend derives from an item in the *Eagle* for 19 July 1848, in reply to the *Brooklyn Advertiser*, which had taunted the *Eagle* for discharging Whitman because he had refused to lend his editorial columns to Hunkerism and because he had kicked an important politician down the *Eagle's* stairs in retaliation for a personal insult. The *Eagle's* rebuttal alleged that

> Slow, indolent, heavy, discourteous and without steady principles, he was a clog upon our success, and, reluctant as we were to make changes, we still found it absolutely necessary to do so. Mr W. cried persecution, . . . Mr W. has no political principles, nor, for that matter, principles of any sort . . . Whoever knows him will laugh at the idea of his *kicking any body,* much less a prominent politician. He is too indolent to kick a musketo.[9]

It is a simple matter to refute the *Eagle's* assertion that Whitman had no political principles (and I suspect that "principles of any sort" is simply a projection of "political principles"). Under Whitman's editorship the *Eagle* forcefully denounced the Nativist movement; in the face of strong Whig and some Democratic opposition in both Brooklyn and New York, the *Eagle* supported the Mexican War and the annexation of Mexican territory; and it consistently opposed the tariff. These, however, were orthodox Democratic principles. The best proof of Whitman's possession of political principles is his support of the Wilmot Proviso, which opposed extension of slavery into any territories acquired by the United States by the Mexican War. This proviso officially was anathema to the Democratic Party; after Whitman's departure from the *Eagle*, the paper's policy became anti-Wilmot Proviso. Whitman himself in *Specimen Days* ("Starting Newspapers") states that his adherence to his political principles lost him his job: "The troubles in the Democratic party broke forth about those times . . . and I split off with the radicals, which led to rows with the boss and 'the party,' and I lost my place." In September 1848 Whitman became editor of the *Brooklyn Freeman*, a free-soil newspaper. He held this position until the following September, when the paper's editorial policy changed. During his stay on the *Freeman*, Whitman's sincere support of free-soil principles was commented upon by several

New York and Brooklyn papers, among them Greeley's *New York Tribune*.[10] It was during this very period that the temporizing *Eagle* accused Whitman of a total lack of political principles or "principles of any sort."[11]

Whitman was described by his old paper as "slow, indolent, heavy, discourteous." Whitman was a larger than average man and deliberate in speech and action; but had he been "slow, indolent, heavy," would he have been acceptable, as he was, as an active worker in the Democratic machine of Kings County? The term "discourteous" seems especially unfitting. Here again such a trait would have made him a liability to a party organization. And almost all personal records of Whitman attest to his steady and kindly courtesy.[12] Doubtlessly he was indolent after hours, lounging along Broadway or a rural Long Island road— but Van Anden's *Eagle* was out.

The *Eagle* bluntly impugned Whitman's journalistic ability in saying that "he was a clog upon our success." It seems unlikely that an incompetent editor would have been kept on for two years by so prominent a paper as the *Eagle*—especially as there were no hints, before the split in the Democratic Party over the Wilmot Proviso, of any incompatibility between Whitman and Van Anden. A perusal of the *Eagle* during Whitman's editorship shows that he put out a respectable paper for the time and that his standing in his profession was good. Whitman became a clog only when his principles interfered with the party line.

Whitman, in 1846-47, was a good example of the progressive type of newspaper editor who seemingly came into being with the advent of Horace Greeley, who founded the *New York Tribune* in 1841. In announcing his new paper, Greeley stated that he intended "to advance the interests of the people, and to promote their Moral, Political, and Social well-being."[13] This statement of purpose could well apply to Editor Whitman. Many of his editorials in the *Eagle* were concerned with health, morals (political, social, and economic), and humanitarianism. He devoted several columns of the *Eagle*, following the lead of Greeley's *Tribune* and Bryant's *Post*, to worthy literary productions. He was interested in the civic improvement of Brooklyn, especially in matters of sanitation, lighting, and parks. He reviewed books, plays, operas, concerts, lectures, and art exhibits. He wrote, in fact, on everything from thunderstorms to young ladies at the exhibit of Hiram Powers' "Greek Slave"; pleasure and instruction for his readers were to be found in all human activity and natural phenomena. True, he engaged, as did all his peers, in political bickering and trifling. But the majority of his political editorials were in support of his basic belief in democracy, America's manifest destiny, and anti-slavery. Rather than compromise one of these principles, Whitman chose to lose one of his "pleasantest sits."

Duties of the Editor

IN THE EARLY 1830s Alexis de Tocqueville wrote: "The inhabitants of the United States have, then, at present, properly speaking, no literature. The only authors whom I acknowledge as American are the journalists. They indeed are not great writers, but they speak the language of their countrymen and make themselves heard by them."[14] In the late 1840s Whitman, in addition to agreeing with Tocqueville on the lack of a native literature, also recognized the influential role of the journalist in forming American public opinion. "In this country," he stated in the *Eagle* on 6 January 1848, "our literature is mainly composed of periodical publications—from daily to monthly; and these give their hue to the minds of the people." Of these publications, the newspaper carried the most weight with the public, for "the people of the United States are a *newspaper-ruled* people." Hence, editors of newspapers had a manifest duty, as a well-circulated paper could exercise considerable influence for good. "To wield that influence," said Whitman in "Ourselves and the 'Eagle,' " on 1 June 1846, "is a great responsibility. There are numerous noble reforms that have yet to be pressed upon the world. People are to be schooled, in opposition perhaps to their long established ways of thought." Unfortunately, many of Whitman's peers took lightly this responsibility to their readers.

Whitman wrote the following in the *Eagle* for 27 April 1846, under the heading "An Important Fact": "There are published in the United States alone as many periodicals and papers as are produced in the whole of Europe. It is no matter of surprise then that America should be centuries in advance of the Old World in point of intelligence and the general diffusion of knowledge." But Whitman was not such a chauvinist as to think American publications were superior simply because they were American. On 6 January 1848 he remarked that periodicals and newspapers in this country "often give a superficial character to the people, and make them light and ephemeral in mind . . . All hands are too fond of making money *directly:* a passion that is ever at war with intellectual completeness; a passion sometimes at war with itself." So far as newspapers alone were concerned, America's intellectual appetite was given a far from satisfying fare. On 29 September 1846, in "American Editing and Editors," Whitman asserted:

> It is a singular fact that while the people of the United States are a *newspaper-ruled* people, we have in reality few, we may almost say no, newspapers that approach even in the neighborhood of perfect specimens of their kind. We have little fine, hearty, truthful writing in our papers. We have (it must be from want of public encouragement) little high-toned gentlemanliness or elegance—little politeness even. Perhaps, however, the want of the refinements of writing in our daily prints is not so strange as the want of depth, force, power, and solidity. The American people are intellectual in a high degree—their brains are clear, and their penetration eagle-eyed. Why then, does not the press which asks their "patronage" present something like the food we might reasonably suppose would be craved by such a mental appetite as comes from a healthy intellectual digestion? Why are our editors so flippant, so superficial, so vague and verbose? Why do they so rarely bring what they write to bear on the light of great principles and truths?

Whitman answered these questions by quoting "one whose name we cannot state" who placed the blame on low wages and low standards ("society has not required more"), which attracted men of low ability and character.

If we are to believe him, Whitman received "good pay" while editing the *Eagle,* and certainly the standards of the paper were relatively high, since William Marsh, in five years, had made it the most prominent of the Long Island journals. Ralph Weld, speaking of the period in which Whitman edited the *Eagle*, remarks: "Brooklyn journalism then, as during the village period, reflected the spirit of the community. Conservative in tone, as a rule it avoided sensationalism. Alden Spooner expressed its attitude, when he wrote 'Brooklyn has a character for morals, if New-York has not.' "[15] Whitman's own character must have been good; no evidence exists that it was otherwise. Finally, his professional ability was sufficiently respectable to draw praise from even the editors of Whig papers.[16] Here, then, in Whitman's case, were none of the causes cited by "one whose name we cannot state" for the failure of American editors to give the proper journalistic food required by readers with "a healthy intellectual digestion."

On 1 June 1846, after having a month earlier moved to larger quarters at 30 Fulton street, the *Eagle* came out improved in appearance as the result of new type. This issue of the paper contained what Emory Holloway has called "Whitman's editorial creed"[17]—the editorial "Ourselves and the 'Eagle,'" already mentioned. In this editorial Whitman referred first, in restrained language, to his paper's political affiliation.[18] "The democratic party of Brooklyn should (*and do*) handsomely support a handsome daily paper.—For our part, too, we mean no mere lip-thanks when we say we are truly conscious of the warm kindness with which they have always treated this establishment." Then he addressed the general reader:

> We really feel a desire to talk on many subjects, to *all* the people of Brooklyn; and it *ain't* their ninepences [the weekly rate for the *Eagle*] we want so much either. There is a curious kind of sympathy (haven't you ever thought of it before?) that arises in the mind of a newspaper conductor with the public he serves. . . . Daily communion creates a sort of brotherhood and sisterhood between the two parties.

Whitman went on to declare, "Perhaps no office requires a greater union of rare qualities than that of a *true editor*." Hence it was not strange that editors "are all derelict, in some particular." What were these rare editorial qualities? First, "in general information, an editor should be complete, particularly with that relating to his own country." Second, an editor "should have a fluent style" but not elaborate, and his articles "should never smack of being uttered on the spur of the moment, like political oratory." Third, an editor should contain his temper with the restraint of Job. Finally, an "editor needs, withal, a sharp eye, to discriminate the good from the immense mass of unreal stuff floating on all sides of him." But though an editor have not all these desirable qualities, and though he have "the duties of five or six," still "much good can always be done, with such potent influence as a well circulated newspaper." Then followed the declaration of editorial responsibility already quoted: "To wield that influence, is a great responsibility. There are numerous noble reforms that have yet to be pressed upon the world. People are to be schooled, in opposition perhaps to their long established ways of thought."

"People are to be schooled"—this was the editor's duty. Just as Whitman later in *Leaves of Grass* equated the poet with the teacher ("By Blue Ontario's Shore," stanza 12), so Whitman here in 1846 equated the newspaper editor with the teacher. Of the various elements discernible in Whitman's writings in the *Eagle*, the didactic element is one of the most pervasive. The citizens of Brooklyn, as Americans, were clear-brained and intellectually curious; and Whitman used his newspaper, while turning out political hackwork and routine news reporting, to contribute to the advancement and education of his subscribers.

In addition to his duty to school his readers, Whitman had, of course, the ordinary duties of the conductor of a small daily in the 1840s. He was both editor and reporter, as had been the late Mr Marsh. Besides preparing editorials (which ranged in number from one or two daily to occasionally as many as three or four), Whitman clipped items from exchange papers, wrote book and periodical reviews, arranged a literary miscellany for the first page, compiled a column or so of local news, and frequently did his own legwork on news stories in Brooklyn and across the East River in New York.[19] In addition, Whitman also edited the *Weekly Eagle*, published on Wednesday afternoons, which contained selected material from the preceding week's daily *Eagle*.

The *Eagle* employed one special reporter during the first half of 1847—a Mr Oliver Dyer, phonographic reporter and teacher. Beginning 8 December 1846 Whitman ran a series of articles by Dyer on the nature of phonography, a species of phonetic shorthand. Early in 1847 the *Eagle* began on Mondays to report sermons in Brooklyn churches. On 10 May 1847 this item preceded such a report:

> The following *full* report, word for word, of a brilliant sermon by Dr Cox yesterday, is made for us by the reporter whom we have engaged for such occasions—Mr Dyer, the phonographist. It tells its own story; and we invite any of the vast assembly who crowded the Cranberry street building yesterday to hear the discourse; we invite them to tax their memories to the utmost—we invite the pastor himself—to discover the least inconsistency (unless some typographical error occur) between this report and the sermon itself.

Dyer left Brooklyn in the summer of 1847 and the *Eagle's* reports of sermons dwindled to occasional sketchy comments by Whitman and accounts sent in by correspondents.[20]

The *Eagle's* correspondents were a constant source of poems, sketches, reform tracts, travel letters, reminiscences, political essays, and recipes. Whitman demanded certain things of their contributions. The following appeared in the *Eagle* on 24 April 1846:

> How To Write For Newspapers—1. Have something to write about. 2. Write plain; dot your i's; cross your t's; point sentences; begin with capitals. 3. Write short; to the point; stop when you have done. 4. Write only on one side of the leaf. 5. Read it over, abridge and correct it, until you get it into the shortest space possible. 6. Pay the postage.

A brief item of 29 July 1846 indicated that many of Whitman's correspondents did not know how to write for newspapers: "The communication of 'Fair Play' is unpublishable in our columns because it is written in very faint pencil mark. A great deal of the MSS. sent us are not attended to, from their illegibility, being written on both sides of the sheet &c." This protest appeared in the *Eagle* on 2 December 1846: "If the gentleman who sends us the report of interments, would write any thing else better than crow-tracks, the names of the diseases would doubtless be printed rightly. If not, not." When the contribution of a correspondent was printed, Whitman usually was careful to indicate his agreement or disagreement with its sentiments if the piece dealt with politics or social conduct. He did not wish to have his personal opinions compromised by any not his own. Of extracts from books and periodicals, Whitman once said in the *Eagle* (30 April 1847): "Amid the extracted articles put in our *Eagle*, there is here and there a sentiment of which we cannot fully approve. *Our own* sentiments are always in the editorial articles proper."

As editor, Whitman was jealous of "*our own* sentiments"; ample proof is his persistence in supporting the Wilmot Proviso against the line taken by the proprietor of the *Eagle* and by the Democratic Party of Kings County. Whitman also was jealous of the freedom of the press. On 16 September 1847 Henry A. Lees, publisher and editor of the *Brooklyn Daily Advertiser*, a Whig and an old adversary of Whitman, was struck by George H. Cooper, local lawyer, for an article Lees had printed. Lees challenged Cooper to a formal pugilistic encounter, with seconds, on the fourth floor of the *Advertiser* building. Cooper accepted and the fight took place. On the next day, the following appeared in the *Eagle:*

> When an editor, in the discharge of his duty to the public, gives in the columns of his paper a simple statement of facts, and that statement contains nothing which can *in any manner* be construed, or tortured into a construction, to violate propriety, or wound the feelings of any individual—when an editor does simply this, and *for this* is assaulted in his own office, we conceive that the rights of the press, its dignity and freedom, have been outraged, and we cannot too strongly express our sympathy for our injured and insulted contemporary, and our unqualified scorn for the perpetrator of the wrong. And we believe that the whole public would justify an editor thus attacked, if he should summarily inflict the most violent punishment in his reach upon the aggressor. In our belief, no punishment could be too severe.

However, Whitman went on to condemn Lees for entertaining "no proper estimation of his dignity and of his position" by lowering himself to defending the liberty of the press in the prize ring. Having done this degrading thing, Lees "forfeits his claim not only to the sympathy, but also to the respect, of all his contemporaries, and proves himself unworthy of the station he occupies."[21]

No account exists of Whitman's having been assaulted as the result of anything he printed in the *Eagle*. As will be seen later, on several occasions Whitman rather persistently attacked prominent citizens of Brooklyn in a fashion calculated to "wound the feelings of an individual." Assault was not an uncommon conclusion to such matters in the hot-tempered forties, and what Whitman would have done had he been confronted with a situation similar to Lees' is a matter of purest conjecture. All we have along that line is a probably apocryphal story of Whitman's kicking a politician down the *Eagle's* stairs.

Though he did not have his time taken up with exchanging blows with enraged readers, Whitman was busily engaged in his regular duties until he had finished reading proof in the afternoon.[22] That he enjoyed the steady grind of putting out a daily paper is evident from the general good spirits he displayed in the *Eagle*. In midsummer, with the liveliness of the city dampened by the excessive heat, he was sometimes bored (but see his later response to New York hot weather in "Hot Weather New York," *Specimen Days*). He wrote 21 July 1847:

> We learn that the rim of Long Island is swarming with the city denizens who have managed to effect their escape, while squads of absentees are perched high on the top of every mountain resort which looms up landward. "Keep cool" seems to be the favorite motto, with all except omnibus horses and the class of beings who for the prescriptive right to use the syllable "we" are doomed for an uncertain time to the prison house of a daily paper. Poor "we" things, how are they to be pitied.

But though he had to work as hard as ever while many of his readers lounged in pastoral breezes, Whitman found gratification in doing his job. An excerpt from an article by Captain Frederick

Marryat, Retired R.N. (author of sea novels and of the notorious
—to most Americans—*Travels in America*, 1839) was printed in
the *Eagle* on 16 March 1847, under the heading "The Toils of a
Newspaper." Marryat complained of the obligation of writing
a lead article day after day and year after year regardless of one's
health, mood, or situation. "To write for a paper," he said, "is
very well, but to edit it is to condemn yourself to slavery." Whitman appended the following to the extract:

> That the labors of an editor are hard enough, is an undoubted
> fact. But for our part, we *like them*. There are many plea-
> sures and gratifications in the position of an editor. More-
> over, we think there has been quite too much of this cant
> about the dreadful things concomitant with the "labors of a
> newspaper editor." The worst of it is, not that the work is
> hard, but that, in this country, one man has to do *so many
> things* in the paper. Abroad . . . half a dozen editors are a
> small allowance for a well conducted daily journal. And one
> is apt to regret the having so much to do, here, because, in the
> multiplicity, each subject cannot be thoroughly done justice
> to. We would not give much however for a newspaper editor
> who is constantly grumbling at and disliking his profession.
> The same rule . . . may hold good in other matters. What
> would you think of a sculptor, or a painter, or a physician,
> who should be ever piercing the wounded air with bewail-
> ments of his hard lot?

Whitman enjoyed his profession and took it seriously. For one
thing, newspaper editing entailed, for a man who tried to be a
"true editor," an earnest purpose—that of educating the naturally
intelligent American. For another, his job allowed, or rather
demanded, that he go among and observe—and absorb—the
myriad activities of his fellow beings. The following lines from
"Song of Myself" (section 42) are descriptive of the young editor
of the *Brooklyn Eagle*:

> This is the city and I am one of the citizens,
> Whatever interests the rest interests me, politics, wars,
>   markets, newspapers, schools,
> The mayor and councils, banks, tariffs, steamships, factories,
>   stocks, stores, real estate and personal estate.

Whitman and His "Contemporaries"

DURING the two years when Whitman was editing the *Eagle*, the Brooklyn public was being served also by two other daily papers, the *Evening Star* and the *Advertiser*, both Whig. Whitman had been employed by Colonel Alden Spooner, proprietor and editor of the *Star*, on two occasions. He had worked as a compositor on Spooner's weekly *Long Island Star* from the fall of 1832 until May of 1835; and he had written for the *Evening Star*, as has been noted, for several months before coming to the *Eagle*. Henry A. Lees, a native of England, had established the *Advertiser* in 1844. Whitman followed the journalistic custom of his day in maintaining a political and professional feud with his two local rivals. However, his tone varied according to which of the two journals he was attacking.

Gay Wilson Allen remarks: "Whether he was piqued because he had lost an inexpensive reporter and special writer, or thought Whitman unequal to editing a daily, or—more likely—resented the political opposition the new *Eagle* editor would give him, Edwin Spooner published editorials ridiculing Whitman's 'weakness.' "[23] Indeed, the last named motive for the *Star's* attacks on Whitman seems the correct one, for verbal blows were not exchanged between the two papers until 1847; and the time element suggests that "would give" should read "was giving." A number of Whitman's editorials in the *Eagle* took to task the *Evening Star* for its reactionary stand on such matters as the national bank, the tariff, the Mexican War, President Polk's administration, and radical democracy. The *Star* retaliated by commenting on Whitman's "weakness" as an editor, calling him a "pig ringer,"[24] describing him as a "country schoolmaster" and "hectoring scriviner," and imploring him to "soar above the low and foetid purlieus of profligate partyism."[25] In return, Whitman was more strongly sarcastic about the *Star's* whiggish political principles (though he sometimes described the paper as a political mongrel), its diction, and its apparent habit of filching copy from the *Eagle*.[26] But never did he impugn, in contrast with his treatment of Henry Lees, either of the Spooners' personal character or integrity—though on one occasion he came near doing so. When he wrote his items critical of the *Star*, Whitman must have been consciously aware that its senior editor was "our old friend, Mr Spooner, one of the best-hearted old men in the State of Long Island" ("Professional Compliments," 4 June 1846). Ordinarily references in the *Eagle* to the elder Spooner spoke of him as "our venerable contemporary of the *Star*" and of the *Star* itself as "our staid whig contemporary." It was the whiggery in the *Star* that Whitman principally aimed at, even when criticizing it for lack of professional decorum in the matter of printing material appropriated from the *Eagle* as its own.

Whitman appears to have been careful in the *Eagle* to credit the sources of those items in his columns not from his own hand. The *Star* did not anger Whitman on this point until the late summer of 1847—the time when its comments on Whitman were sharpest. On 27 August Whitman said: "Since the Brooklyn *Star* is so nice in its sense of editorial decorum, will it once in a while give this print credit for the lengthy reports, prepared with care, which it often copies from us, and prints just as if they were original to it?" On 30 August Whitman came his closest to dealing in personalities.

> The *Star*, which is too mean to get local reports, takes ours, and instead of crediting our paper, attributes them to third parties. None but a sneak, as stingy as obtuse, would descend to such a petty subterfuge. All local reports come from some writers, of course—but no one except an innate vulgarian would go behind the paper, to refuse credit on such flimsy grounds.
>
> The *Star* has made itself the laughing stock of Brooklyn, by its ridiculous and sleepy management as a newspaper, without enterprise, without even common talent, and without any fixed tone. It seems disposed to go a step lower, and spatter with its low impudence, those through whose labors it makes occasionally even a tolerable page of reading.

On 14 September Whitman noted that the *Star* had reprinted a brief extract the *New York Tribune* had made from the *Eagle's* account of the Brooklyn charter convention and had credited it to the *Tribune*. "Our contemporary," said Whitman, "ought to have more local spirit than to rely upon foreign papers for its accounts of local occurrences." Whitman's final protest against the *Star's* purloining practices came on 3 November.

> Our venerable contemporary of the Brooklyn *Star* in its yesterday's issue, took advantage of our paper being printed two hours in advance of the usual time, and cribbed from us an account of the murder in Leonard street, New York, which we took special pains to go over during the morning, and collect by our own personal trouble. The *Star* not only cribs this from us, but uses our own words in rendering the account—and publishes it as if it were original. Since we have commenced this matter, we are determined to expose our venerable contemporary every time it does this very wicked newspaperial wrong. It has long cabbaged our local reports, and palmed them off as original; and now it seems determined to have our latest items of special news.

Perhaps after this cry for justice by a busy editor, the *Star* did not repeat this "very wicked newspaperial wrong." At least there were no further references of importance in the *Eagle* to the Spooners' paper; and soon Whitman was no longer connected with the *Eagle* and its quarrels.[27]

Whitman's wrangle with Henry Lees' *Advertiser*, though its peak of intensity was reached in 1847, began earlier than that with the *Star* and was continued on the same level of virulence by Whitman's successor on the *Eagle*, S. G. Arnold. Whitman's disputes with the *Advertiser* had their origin in political differences which quickly degenerated into mutual denigrations that were intense, personal, and often in remarkably bad taste.[28] Strangely, Whitman never accused the *Advertiser* of stealing copy from the *Eagle*. But he did accuse it of being a carbon of such New York Whig papers as the *Morning Express*. On 22 May 1846 Whitman spoke of the *Advertiser* as attributing to the *Express* an article condemning the Mexican War, and added:

> Heaven forbid that we should charge the *Adv.* with *originating* this thing . . . its cant and impertinence are mostly copied from one or two prints on the other side of the river. When they rave in the morning, the *Adv.* raves in the afternoon; and when the rising of the sun witnesses their attempts to be

funny at the idea of American courage, the setting of that luminary beholds the Brooklyn *Adv.* close at their heels, snivelling and whining its whiffety bark, to the same tune . . . insulting to our people . . . when every true patriot stands up by his government, and has a hand and voice of sympathy for our soldiers in the south-west.

Whitman's standing complaints against the *Advertiser* were that it was a subservient party tool, was edited by a "cockney" Englishman devoid of any vestige of patriotism for his adopted country, and was a corrupting influence on the American press. Perhaps party jealousy alone did not dictate this attitude toward the *Advertiser* and its editor. On 14 April 1847 the *Eagle* quoted the *Star* as saying the following about its brother Whig in reference to party servility: "In this the *Daily Advertiser* has no rival on this side of the Atlantic. The thought is not altogether uncomfortable that there is not a drop of American blood in the veins of the editors and reporters who scribble the contents of that paper."[29] An editorial in the *Eagle* on 12 July 1847 provides a compendium of Whitman's opinion of Lees and his paper.

To hear such a print as the Brooklyn *Advertiser* say, "we have none to call us to account for what we advance, and are responsible only to the public," is one of the best jokes of the age. . . . Its body belongs to the most selfish and reckless of cliques; soul it has none to belong anywhere. The gutter-dirt that is washed into the dock by a shower, might as reasonably talk of *its* impudence. . . . And though it *may* be a very reasonable thing for the nest of English cockneys, who, as they boast so perpetually, "own the paper" they "edit," to come over here and enlighten the free people of Brooklyn with their effusions; we must say we can't realize that alleged fact. Quite on the contrary—for while always glad to receive the many good specimens from Old England, such samples as the *Advertiser* are alike unfair to their native country, and degrading to this. What vile elements these meaner sort of Englishmen, over the land, have introduced into our American press! Nearly all that is low and morbid, that corrupts and violates the rules of taste, as far as newspapers are concerned, have been infused among us by these migrating gentry from the stews of the English cities. And the worst of it is, that, in reality, they have little but hatred toward the country that affords them a living.

As for Lees himself (according to the *Eagle* on 3 November), he was "an English cockney, of fifty-sixth mental calibre, deficient of an original idea in his head, or the capacity to write a sentence without the grossest blunders in grammar, and even in spelling!" Lees must have retaliated for this unflattering picture of himself in the next day's *Advertiser*, for on 5 November Whitman defended himself against the *Advertiser's* charge that he used bad grammar himself. He began first by sounding the old theme of the Whig paper's contempt for American institutions, its "obscene stories and allusions," and its "daily martyrdom of our language"; then he explained his philosophy of grammar.

> What our style and "grammar" are, the readers of our columns can see for themselves. As to the style, we simply endeavor to be clearly understood: as to our "grammar," it is of course perfectly correct, or we shouldn't presume to write for an intelligent community. We say so plumply, because we consider the very least requisite of an editor is not to violate philological truth. We never sacrifice at the shrine of formal construction, however; and it is well known that a numbskull with a grammar *book* in his hand, but not the least idea of the general philosophy of the science in his head, can pick flaws in any idiomatic sentence, and parade his stupidity by calling incorrect what is frequently the best merit of the composition.

Lees' obvious answer for Whitman's monotonous epithet of cockney was to accuse the editor of the *Eagle* of being a Nativist—a term of particular approbrium in Brooklyn, where the rapidly increasing Irish (and German) population was courted for its votes by both the Whigs and the Democrats. Whitman's answer to this charge was, as on 8 August 1846, that "for the *Advertiser* to identify itself with any of the European nations, is unfair even to the wickeder phases of those nations' character"; as for being anti-foreigner, the editor of the *Eagle* "would banish" the word "foreigners" from the press of this country if he could.

On another occasion the *Advertiser* indulged in a bit of irony in its remarks on the following paragraph which appeared in the *Eagle* on 12 January 1847:

> MONKEYISM IN BROOKLYN.—Among the sights that go to make a man's stomach qualmy, is that monkeyism of literature, involved in a few gentlemen (very well in their places, but very silly when they reach higher) getting together, and "adoring" and "doting" on Byron, Scott, and "sentiment"— making pretensions to criticism, with about as much ability that way as a smart little counter-jumper might have to rule the Treasury Department.....At the anniversary of the *Hamiltonian Literary Association* last evening, after a long string of toasts of a character the very opposite of American, one of the guests—a citizen of New York—had the audacious vulgarity to think that it might not be out of time to remember (the low-bred fellow!) that there was such a republic as his own on the surface of the earth—and accordingly gave: "The United States of America—an independent country, *not* a suburb of London"—which was partially *hissed!* Is it too much to say that this was a specimen of the monkeyism of literature?[30]

On 14 January 1847 Whitman briefly noted that the *Advertiser* had taken the article on "Monkeyism" as an insult to itself and had used in rebuttal "such arguments as are involved in repetitions of the overwhelming phrase, 'poetical editor of the Eagle,' and 'poet editor, looking down from his Parnassian heights.' " Whitman avowed that he found these arguments "quite unanswerable."[31]

Whitman's verbal exchanges with his New York contemporaries were fewer and much milder than those with his Brooklyn competitors and usually were concerned only with political differences. That Whitman thought well of the New York press on the whole is indicated by the following which appeared in the *Eagle* on 6 January 1848:

> We possess infinitely more newspapers, of course, than the English; and, in the way of getting late news the New York *Tribune, Sun,* and *Herald,* are fully equal in forethought and outlays to any journals in England. The London papers,

though their "leaders" are choice specimens of force and pungent style, have oftentimes sad trash in their editorial columns. In the way of elegance of composition, none of them prints articles equal to those which proceed from Mr Bryant's pen, in the *Evening Post*—and none that in dashy strength and freedom and clearness, are like Leggett's old editorials in the same paper.

The New York press . . . affords many peculiar features, both in literary and other points of view. We are no admirers of the *Herald's* flippant, sneering, exclusively selfish and sordid method in its editorial department; but still consider that that print has done an immense advantage to the American press, in the way of offering it an example of newspaper enterprise and activity. Not until the advent of the *Herald* did the "Wall street press" get the wind taken out if its sails; for previous to that time, the cheap papers were purchased merely because they *were* cheap; afterwards because they were *better. . . .*

Taken altogether, there is a vast amount of good reading, and writing, in the New York newspapers.—Only think of the *haste* of preparation, and the *amount* needed; and one will be ready to excuse the frequent want of condensation, and the looseness of style, noticeable in many editorial articles. Great is the estate of the press! and in it, great are the newspapers of New York!

But these great New York newspapers could be as guilty as the *Brooklyn Star* of petty filching from the *Eagle*. On 16 June 1846 Whitman remarked that Bryant's *Post* "is in the frequent habit . . . of taking bodily our local news, and publishing it as original. So are nearly all the New York newspapers, with the exception of the *Tribune* and the *Express*. . . . Professional brethren, we presume, must notice in the *Eagle* that *we* render unto Caesar, &c." At times the New York press spoke slightingly of matters in Brooklyn, and then Whitman would respond as he did on 10 April 1847: "One could better swallow even that 'brine' which lies between Brooklyn and New York than such a nauseous dose of insipid milk and unclean water which the *Evening Mirror* serves up, entitled 'Brooklyn affairs.' "

Sometimes the *Eagle* warned its subscribers against fraud in the press across the East River. Not awed by the *New York Sun's* daily circulation of 30,000, Whitman advised his readers on 20 May 1846 that the *Sun's* extras were "humbugs . . . half the time full of the most ridiculous blunders and misstatements. We have been 'shaved' several times with them, and consider it our duty to put our readers on their guard."

From time to time the New York papers were critical of certain of Whitman's stylistic idiosyncrasies; he ordinarily begged the question by being "cute." Often, when discussing the beauty or salubrity of Brooklyn, Whitman would speak of the "grateful Brooklyn air." On 14 July 1846 he noted: "The *News* wants to know what the Brooklyn air 'is grateful for.' For not being confined, like its sister air, in the odious precincts of New York, to be sure! No dire penance, threatened by the angry Prospero to his 'tricksy spirit,' were half so terrible as *that*."[32] Early in November 1846 Whitman instituted a column of New York City news with the somewhat ambiguous heading of "New York City: &c." On the sixth of that month he remarked that "The *Tribune* 'wants to know' if the '&c.' in the above head line stands for Brooklyn. Yes, it may, if we write head lines on the same principle that a lady writes a letter, and puts the best and sweetest part in the postscript." The "&c." stayed in the heading and the Brooklyn air continued to be "grateful."

In "Song of Myself" (section 4) Whitman wrote: "Backward I see in my own days where I sweated through fog with linguists and contenders." Perhaps he was thinking of his *Eagle* days when he contended with his contemporaries every day but Sunday and found it good. Doubtless the young editor sweated, but he gave no sign of being troubled by the fog.

Town and Country: the Setting

FLOYD STOVALL has remarked, "What we feel most in *Leaves of Grass* . . . is the sense of life and the photographic impression of reality in scenes of the street, shop, and countryside."[33] To a perhaps lesser yet still positive degree, Whitman's genuine interest in the spectacle about him is apparent in the columns of the *Eagle*. Editor Walter Whitman was a traveled man—in Brooklyn and its rural environs, in New York, and on the

East River. After business hours, and often during them, he strolled the streets or rode the omnibusses, stages, ferries, and sometimes the Long Island Railroad. Some of his rambles were aimless saunterings to see what he could see up some street or down another; others were purposefully directed toward an exhibition, a picnic, a ship launching, or a parade. In the *Eagle* Whitman told his subscribers what he had seen on these excursions. And since the *Eagle* was a Brooklyn paper, the Brooklyn scene predominated greatly over the New York scene in those accounts.

As the editor of a local newspaper, Whitman was perforce a Brooklyn booster. He spoke for the superiority of Brooklyn over the "Gomorrah," as he frequently dubbed New York on the opposite side of the river.[34] But New York surpassed Brooklyn in one thing, as Whitman admitted on 30 September 1846.

> N. Y. Broadway is about the only thing that we will confess to "beat our time," in Brooklyn.—We have a healthier, pleasanter, more orderly, cleanly, "nice" city than N. Y.; we have as elegant private dwellings—as commodious omnibusses . . . but we have no Broadway!.....The shops of Broadway are world famed. Stewart's new place is just now all the rush in the "dry goods line." And 341, Thos. Crane Banks's, is just as famous in another and perhaps more beautiful line: the windows alone are a study. There are all kinds of dazzling and expensive knick-knacks—bracelets, whose worth is equivalent to a comfortable house and lot—necklaces that balance an editor's ten years' salary—cameos on which the genius of art has taken pride in substantializing gorgeous thoughts—finger rings of rare worth and brilliancy . . . We were shown, by a friend there, the other day, a wristlet of heavy gold the weight whereof on a lady's arm we would call "aggrawatin"; it enclosed a costly gold watch, set in diamonds, and in many other precious things besides.....A man can edify himself for hours by looking in the shop windows of Broadway—and learn no little of human nature in the operation.[35]

Indeed, the spectacle of Broadway, its stream of humanity fed by 400,000 New Yorkers, so stimulated the young editor of the *Eagle* that he saw in it the epitome of all great American thoroughfares and a symbol of the American spirit. The following, "Gayety of Americans," was the lead editorial in the *Eagle* on 23 September 1846:

> The passed morning has been very beautiful. . . . We had occasion to pass through Broadway, in N. Y.; and never have we seen that famed thoroughfare present a brighter aspect. Walking there, if we had been asked to mention the particular characteristic which would in all probability first impress a stranger visiting New York, we should reply that it was a *gay activity*. This is surely the most striking feature of the population. We have often wondered, of a bright morning, how every body could dress so well,[36] and where on earth they could find business enough to employ them, and make it necessary for them to hurry along at that helter-skelter pace.
>
> We are not sure but it is unjust to this country after all, to attribute the want of "fun" to it, which most European travellers attribute. Go through the streets, and see for yourself, almost any where, in pleasant weather, particularly at the beginning of "business hours." For the early time of the day, there is, too, an aspect of *youth* impressed upon N. York. Two thirds of the persons you meet in the street are young men or boys nearly grown—clerks, apprentices, office-boys, and so on. These with their bright faces, and their exact attire, form by no means the least agreeable part of the scene. Dull and torpid must that man be who can walk any distance in the streets of the metropolis, of a morning, and not become imbued with the cheerfulness so evident everywhere around. . . . the gayety we speak of is quite different from the flippant gayety of the Parisian population. . . . Ours, we think, is more the disposition to make business a pleasure—to work, but work with smiles and a bright heart. Theirs is a repast, all flowers and fine dishes, but with little for the appetite; ours forgets not the ornamental part of the feast, but retains the solid, too.

Foreign travelers, Whitman continued, gave the Americans too much credit for a feverish pursuit of wealth and too little for a capacity for enjoyment. There was admittedly too great an eagerness for wealth among the Americans; but there was at the same time a marked element of cheerful liveliness in the national character.

> What can afford a livelier spectacle for instance, than the lower part of Fulton street, or of Atlantic st., Brooklyn—than

Broadway, the Bowery, Grand street, Canal street, and nearly all of the large N. Y. thoroughfares, on a fine morning or afternoon? Of course, many of the persons who look so gay there have their own special troubles and cares . . . But, for the hour, they have forgotten them. Sunshine of the mind beams over their faces, and they find relief in the excitement of so much bustle and noise—the spectacle of so much fashion and beauty. And, indeed, all through the day, in almost all parts of New York, this activity never flags. Surely there can be no town on earth that has less of a sleepy look than that. It is always "wide awake," and the throbbings of its pulse beat forever. . . . Life is short enough to make the most active hands, joined with the quickest brain, slow to do what ought to be done—and dark enough to render all that throws sunshine around us welcome indeed. We might . . . offer some suggestions of improvement; but to tell the truth, we are not among those who prefer to dwell on the deficiences of a community, than on its merits; and we are quite satisfied with Brooklyn and New York character as it is—confident that though it might be better, there are hardly two cities elsewhere . . . in which it is as well.

If one may judge from the references in the *Eagle* to Broadway, Whitman was particularly impressed by the street's show of wealth and luxury. At times he may have felt that an admirer of Tom Paine, who also was a mere journalist from a poor family, had no business taking pleasure in monied display, for he sometimes coupled his praise of the Broadway pageant with depreciation. In "Matters Which Were Seen and Done in an Afternoon Ramble," 19 November 1846, he remarked:

> What a fascinating chaos is Broadway, of a pleasant sunny time! We know it is all (or most of it) "fol-de-rol," but still there is pleasure in walking up and down there awhile, and looking at the beautiful ladies, the bustle, the show, the glitter, and even the gaudiness. But alas! what a prodigious amount of means and time might be much better . . . employed than as they are there!

On the whole, however, Whitman's delight in the splendor of Broadway was unqualified, and its fascination drew him whenever he set foot on Manhattan's shores. The *Eagle*, 25 January

1847, announced that New York had received news that morning at ten, over the magnetic telegraph, of the arrival at Boston of the long-overdue British steamer, the *Hibernia.*

> So this beautiful morning—the sun shining so gaily, and the air so pleasantly tolerable, for winter—we strolled over to the Gomorrah on the other side of the water, to hear what we could hear, as well as to "see things." How fine the river breeze, standing to feel it on the forward part of the Montauk! How active and inspiriting the spectacle of so much passage and life, on the river and bay!—How innumerous the tides of humanity that swept along the streets adjacent to the shore! Broadway, too—for even thither wended our steps—was "out" this morning, in all its splendor and joy, and glitter, and frivolity, and richness and pride! The rolling carriages—the groups of elegantly attired women—the showy shops—made up a scene, which is met with *only* in Broadway!

"Mannahatta," which first appeared in the 1860 edition of *Leaves of Grass,* contains this line: "Trottoirs throng'd, vehicles, Broadway, the women, the shops and the shows." Thirteen years earlier Broadway had evoked the same associations for the young editor of the *Brooklyn Daily Eagle.*

New York had another spectacle which attracted Whitman as much as Broadway—the theatre. In "Matters Which Were Seen and Done in an Afternoon Ramble," Whitman's stroll ended at the Park Theatre, where he saw the Keans in "a counterfeit presentment of 'The Troublesome Raigne of John, King of England.' " Numerous accounts in the *Eagle* of plays, operas, and ballets seen in New York attest to the frequency of his excursions to that city (Brooklyn had no theatre) to see its stage productions. Whitman's response to these entertainments will be discussed in a later chapter.

Notably absent from the columns of the *Eagle* were comments on P. T. Barnum's popular American Museum in New York. Why, it is difficult to say. About two months after Whitman came to the *Eagle,* Barnum and his greatest exhibit, General Tom Thumb, returned to America after a successful European tour which included the presentation of the General to Queen Victoria. The following appeared in the *Eagle* on 25 May 1846:

Despite Barnum's laudable republicanism, and despite the frequent advertisement the *Eagle* carried announcing General Tom Thumb's five performances daily, Whitman never recorded for his readers any visit to the American Museum. Perhaps he considered the place a total humbug, for he labelled as one of Barnum's hoaxes a purported Chinese junk which visited New York in the summer of 1847. On 14 July the *Eagle* reported, under the heading of "That Tallest of Small Potato Humbugs, The 'Chinese Junk,' " that, according to "undoubtedly authentic information," the junk "was built recently near the city of Philadelphia, under the direction and superintendence of a man who belongs to that city of humbugs, New York, and has been notorious for humbugging the people by old negro women and mermaids for several years past, for a two-fold purpose—first as a speculation and then as a hoax." Whitman described the crew as a mixture of whites and mulattoes, and the junk as "a humbug from stem to stern and from topmast to keelson." But for the New York populace the junk was a genuine exotic. Whitman's article continued:

We happened in the neighborhood of 17th street and West street yesterday afternoon on business, and observing thereabout a prodigious throng of men, women, children, and vehicles of all kinds, colors, and shapes, we were led to inquire what meant all this commotion? when we were informed by a man with a long beard and a very dirty shirt, that the "Chinese junk" was in sight, with her "latteen sails" all set, coming up . . . at the foot of 19th street.—We stood some thirty minutes at this point and counted eight hundred and thirteen deluded ones, as they passed down to the "long wharf." . . . and should judge the number on this wharf and pier alone about five thousand. . . .

We hope none of our Brooklyn citizens will be gulled by this ridiculous imposture—for such it surely is.

But by 6 August, however, Whitman apparently had accepted at least the crew of the junk as authentic. On that date "The Chinamen on Long Island" appeared in the *Eagle* describing the reactions of "Hesing and Sum Teen, the two principal dignitaries of the Chinese junk," to the Long Island Railroad while guests of an excursion of the American Institute (a New York agricultural, commercial, and industrial society) to Greenport, Long Island. The two Orientals, Whitman reported, "for the first time since their arrival, exhibited astonishment and delight. . . . The speed of the train absolutely brought their queues to a complete perpendicular with fright." On 2 October the readers of the *Eagle* learned that twenty-six of the thirty-one members of the crew had returned to Canton at the expense of Captain Kellet, commander of the junk. "Gone at Last," said the *Eagle*, when the junk left for Boston and further exhibition on 23 October.

A very different sort of vessel attracted Whitman's attention earlier in 1847. On 30 January the *Eagle* printed the following:

LAUNCH THIS MORNING OF THE WASHINGTON STEAMSHIP.— This bright and breezy forenoon, at and about the foot of Seventh street, New York, was gathered such a congregation of humanity of both sexes, as is seldom seen on any occasion. The coming forth of these thousands was induced by the announcement that the first American ocean steamer would, at 9 o'clock, leave the wooden cradle wherein her strength was matured, and be henceforth "rock'd in the cradle of the deep."[37] At the appointed time, the last wedges were knocked away, and the giant ship commenced her movement. . . . Cannons were fired, drums beaten, and all the people shouted . . . The stern of the noble vessel plunged deeply into the yielding element . . . but as her whole body moved swiftly into the water, she gained her equilibrium with a bound, and was *afloat!*

In the fall of 1846 Whitman went several times to the American Institute Fair at Castle Garden off the Battery. On his first visit, 6 October, he found the carpenters and exhibitors still busy preparing for the public, who had arrived already. But Whitman saw enough in the confusion to assert that the displays proved America's capacity to produce cheap yet excellent products which had no need of a protective tariff. He visited the fair again on 16 October: "A 'large and respectable' quantity of ladies and gentlemen filled the great amphitheatre of Castle Garden this morning . . . We listened a moment to some one playing on the superb piano . . . edged our path amid bedsteads, shower-baths, and five hundred etceteras—and so came away."[38]

Whitman attended the fair again in the following fall. The *Eagle* for 13 October 1847 described its editor's reaction to "The Current Exhibition at Castle Garden." There was, Whitman said, more matter "for rational curiosity as well as entertainment, in one of these exhibitions, than in many very pretensive books, and many literary, theatrical, or musical performances." The articles on display illustrated a functional esthetic.

> After threading one's way through the covered bridge to Castle garden . . . lined with all sorts of agricultural implements, carriages, washing machines, boats, etc., the first impression . . . at entering the great rotunda hall, will be the impression of magnificence and richness. There is nothing like it in New York—which is equal to saying there is nothing like it in America. The wares of glass, polished cabinet work, plated articles, and a thousand other things, make a glitter and a sparkle that very happily set off the rest. One could ramble for days among these beautiful, useful, and *not* costly fabrics, without tiring. At least one who *thinks* can do so. That new and powerful steam-engine, alone, is an almost *sublime* subject for observation.

Whitman then enumerated the exhibits of Brooklyn manufacturers, among which he especially liked "the simple elegance of the bell handles" made by George W. Jackson. And the cut glass of the Brooklyn Flint Glass Company was "ahead of English glass—which is ahead of all the rest of the world—except us. (Or paraphrasing what Hackett said, last night, in the Kentuckian, 'Brother Jonathan's father can lick any man on airth, and Brother Jonathan can lick his father.')"

Some of Brother Jonathan's children had been called together by the Mexican War. The *Eagle*, 17 September 1846, told of its editor's visit the day before to Governor's Island to see Governor Silas Wright inspect the regiment of volunteers for California encamped there. The governor did not appear, so Whitman made his own inspection of the gypsy-like tent encampment. "We regret," said he, "that we cannot speak in very high terms of praise for the general appearance of the regiment, in regard to *physique*." But he supposed they were fitted for the job planned for them, and they seemed eager to be up and doing. He noted that "in nearly every tent was conspicuously displayed one of the bibles recently presented to the men; but they seemed, with their gilt bindings, to be mere matters of ornament; for whenever a Californian was reading, he seemed to be intently engaged in devouring the contents of a 'cheap publication,' which required no great stretch of imagination to determine might be an emanation of Eugene Sue or Paul de Kock." Whitman was "charitable enough to suppose that our visit was not made during the time appointed for devotional reading." He professed to envy the volunteers the "nutritious dish, pork and beans," that a number of women, probably wives, were preparing in "seething cauldrons, erected upon primitive furnaces, built of loose stones, near the water's edge." Colonel Stevenson, commander of the regiment, was present to supervise the first monthly payday of his men—seven dollars each. On 29 August the *Eagle* recorded another visit to the California volunteers and rhapsodized upon the theme of great new states along the Pacific coast. On 26 September Whitman watched the squadron of ships carrying the volunteers down the bay and wished them "success in all their 'good intents'!"

One of the main New York waterfront streets was South street where the rigging of the prows of the merchantmen overhung the seaward side of the pavement. "If anybody wants to see the activity of commercial life," said Whitman on 14 March 1846, "let him take a walk along South street, in New York, just at this time, and observe the shipping. Crowds of stevedores and laborers are constantly engaged in loading and unloading the vessels. Cartmen bring loads, and carry loads away, so thickly that the wharves are blocked up, and passengers are frequently impeded in crossing the street for ten or fifteen minutes." On occasional Sunday afternoons Whitman "sauntered" (a favorite word with him) along South street looking at the shipping and talking with crewmen. On 9 March 1846, under the heading of "An Hour Among the Shipping," the *Eagle* reported: "We spent an hour or two yesterday afternoon, sauntering along South street . . . and 'boarding' some of the lately arrived packet ships. The gales . . . since the middle of January, have detained more vessels, and raised anticipations of more marine disasters, than ever before in the same space of time." One of the battered vessels along South street especially attracted his attention.

> The *Roscius* was really a pitiful sight. Just before her last voyage, we had noticed and admired this beautiful and favorite packet—and the contrast presented by her present appearance, with her appearance then . . . puts one in mind of a dripping, half-drowned Chanticleer. . . . One of the crew told us she had been carried by contrary breezes over four hundred miles to the south; which . . . thawed the frozen ropes and rigging, previously encrusted in ice.

A week later, Whitman took a "Stroll Along South Street." "Some idea," he remarked, "may be formed of the swarming state of the wharves when we mention that there are between sixteen and twenty Mobile and New Orleans packets to sail today! Other ports 'in proportion.' " Then he described his Sunday stroll.

> We noticed as we sauntered along, that fully four-fifths of the vessels had more or less of their sails spread to dry. This gave the crowded shore somewhat the appearance of an immense fleet, under sail. Moreover, though it was the Sabbath, many of the crews were at work . . . The late storms . . . have turned every thing topsy turvy . . .
>
> The poor *Roscius!* She has her masts clipped, her spars cut away. . . . We promise, however, that she gets as smart as any of her sisters in less than a fortnight!
>
> About that part of South street, near the Battery, is the great rendezvous for the flour trade, the canal boats, grain,

and so on. You will observe divers sloops and schooners, of a dirty green, with such information as this chalked on an old slab of board and hung up conspicuously:

> "Jersey Corn,
> Canal Oats, and
> Ship Stuff."

About the same neighborhood may be noticed some of the largest kind of freight barges—such as the *Indiana,* now lying at Old Slip. It would almost seem as though the capacious paunch of such a boat could bring down enough pork and flour to supply all New York! Yet, during the "session" of the canals, scores and scores of such barges may be sometimes seen there, all at once, within a few rods of one another —some coming in deeply laden, and others taking in return freight.

At 11 o'clock the *John R. Skiddy,* a Liverpool packet, hauled in near Fulton ferry, her decks covered with emigrants. We felt glad, on their account too, that the day was so fine, and that their "first impressions," of the strange land they had chosen for their home, might thus be brightened with sunshine and clear mild air. They were a robust good looking set, mostly Hibernians; and, spite of Nativism, we sent them a hearty welcome to our republic, and a wish that they might indeed find "better times acoming!"

The *John R. Skiddy* docked near the New York terminal of the Fulton ferry, whereby, it may be assumed, many of her Irish passengers made their way to the large Irish colony in Brooklyn. The ferries, according to Whitman, best served as an escape from an oppressive New York to a "delicious" Brooklyn. On 9 July 1846 the *Eagle* retorted to the *New York Express's* description of Brooklyn as a city of pigs and dirt (New York had its share of the same): "We confess the pigs; but as to the dirt, we have hardly any at all except what comes from New York— brought on the heels of the thousands who so eagerly rush over our ferries, out of that stifling place, to enjoy *our* delicious goodness here."

One inevitably associates ferries with Whitman, and they were indeed precisely a passion with him, as he says in "My Passion for Ferries" (*Specimen Days*):

Living in Brooklyn or New York city from this time [1841] forward, my life, then, and still more the following years, was curiously identified with Fulton ferry, already becoming the greatest of its sort in the world for general importance, volume, variety, rapidity, and picturesqueness. Almost daily . . . I crossed on the boats, often up in the pilot-houses where I could get a full sweep, absorbing shows, accompaniments, surroundings. . . . Indeed, I have always had a passion for ferries; to me they afford inimitable, streaming, never-failing, living poems.

The Brooklyn ferries were often mentioned in the *Eagle*, and on 13 August 1847 Whitman devoted an editorial to the "Philosophy of Ferries."[39] "Our Brooklyn ferries," he said, "teach some sage lessons in philosophy, gentle reader . . . whether you ever knew it or not." The ferry functioned like destiny.

Passionless and fixed, at the six-stroke the boats come in; and at the three-stroke, succeeded by a single tap, they depart again, with the steadiness of nature herself. Perhaps a man, prompted by . . . delirium tremens, has jumped over-board and been drowned: still the trips go on as before. Perhaps some one has been crushed between the landing and the prow . . . still, no matter, for the great business of the mass must be helped forward as before.

The mad rush of people to catch a departing ferry or to dash off an incoming ferry before it was securely tied up was to Whitman illustrative of the American trait of hurry in all things. "If the trait is remembered down to posterity," Whitman told his readers, "and put in the annals, it will be bad for us."

On the Brooklyn side of the Fulton ferry was a sign warning passengers not to leave the boat until it had been made fast. Fatal accidents sometimes happened to over-anxious patrons of the ferry. One of Whitman's secondings of the ferry company's pleas for safety is the following, which appeared in the *Eagle* on 17 July 1847:

Some of the New York papers continue their ridiculous tirades against the Union ferry company for keeping the chains up to prevent people from falling overboard. We think the company are the best abused body of men in this country.

> First they are anathematised for not having safeguards for passengers; but the moment they provide the chains they are abused for putting up traps which trip people overboard. It makes no difference whether a man jumps overboard in the middle of the river, or whether he plumps into the dock while leaping several rods after a boat, the company are represented to be wilful murderers, and harborers of malicious designs against every passenger who goes on board of their boats.

Whitman ironically advised his readers that the ferry company had decided to padlock each passenger to a "stout dog chain" attached to the side of the cabin; in the event any passenger broke his chain and fell overboard, "the pilot is to be directed to vacate his post, and the management of the boat delivered up to sixteen of the most vociferous of the passengers, who are always wiser on these occasions than any pilot can possibly be." It was hoped that eventually no crews would be necessary on the ferries.

When Whitman witnessed a ferry passenger going overboard (he had an excellent view of the ferry slip from his editorial window at 30 Fulton street), he often recorded the event in the *Eagle* and in a generally humorous way, as on 21 October 1847.

> UNFORTUNATE.—A colored Adonis attempted to leave the ferry boat Montauk night before last, before being "made fast to the bridge," missed his footing and liked to have gone to Davy Jones' locker. After swallowing a quart of the east river . . . he crawled out in a highly saturated condition, entirely fire proof for the time being, and made rapid tracks for home —unknown, unhonored, but not unsung.

But once (24 June 1846), perhaps because the accident occurred on the New York side of the ferry, Whitman was indignant—but not at the carelessness of the unfortunate victim.

> APATHY OF A CROWD, IN CASES OF INDIVIDUAL DISTRESS.— A poor strawberry woman, coming over to Brooklyn from New York, accidentally fell into the ferry dock, on the latter side, yesterday afternoon about four o'clock. She was . . . extricated without any serious damage, farther than the fright, the cold bath, and a slight contusion of her hand.—The poor creature, being lifted safely on terra firma, thanked God, and

sat herself down—thoroughly exhausted, of course—to dry in the sun. Then saw we a practical exemplification of a crowd's heartlessness. At least a hundred well dressed people surrounded the dripping woman—people, doubtless, with five dollar bills in their pockets—and not a soul offered the least assistance! For a while, even not a word of kindness! A lot of mere "stupid starers," stood they; though at last one person, enquiring her residence, was leading her to a carriage, to be transferred home—when a young gentleman (for so he *is*), attached to the Ferry establishment, relieved him of the duty by taking charge of the woman himself, and promising to have her conveyed to her domicile in Cherry st.

Whitman at last came up with a solution for the problem of deterring passengers from wantonly leaping off and on the ferry boats. On 31 August 1847 the *Eagle* noted, under the heading "An Anecdote With a Moral," that on the preceding night at the New York Fulton ferry slip, a hurried gentleman jumped ashore, as he thought, but landed in the water between the dock and the moving prow of the ferry. He managed to scramble up the dock in time. This account merely was Whitman's prelude to his "anecdote with a moral": the tale of the fourteen-year-old son of "an acquaintance of ours" who attended school in New York and commuted on the South ferry. It was the boy's practice to try to be first on and first off the boat. His mother remonstrated with him, but to no avail. At last she "prepared a pretty vivid drawing, with plenty of red blood about it—laying the scene thereof at the ferry landing, and making a crowd of people just stand aside enough to afford a view of a mangled body, and a pale face bending over the same." This drawing was shown to the boy each morning as he left for school. "He is now thoroughly 'reformed,' " reported Whitman. Then he suggested that the Union Ferry Company "get a few paintings— (they can take the subject from life, at their own wharves, if they wait a little)—of mutilated human trunks, with the gore trickling from the same—all caused by the rash haste to save a few seconds . . . and . . . put these pictures up so that everybody on board will be likely to see them. They will be useful . . . if not ornamental."

50

The *Eagle* conducted a lesser crusade against smoking on ferries. On 17 April 1846 Whitman had "A Word to the Fulton Ferry Company," which echoed the criticisms of Mrs Trollope, Dickens, and many other visitors to America.

> Nineteen-twentieths of the persons who cross your ferry are annoyed, sickened, and disgusted, by the tobacco smokers and spitters who form the other twentieth. As to the spitters, there is perhaps no deliverance from them—but the smokers (who are the worst) should be stopped altogether. No person ought to be allowed on the boats, at all, smoking a cigar.

Nevertheless, Whitman came to the defense of his favorite ferry when the *New York Express* alleged that on the Fulton ferry "loafers were allowed to smoke in the ladies' cabin without remonstrance." Whitman asserted on 6 May 1846, "Every one who knows anything at all about the ferry in question knows this to be false. Our contemporary should be careful about publishing ill natured rumors against *the* best conducted ferry in the world." But from time to time the *Eagle* continued to print indignant little squibs against smoking on ferries, with its special anathema reserved for men who, selfishly indulging themselves, smoked their cigars while standing at the open end of the ladies' cabin.

Whitman championed the ladies in another matter connected with the ferries—that of fares. On 14 May 1846 he noted that a large number of young working women commuted daily to New York and back on the Fulton ferry. Since many of them supported aged parents or younger brothers and sisters, the ten dollar yearly rate for ferriage was a burden. "We are refreshed every day by the sight of their pleasant faces blooming with health and intelligence," said Whitman, "and if *we* were the toll taker, we couldn't have the face to charge them any thing more than a look into their bright eyes." He suggested that the annual rate for women be reduced to five dollars and asked, with wretched syntax, the Union Ferry Company (which owned the South ferry and had recently acquired the Fulton ferry), "Will you act as we suggest, forthwith, and gain the gratitude of those, one kind look from whose faces, there is hardly any thing *we* wouldn't do for?" Whitman suggested from time to time that the ferry company reduce its rates for all passengers, especially urging that the two-cent charge for foot passengers be lowered to one cent (which was finally done in 1850). However, he did not consider the ferry company extortionate. The following appeared in the *Eagle* on 12 March 1847:

> Every time we pass over the Fulton ferry we cannot help being struck with the very great change and improvement which have taken place since the present company assumed the charge. . . . passengers are now quietly propelled across the East river, while seated in apartments combining all the substantial comforts in the most splendidly appointed parlor. And for these advantages we are all indebted to the desire of the present ferry company to subserve the interests of the public instead of their own purses.

In the fall of 1846 the Union Ferry Company acquired a new boat, the *Montauk*, for the Fulton ferry. Whitman attended the christening excursion of the vessel on 1 October and duly reported it the next day. The *Montauk* with Granger's Brooklyn Band, which "greatly astonished the porpoises who rolled about in great delight at the fine music," had sailed down the bay to the Narrows and back again to Brooklyn. The "gay party" of two hundred ladies and gentlemen "whirled away the time in conversation, or amused themselves in looking at the pretty gothic cottages on Long and Staten Island"; and finally all joined in an oyster feast.

In the following year, the *Wyandank* was added to the Fulton ferry's fleet. Her maiden trip across the East River added to the color of the scene outside the editorial windows of the *Eagle* on the morning of 19 April 1847.

> There is a great rush this morning among passengers to make their trip across the river in the Wyandank. On their approach to the ferry, the moment they catch a glimpse of her new tints, streamers and flags, presto! away they go, pell mell . . . running down all the smaller specimens of humanity on the road, over applestands, carts, and carmen, until they bring up safely by a perilous leap on the deck of the new boat.

52

The readers of the *Eagle* were often reminded of the nearness of the Fulton ferry's landing to the newspaper's office. If Whitman commented on a foggy morning, he was almost certain to mention the constant ringing of the bells on the ferry landing to guide the boats in. Persons running past No. 30 Fulton street in the morning to catch a boat were often ridiculed that afternoon in the *Eagle*. Occasionally the passengers moving to and from the ferry landing inspired bits of whimsy, as on 3 December 1847: "UMBRELLAS.—From our 'loop hole of retreat,' we see nothing, this morning, but a vast mass of moving umbrellas. It looks funny . . . to see the umbrellas rushing down to the ferry, and up too, without a squint at those concealed under them."

Not only the ferries but also the river steamers running from New York to Albany furnished copy for the *Eagle*. Such copy, however, was taken from exchange papers, for Whitman does not appear to have taken the trip up the Hudson during his stay on the *Eagle*. He did, nevertheless, attend the housewarming of a new river steamer, the account of which he turned into a humorous comment on the bibulous habits of his Brooklyn peers.[40] The *Eagle* noted on 10 April 1847 that "in the handsome saloon of the *Roger Williams*, at the foot of Warren st. N. Y. was collected yesterday afternoon, a merry gathering enough." Among those invited to the celebration by Captain De Groot was "a party from Brooklyn, including our humble selves." Whitman continued:

> All was life and jollity. We *thought* we observed in a distant part of the room, a pretty considerable quantity of bottles, and champaign glasses—and heard a strange pop! pop! pop! continued without any intermission all the while we were there. Indeed, when we come to remember the looks of a portion of the party, and get their testimony this morning, we shouldn't wonder if there were wine, *some*—and the tallest nicest sort. We understand that two representatives of the press of Brooklyn—not democratic—had to be left in charge of Captain De G.

Ocean-going steamers also came in for their share of notice in the *Eagle*, though the citizens of Brooklyn no longer were excited by their sight. On 25 October 1847 the *Eagle* remarked that the French steamer *Missouri* had passed down the East River that day at noon on her outward voyage. "These large steamers attract little more attention now than our ferry boats," Whitman commented. "Four or five years since the town was all agog and the shores lined with anxious spectators whenever one arrived or departed. Steam navigation has made a monstrous stride within the time above mentioned." Whitman himself was an interested spectator of the shipping which could be seen from the Brooklyn docks or from the ferries as they crossed the East River. Usually his comments on these ships were brief descriptions such as this one on 10 November 1846: "The new ship, the New World, has been enlivening the river off against our shores this morning . . . with the sonorous 'heave-eo!' of a gang of sailors, &c., hoisting her anchor. She is a huge sea-monster—and not deficient in grace and beauty, withal."

Though as a rule Whitman found something which pleased him in each ship he saw in the Brooklyn waters, on one occasion (29 May 1846) the British steamer *Great Britain* aroused his total disapproval.

> The great interminable length of this gigantic monster came crawling up the bay just before eleven o'clock this morning, in her usual sulky style . . . Her decks were covered with people; and we noticed that her number of masts were minus one—having now but five . . . What a ponderous looking creature she is! . . . Vastness, heaviness, unwieldliness are the peculiar attributes of this monster vessel. As she drew her dark stretch of hull along our Brooklyn shores this morning, we thought of sea-serpents, hippopotami, and such like interesting specimens of marine life. The smoke from her mighty pipes blackens her rigging and every thing about her—makes her very flags look singed . . .
>
> Talking of the Great Britain's flags, we observe a somewhat singular custom her commander had this morning—and on her previous passage, too—of quartering a little bit of American stripes on the same piece of bunting which has the English ensign *over* them, and flying the whole in one flag at the peak! . . . It smacks a trifle of cool impudence—and we see no reason why the captain of this craft, big as it is, should amuse himself at our expense. It is somewhat the more singu-

lar when we observe that a large beautiful Union Jack was
flying at the stern of the steamer. There were plenty of masts
also to run up the Star Spangled banner—which has been
borne over prouder worthier decks than this smoking looking concern, we wot!

Whitman could have mentioned that the impudent English captain would soon discover that Americans could build great ocean
steamers too, for the *Eagle* had remarked on 10 March 1846:
"AHEAD OF THE WORLD!—Quite a public interest is felt in the
construction of the new ocean steamers lately contracted for by
the government. It is the ambition of the builders that they shall
be as much ahead of all previous steamers in the world, as American ingenuity is ahead of that of other nations." On 30 January
1847, as has been noted, Whitman witnessed the launching of
the first of these steamers, the *Washington*, the United States'
first transatlantic steamship.

Probably Whitman gazed censoriously at the *Great Britain*
from the dock of the Fulton ferry at the foot of Fulton street,
Brooklyn's principal business thoroughfare. The foot of Fulton
street was the focal point of the city since its ferry was the largest
and most patronised of all the local ferries; and for the editor of
the *Eagle* its interest was enhanced because his office windows
looked out upon it. Whitman commented on this location on 4
June 1846 in an editorial, "Fulton Street, Brooklyn." There were
a number of new four-story brick buildings on the right as one
came up from the ferry. "One of the first that strikes you, coming
up from the boat," he said, "is the '*Eagle Building*,' the domicile
of this veracious print, and all that it inherit." Earlier, on 6 May
Whitman had written a long editorial on "The Foot of Fulton
Street," which began with childhood reminiscences of that lo-
cality.

Of all the busy scenes to be met with in this busy country—
scenes which place it beyond the power of a foreigner to deny
that we are the "tarnalest" nation in the world, for energy and
activity—we have yet observed none that go beyond the foot
of Fulton street, Brooklyn. We well remember this spot, a few
years ago—how much narrower it was than now, and how
the Old Long Island stage houses ranged sleepily on each

side, with the look of portly country farmers, well to do in the world, but not caring much for appearances. We remember Coe Downing's huge sign stretching over the side-walk (there were no laws against "obstructions," then), inscribed with the names of all the places on Long Island—half of them decent christian terms from the Bible, and the other half heathenish words, such as Quogue, Hopaug, Speonk, and so on. By the by, what has become of that old sign? Capt Basil Hall copied it verbatim and literatim in his book of American travels [*Travels in North America* 1829]; and if we had on this island a museum sacred to the relics of our own territory and people, *that* would be worthy a place by no means the least conspicuous in the show.

We remember Old Mr Langdon, as he used to sit in his gouty chair (we don't mean that the *chair* had the gout), and what a marvellous piece of mechanism it seemed to us, wherewith he moved the said chair by turning a little twisted handle. We remember how the marketmen used to come jogging along (by no means on the locomotive principle of the present time) in their canvass covered wagons painted with lamp-black, the smell of which made us sick. There was Smith & Wood's old tavern, too, with its snug bar in the corner, and the queer cast-iron stove set in the wall, so as to throw its heat in two rooms at the same time—and the high wooden press of the public room, in which the farmers hung their stout homespun overcoats, their whips, &c., all without fear of theft, for the world was more honest in those days.[41] Oh, that race of jogging country-stage men has pretty much passed away! We see one of them at rare intervals, in a wagon of the old sort, but somehow *he* has not the old sturdy comfortable look. He has no one to keep him in countenance: the Long Island Railroad has quelled the glory of his calling.

Whitman remembered, too, when the ferries were powered by horses and he was "lifted up to the ocular demonstration thereof, by a pair of parental arms." The old ferry house only recently had been supplanted by a new one, and several of the persons employed there still looked just as they had in 1830.

But the foot of Fulton street, *now*, presents a very different scene. In the morning, there is one incessant stream of people —clerks, merchants, and persons employed in New York on business—tending toward the ferry. This rush commences soon after six o'clock, and continues till nine—being at its climax about a quarter after seven. It is highly edifying to see the phrenzy exhibited by certain portions of the younger gentlemen, a few rods from the landing, when the bell strikes three, the premonitory of the single stroke that sends the boat off. They rush forward as if for dear life, and wo to the fat woman or unwieldy person of any kind, who stands in their way! How astonishing it is that they do not remember them of another boat, to start right off, in less than five minutes!

"Several handsome lines of omnibusses" ran from the foot of Fulton street to the outskirts of Brooklyn, as did a number of stage lines to nearby villages despite the Long Island Railroad.

There are divers old fashioned folk, ancient ladies and those under their charge, who cannot get out of their minds a dim connection between the steam-engine and Sathanus—who eschew modern innovations and wish to be taken in Christian style, by the aid of horses' legs, to the very door of their destination. These keep up a patronage of the stages; and indeed, of a pleasant un-dusty day, when the rate of peregrination is not *too* slow, we ourselves never find it amiss to traverse this beautiful Island in the same manner—prefer it, even, to the whizz and whisking of a locomotive.

The morning of 27 May 1846 found Whitman unprepared for his lead editorial, so he looked out his window at the foot of Fulton street and wrote what he aptly called "Some Afternoon Gossip."

The war excitement which swallows up everything else, makes dull times, notwithstanding, during the intervals.—It is like the appearance of a great actor, half the week: all the "off nights" are heavy, and the players mouth it to empty benches. When we have nothing to tell from the southwest, we hardly know what to make our "leader" of. . . .

The violent storm of last night has subsided into a perpetual dripping chilly rain—this morning, dark and dreary . . . Talking of rains, the scenes presented at the lower part of Fulton street, on the coming up of a sudden heavy shower, it is curious to see. To say nothing of the ordinary hurry-skurry of pedestrians, the alarm of fat men, aged matrons, and gossamer dressed virgins, the *street* is then a truly "interesting spectacle." It is changed into . . . a very respectable river.

> The tide . . . bears trophies on its swelling but somewhat dirty breast, viz., stray boards, fruit from surprised apple-stands, dead cats, and so on.

Perhaps Whitman should have given Swift and his "Description of a City Shower" some credit for the above picture; but gutters and their contents had changed very little in many American cities from the gutters and said contents of the London of the early 1700s. But, to return to "Some Afternoon Gossip," had the morning been clear, said Whitman, instead of dark and rainy, then the foot of Fulton street would have presented a scene of confusion almost equal to the "equestrian pandemonium" seen there on race day.

> A race day on Long Island—and a great race day withal! No other spot, perhaps, can give just exactly such a spectacle, as Fulton street, then—particularly at the foot of it. Crowding over the ferry from the very earliest day-dawn, come vehicles of every supposable description, and some that are not supposable . . . Then may you see the "b-oys" in all their glory. Then the exstatic lessee of a "three-minuter," cometh and goeth rejoicing on his way—the envy of all more luckless wights. Then flaunts vice: then prepares temptation its damnable gambling wiles: then reckon the sons of darkness how many simple ones they may delude into their grasp.

The rain still pattered against Whitman's office window as he gossiped to his readers; the rain drops reminded him of cold water and the temperance movement, but he fancied that even temperance reformers failed to appreciate the full merits of pure water. " 'In heaven,' says he whose grave is now verdant in Greenwood, poor McDonald Clarke, once said to us, 'In heaven we shall find plenty of flowers, of little children, fine air, and pure water.' "[42] Pure water, fresh or salt, was a blessing here on earth to the editor of the *Eagle*, who reminded his readers of the delights of bathing. Then he closed his rambling essay on a note of sentimental pathos.

> The rain having "suspended" a while, we observe . . . four ragged boys and one gentleman whose forefathers ate plantain in Africa—the said boys and gentleman profoundly

wrapt in some deep inquiry, with down-cast eyes and slow-dragging steps, promenading in the very middle of the street. Poor creatures! they are in hopes the flood has swept down some little trifle, which they may find in the gutter.

The foot of Fulton street was at times the setting of tragic sights other than that of five indigents searching the gutters. Items such as the following (11 June 1846) were frequent in the *Eagle:*

> RECOVERED.—The body of the boy John Wallen, who was drowned near Fulton ferry on Friday last . . . was yesterday discovered by Pat'k Lynch, a lighterman, floating about a quarter of a mile from the wharf at the foot of Dock street.

Not remarkably, most of the persons drowned along the Brooklyn shore were boys. On 5 June 1846, in "Accidental Sudden Deaths," Whitman dwelt mostly on drownings, particularly of young boys. "The most touching part of Hamlet (the most touching play ever written) is," he said, "the sequence that comes after the drowning of Ophelia, and the description of that hapless accident. What a world of agony . . . is there in the two little words, 'Drowned! drowned!'" He noted that now was the beginning of that season when deaths by drowning were usual occurrences: "Boys roam down to the docks to bathe . . . they venture . . . out to a distance in the river, or emulate their companions in diving . . . Many a death occurs in consequence of their boyish rivalry. The proper place for boys to swim is the bath," such as Whitman's favorite, Gray's Bath near the foot of Fulton. Whitman imagined a mother whose spirited young boy was late in returning home; "A knock is heard at the door." The knock, of course, was the omen of the news that immediately followed—her son was drowned. And the mother's grief was pictured with that sentimentality which pleased the readers of the time.

By a peculiar coincidence (as the *Eagle* reported the next day) Whitman witnessed on the very evening of the day that "Accidental Sudden Deaths" appeared in his paper, the emotions of a father and mother whose son had been drowned—of the parents, indeed, of John Wallen, whose body was to be found five days later by Patrick Lynch, lighterman.

"A BOY DROWNED!" was the answer given to our inquiry
about a large crowd rapidly gathering at the dock, just south
of Fulton ferry, at five o'clock yesterday afternoon. We moved
with the current to the spot. There they were, peering over
the great beam that borders the wharf—some few with a
little excitement . . . but most of the crowd in that singular
state of apathy which masses of men will sometimes exhibit,
when collected together on such business.

Whitman was surprised to learn that nothing had been done to
recover the body at once. The boy's cap lay on the dock—he
had been fishing with some other children, who ran away when
he fell in the water—and it was not certain who he was. There
was considerable alarm in the neighborhood among those parents
who had small sons, but it was soon discovered that the boy
drowned was "an Irish lad of nine or ten years, named Wallen."

Presently his father, a stalwart young Irishman, came along.
It was pitiable to see his tears and wailing when he took the
little cap! That was *fatal proof* enough. Great drops gathered
on his forehead—and he wept and wrung his hands, and
acted like an insane man. But his grief was nothing compared
with the mother's; for presently she came down too. Poor
thing! our pen could do little justice to the scene, as far as she
is concerned; and besides a mother's sorrow is something
almost too sacred for idle description. We noticed when we
returned to the spot half an hour afterwards, that the *man*
had become comparatively calm again: but the mother had
been carried home under the exhausting agony of sorrow that
would not be comforted.

"It was melancholy (many might have beheld only the ludicrous
points in the picture, but we could not do so)," said Whitman, "to
see the number of women who gathered so quickly there—each
apprehensive of some danger to *her* little boy." As he had gone
toward the crowd on the dock, he had seen a "withered, aged
dame" hobbling as fast as she could toward the wharf, "her
wrinkled face moist with agitation." The next instant, she was in
the midst of the crowd. "Immortal beauty of woman's affection!"
exclaimed Whitman, "how it outlasts the green and very autumn
of life! how it ennobles the commonest characters, and makes
graceful things which would otherwise be rude!" "*When it was*

too late," some boat hooks were gotten. "It was not entirely un-singular," he mused, "that at the very time that article ["Accidental Sudden Deaths"] was being distributed among our readers, the grief we depicted as filling a parent's mind at the sudden accidental death of a beloved child, we were called upon to see in one of the most affecting phases of development." In conclusion, Whitman blamed the many Brooklyn drownings on the failure of spectators to rescue drowned persons as quickly as possible and to apply proper methods of resuscitation. Among other things, he suggested that "a moderately persevered in attempt to inflate the lungs with a bellows inserted mildly in the mouth frequently produces a good effect."

One of the most eventful sights at the foot of Fulton street during Whitman's editorship of the *Eagle* was the arrival of President Polk on the Fulton ferry on 26 June 1847, for an hour's visit in Brooklyn—a visit duly reported by the *Eagle* on that date under the heading, "The President in Brooklyn." Before nine o'clock a large crowd had gathered at the foot of Fulton street, including "the city Guard, spirited little companies of firemen in uniform, with a corps of mounted dragoons, all with bands of music." Under a subhead reading "One O'Clock.—Arrival of the President at Brooklyn," Whitman wrote:

> The president has arrived at the Fulton ferry.—His passage over the river was announced by the thunder of cannon; and his appearance on shore, after landing from the boat, was hailed by the most vociferous cheers from the assembled multitude.—The president's passage through the dense mass of persons was impeded by the great concourse—hundreds of citizens crowding to the carriage where he was, to grasp his hand, or speak to him. He stood erect, and bowed to the people as he passed. The story in some of the whig prints that he looks jaded and bowed down with care, is all bosh . . . His eye, particularly, is full of fire and vigor—and we liked well his massive intellectual-looking face. It is traced with his high responsibility, of course—but, to our mind, has every evidence of both bodily and mental health. To the ladies— who were in every window—he bowed with marked courtesy.

Polk rode several blocks up Fulton to a point opposite the carriage of the Whig mayor of Brooklyn, where both gentlemen

61

made brief speeches. Whitman was unable to hear the mayor, "partly from the low voice" in which he spoke. Polk "happily" alluded to Washington and the Battle of Long Island. "The elocution of Mr Polk is hearty and clear," stated Whitman. At two o'clock the President returned to the ferry and steamed back to New York. "Our Brooklyn military, and the firemen, looked fine, and marched superbly."

The trees had gone from the lower end of the busy street up which President Polk had ridden, but at its upper end, and over most of Brooklyn, they were flourishing; and Whitman championed their preservation. On 4 June 1846, in "Fulton Street, Brooklyn," the editor of the *Eagle* gave his readers an inventory of the business places which lined the street. He noted that an old residence on upper Fulton was being removed to make way for several stores and the new home of the Brooklyn Savings Bank, and he hoped the proprietors of the bank would "preserve those beautiful trees from the least harm. We shall be very, *very* sorry indeed to notice that the building is allowed to encroach upon them, trunk or limb. The beauty of Brooklyn is in its trees." Slightly more than a month later, on 11 July Whitman recorded the death of the trees on the site of the new bank.

> BROOKLYN TREES.—The beautiful large trees that stood so long on Dr Hunt's old place, corner of Concord and Fulton streets, were cut down the other day, to gain a few inches more room, to build brick and lime walls on. Now, though we hold to as little intermeddling as possible, by the press, with "private rights," we pity and denounce this work of death. Why didn't they let the trees stand—and build their fine edifice a few feet farther in?
>
> We remember those beautiful trees from our childhood up. One of them was indeed a beauty—the great horse-chestnut, with its magnificent bulge of verdure . . .
>
> But a few years ago there was also a splendid row of towering elms on the opposite side of Fulton street, from James B. Clarke's old place, up to Clinton street. One or two yet stand in front of the Rev Mr Jacobus's church; but all the rest have been *slaughtered.*
>
> It is perhaps expecting too much of those who new-come or new-buy in Brooklyn, that they should look upon such things with the regard of love and sorrow. *They* never played

under them in childhood. *They* don't remember them, identified with many a boyish spree, and merry game. . . . But new-comers and speculators might at least have their eyes open to the *highest profits:* for, even by that sovereign rule, it is better to preserve the good looks of Brooklyn. . . . We have for a long time observed this practice of cutting down fine trees, to gain sometimes twenty inches of room! In the name of both the past and the future, we protest it!

Whitman advocated positive countermeasures against this arboreal slaughter. Time and time again his newspaper urged the planting of trees in those sections of the city in which expanding construction was especially destructive of trees. But despite all the building and chopping, Brooklyn remained a city of trees, as witness the *Eagle* on 3 May 1847.

How Brooklyn Will Look, Soon.—Already, this beautiful morning, the horse-chestnuts have burst out their bright green leaves—the peach trees and the early cherries are in bloom—the lilacs have donned their umbrage—and the moist fresh grass is thick enough, wherever the earth will allow it to grow in any fertility! Yes; spring is at her maturity, and will soon yield to the more warm-breathed summer. Then Brooklyn will be in its pride and glory. Then in all the blocks between Fulton street and the heights, will lie a dreamy shady quiet, under the trees that line the walks there, and through the ample yards. Then Brooklyn will have its green robes about its shoulders, and its skirts will be not a little draggled with the wet dews when it walks out in the morning.

The various seasons of the year were so amply reported in the *Eagle* that it would not be difficult to prepare from its pages a general weather almanac ranging over the two years of Whitman's editorship. Of the seasons, spring and autumn were Whitman's favorites. Winter days pleased him when they were mild enough for such saunterings as those he took along South street in New York in January 1847; but wintry days ordinarily led him to write brief paragraphs about heavy clothing, blue noses, and tearful eyes. His references to the sound of sleigh bells in the streets and to omnibusses temporarily on runners were lacking in any sort of enthusiasm. Winter had its nuisances. On 7 March 1846 Whitman wrote: "The practice of boys sledding down the declivities on the sidewalks is a general and abominable nuisance. The easiest way to abate it is to sprinkle ashes where there is ice, and we advise all not to be very economical thereof." Winter in Brooklyn was not the season for those who enjoyed their pedestrianism. And winter scenes are rare in *Leaves of Grass*. Autumn, on the contrary, invoked such paeans as this, which appeared in the *Eagle* on 9 October 1846:

> OUR CHARMING WEATHER continues yet! Both the days and nights are beautiful exceedingly—the days with their brilliant freshness and elasticity, and the nights with their clear shining full moon, and the moistness in the air. It is hard to drudge at one's work these sweet autumn times—much harder, of course, than when the sharp frosty air we are going to have surrounds every thing that is not housed.—We therefore take the liberty of advising the gentle reader . . . to steal away a day or two—or a few hours at least—now while the Heavens invite him (or her) and commune with what he will see outside of cities. We advise the ennuyee, the dyspeptic, the sour man, the grumbler, the dawdling lady too, to go forth in the neighborhood of trees and where nothing intercepts the broad view of the sky up above; go to the outer wards of Brooklyn, to farther East Brooklyn, to Greenwood, to Flatbush—to Hoboken, or Staten Island—and inflate the lungs with the purest of air, once in your life at least!

Spring as well as autumn invoked paeans. On 9 March 1846, two days after its having denounced the practice of boys sledding on the sidewalks, the *Eagle* showed a better humor with the world.

> APPROACH OF SPRING.—Yesterday was a sweet day; and though the "going" was bad enough, nearly every body who could get out, walked into the open air to enjoy its warmth and freshness. The arrival of a fleet of long due vessels . . . and the lifting up of the ice-finger that has been chilling us so much of late—combined with the spring-like beauty of the day—contributed to infuse among the community an unusual exhilaration and cheerfulness. Welcome, loveliest of seasons—young Spring! Your birds will soon be "singing blithe and gay," for even now the signs all around (except the dirty snow—but that is fast melting away) prove that you are indeed "coming, coming!"

And spring came in 1846, and again in 1847, with the editor of the *Eagle* reminding his readers from time to time of the beauty of Brooklyn and Long Island in that season.

But with July came the oppressive heat of the city (though Whitman often spoke of Brooklyn as a veritable summer resort compared with New York and its heat), and Whitman recorded in the *Eagle* the departure of his fellow Brooklynites for cooler regions. On 5 August 1846 he noted that "yesterday the City Guard evacuated the place; and this morning that numerous body, the Daughters of Temperance departed for up the river, and the first detachment of the numerous Fire Island party 'put out' for their cool destination." As one who could not leave the city, Whitman found solace in the occasional cool mornings, as on 13 July 1846: "THIS MORNING the air is grateful again! What a relief to the sweltering city! . . . The frolicsome wind comes coolly over the Heights this morning . . . How blessed is the wind!" More often Whitman's comments on summer weather had the tenor of the following from the *Eagle*, 14 August 1846:

> THE HOT DAYS are again upon us. The air is dry and feverish, and the glaring sun comes down *so* spitefully at one! It is not so much the warmth, perhaps, but the glare, which makes this August atmosphere almost unsupportable.....How lurid the sun was, when he went down last night! We watched him from the Fulton ferry as he hung like a great red ball over the roofs of Gomorrah on the other side of the river . . . like one of the play demons, on the Chatham stage (in pieces which, to please one pit, represents another, whereof the denizens of the first may perhaps know one day somewhat nearer), with eyes of fiery crimson glass.

But warm weather brought variety to the scene, as Whitman noted on 4 June 1846. "The present weather brought the woollen and flannel trade to an abrupt termination. There is a regular forest of white pants passing along opposite to our office."

Other areas of Brooklyn than Fulton street were perambulated by the *Eagle's* editor—regardless of the season. Usually Whitman's observations centered on the evidences of Brooklyn's rapid growth—an obvious matter for comment, since Brooklyn almost doubled in size during the two years he was with the

Eagle. On 14 September 1847, in a paragraphed headed "Residence in Brooklyn," he remarked that "blocks of splendid dwellings have sprung up in every direction, as by magic; and large private residences, almost palaces; and commodious houses for the 'bone and sinew' portion of the community, are met with in all parts of the city, even to the very outskirts." New York businessmen were finding it pleasant to live in Brooklyn and commute to their work.[43] In addition, other streets were becoming challengers of Fulton street's position as the principal business street of Brooklyn. One of these was Atlantic street in rapidly-growing South Brooklyn. On 28 September 1846 Whitman remarked that "passing through there [Atlantic street] on Saturday evening, we were surprised as well as gratified to witness the great amount of business done in that section of Brooklyn. From the brilliant and busy appearance of the stores and shops, we could almost imagine ourselves in Fulton street, or N. Y. Broadway." On 25 March 1847 the *Eagle* asserted of South Brooklyn: "Perhaps . . . the republic does not present a greater evidence of the go-ahead spirit of the American people than that same section of our city—joined with what may be seen at East Brooklyn."

Whitman was especially interested in a project under construction in South Brooklyn—the Atlantic dock and basin—and frequently and correctly prophesied its future commercial greatness. On 24 July 1847 he devoted an article on South Brooklyn almost entirely to a description of the piers, warehouses, grain elevators, steam engines, and railroads which had been completed at the dock to that date. Exactly a month later the Atlantic dock was still a stimulating sight.

THE GREAT WORK AT SOUTH BROOKLYN.—We have of late years seen in the newspapers and magazines a great many poems on "the sublimity of labor," and such like topics; but the most potent argument possible in that line is furnished by the Atlantic dock, still in process toward completion in South Brooklyn. We spent some hours there yesterday afternoon— and under the polite guidance of Col. Richards, as well as by our own investigations, we saw enough to make us wish to go many times again—which, indeed, will be necessary before a man can get the whole of one of the most stupendous and

uniform commercial conveniences of modern times, fairly in
the scope of understanding.

He concluded the paragraph by marvelling at the "incomprehensible process" by which grain was conveyed by "steam en-
ginery" from the vessels to the warehouses at the dock.

In North Brooklyn, Whitman sometimes visited another
shore-line installation—the Navy Yard. Here on the morning of
27 June 1846 (as he reported in that afternoon's *Eagle*) he saw
the launching of the U.S.S. *Albany*. The sloop slid into the water,
"like a duck from a pond shore, *into* said pond." Apparently
"pond" was an exact term, for the sloop was prevented by the
mud at the end of the ways from going past the end of the dock.

At intervals Whitman took his subscribers along with him
on a stroll along a particular street, minutely describing its sights.
Some streets, like Joralemon and Willoughby, were wide, shaded,
and lined with "tasty" residences, schools, and churches. But
others were a more varied and interesting spectacle because they
reflected the city's remarkable expansion. Such a street was
Myrtle avenue, which Whitman described in a long editorial on
16 August 1847. It stretched for three miles east of Fulton, and
Whitman began his promenade at its eastern end and guided his
readers to its conjunction with Fulton. At its eastern extremity
Myrtle avenue had "the appearance of a country road," and
along it were quite a number of "milk manufactories" that re-
pelled Editor Whitman because of the wagons outside them
loaded with the swill from the breweries and distilleries that
formed the staple diet of many dairy cows around Brooklyn. In
the general vicinity of these dairies, and "still coming westward,"
were large tracts of land "all properly laid out on the city map,
and the proper grade fixed, but still unoccupied by houses." The
land was laid out in lots of 25 by 100 feet, selling from $100 (or
even less) to $400; and Whitman suggested that the Brooklyn
mechanic, who paid from $100 to $150 a year rent, would do
well to buy one or two lots, build a small cottage, and so live
healthier and cheaper.

A mile from its eastern end Myrtle avenue changed from
a country road to a street "regulated, paved, lighted and *pumped*,"

67

on which, it may be assumed, were located modest new homes and "thrifty shade trees"; these at least were the features of the side streets which at this point began to intersect Myrtle and down which the editor of the *Eagle* abruptly turned with his readers. Eventually Whitman returned to Myrtle where it crossed Fort Greene, the contemplated site of Washington Park. He was instantly reminded of his fight to make the park a reality and asserted that "no one with common judgment can fail to see that stretching far and wide the streets here are, in a few years, to be filled with a dense mass of busy human beings. Shall there not be one spot to relieve the desolating aspect of *all* houses and pavement?"

Moving still farther westward on Myrtle, Whitman came upon one of the effects of the potato famine in Ireland on many northeastern American cities.

> Descending Fort Greene one comes amid a colony of squatters, whose chubby children, and the good-natured brightness of the eyes of many an Irishwoman, tell plainly enough that you are wending your way among the shanties of the Emeralders. They are permitted by the owners, here, until the ground shall be wanted, to live rent free, as far as the land is concerned. To the right, descending, you catch a view of the burying ground, Potter's field, which is seldom, this summer, without some activity going on inside its low paling; for sickness and death are rife, lately, among the poor immigrants. . . . To the left rise the brown turrets of the county prison.

Leaving the county prison behind, Whitman approached the western end of Myrtle avenue, where "all is the clattering din of traffic, turmoil, passage, and business." The street floors of the buildings on each side were occupied by "groceries, clothing and tailoring stores—dry goods, hat, boot and shoe, and book stores—places for selling tinware, wood-ware, fruit and vegetables, lace, hosiery, cabinet furniture, confectionary, watches and jewelry . . . bakeries, butchershops." However, "one . . . edifice is wanting in this three-mile st.; and that—strange to say in this 'city of churches'—is a house of public worship! . . .

68

There are a great many public houses on Myrtle avenue—but not one church."

A year earlier on 19 August 1846, Whitman had told his readers of a stroll he had taken the day before in East Brooklyn along some of the streets which intersected Myrtle avenue. He had "found surveyors marking out locations for houses . . . recent purchasers with their eyes gloating in anticipation." It made him envious, he assured his subscribers; and on his return down Myrtle he saw, at the new homes already occupied, more matter for envy.

> What an agreeable picture of domestic life is it to see a pretty wife upon the piazza, anxiously peering at intervals down the avenue in expectancy of the evening return of her husband, while the children, accompanied by the spaniel, are gambolling about it in front, ready to run and hasten the near approach of their father; while as you pass, your eye unconsciously peers in at the basement window and takes a rapid inventory of neatly arranged furniture, and a well spread board, rejoicing in all the glories of pure white china and spotless table linen. These are the incidents which make life rationally agreeable; and these we witnessed in abundance on our return.

Whether this passage expressed a sincere longing on Whitman's part or merely served as an agreeable and conventional vehicle for journalistic rhetoric is a matter for speculation.

Whitman's saunters in rural Brooklyn were almost all summer expeditions, and were, after their fashion, surrogates for the few weeks in the country or on the seashore enjoyed in that season by those less bound to the daily exercise of a business or profession than was the editor of a daily newspaper.[44] It was not Whitman's usual custom to stroll to the end of such a street as Myrtle avenue and back again. On the contrary, he combined two pleasures, as he explained on 26 August 1846.

> The East Brooklyn line of stages is among the "good things" of the age and day. After our editorial morning toils are over —weary and fagged out with them—we have no greater pleasure than to get in one of these handsome easy carriages

. . . and drive out to some of the beautiful avenues beyond Fort Greene (*are* we to have that Park?) and there alight, and walk about—stretching over the hills, and down the distant lanes—till after sunset; and then walk home with a tremendous appetite for supper, and limbs that invite sleep.

The East Brooklyn line of stages, operated by Messrs Husted and Kendall, occasionally dropped Whitman off in the afternoon at one of the gates of Greenwood Cemetery, a suburban showplace near Gowanus Bay, about four miles southwest of the Fulton ferry, on the outskirts of South Brooklyn. The *Eagle* for 13 June 1846, in "An Afternoon at Greenwood," described, in terms of conventional sentimentality, its editor's perambulations among the graves at that rustic spot. A year later on 14 June 1847, the *Eagle* again recorded an excursion to Greenwood, but this time its editor was not alone.

On Saturday afternoon last, Messrs Husted & Kendall, with a kind hearted liberality which we should be glad to see imitated, not only placed their large new omnibus "Excelsior"[45] with six horses, and another with four horses, at the service of the orphan asylum, to take the children on a ride to Greenwood cemetery—but themselves accompanied the party. At about 2 o'clock . . . we all started from the Fulton ferry—seventy blessed souls, most of them of a juvenile description . . . The big stage, and especially the six white horses attached to it, created what the writers call an "immense sensation," all along the road. Col. Spooner, gracious and talkative, was inside, at times completely hidden by a clustering mass of feminine juvenility. . . . Arrived at the cemetery, the children wandered over the beautiful grounds there to their hearts' content. We listened to the songs of the birds . . . paid our respects to the pollywogs in Sylvan water —learnt for the first time that De Witt Clinton's remains were deposited in the cemetery . . . rested awhile on the grass in the shade—and then prepared to return. . . . At Mr Husted's house, in Myrtle avenue, the vehicles stopped; and there . . . in an arbor a large table was laid with lots of delicious strawberries, cakes, lemonade, and other refreshments.

Whitman commended Messrs Husted and Kendall's generosity, "for seldom have those little people—without their natural protectors and the indulgences of a mother's love . . . seldom have they cause to know that the outer world yet remembers them so kindly!"

Jamaica, about eight or so miles east of Brooklyn, was a favorite spot with picnicking Brooklynites; and the *Eagle's* editor gave accounts of two Sunday-school picnics which he accompanied to that sylvan spot. "A Day With the Children," 25 June 1846, told of the excursion of the Sunday school of the Unitarian Church of the Saviour on the previous day. "An interesting group of some *four hundred* persons," including Whitman and a great many children, embarked on the Long Island Railroad. "On, on we sped," he reported, "for a half hour or so, after a fashion that Mazeppa's far-famed Ukraine charger might have advantageously imitated; and at length were set down in the vicinity of the pleasant, sleepy, old Dutch village of Jamaica." The party "gaily marched to the inspiring strains of the 'grand march from Norma,' " supplied by an accompanying band, to a grove.

> It would be idle to tell how each of the four hundred engaged in their different modes of spending the day . . . under the shade of trees whose graceful foliage, rustling in the gentle wind, discoursed a strange and agreeable music to the thoughtful; or follow the wandering footsteps of several groups who preferred to roam over the adjoining copses, on botanizing and geologizing excursions . . . or describe the buoyant hilarity of the innocent young hearts who devoted themselves to the various swings with which the grove was plentifully bestowed; or attempt to paint the charms of those bright eyed damsels whose een wrought so vivid an effect upon sundry young gallants; or how some saltatory exhibitions were gotten up, to the accompaniment of the "pipe and tabor," despite the vehement injunctions of sundry prudent and staid matrons.

The grand event of the day was the feasting upon fowl, ham, beef, lobster, pie, pudding, and cake. This feast was followed by speeches by two reverend gentlemen, "the drift of which was somewhat enigmatical, as bearing allusions for the most part, to some previous circumstances whereof we for one did not happen to be in the secret." After "more lounging, strolling, dancing, and swinging," the group returned home, arriving in Brooklyn at six in the evening.

A month later on 13 July, Whitman went again to Jamaica on a Sunday-school picnic, that of the Episcopal Calvary Church. Again some four hundred adults and children feasted in the same grove of trees and engaged in "rural sports." Writing an account of the picnic for the next day's *Eagle*, Whitman expressed approval of that popular institution, which had "a most valuable, moral and healthful tendency," furnished "children, teachers, parents and friends the opportunity to become better acquainted with each other," and strengthened "the attachments of the children to their school and their teachers."

Not all the picnics attended by Whitman were of the Sunday-school sort. On 14 July 1847 some sixty adult Brooklynites, ladies and gentlemen, including Whitman, rode Messrs Husted and Kendall's stages to Coney Island for a clambake. While waiting for the clams to roast, the party swam in the ocean. "The beautiful, pure, sparkling seawater!" exclaimed Whitman the next day, "one yearns to you (at least we do), with an affection as grasping as your own waves" (and I think of the opening lines of section 22 of "Song of Myself"). After the clams were eaten, "the champaigne (good stuff it was!) began to circulate," and divers healths were drunk. The eight-mile return trip to Brooklyn in the evening was pleasant because of the cool air and the odor of the new-mown hay. Whitman concluded his account of the excursion by thanking "the contractors of the new city hall! to whose generous spirit we were indebted for yesterday's pleasure."

The stages of Messrs Husted and Kendall and the cars of the Long Island Railroad were not the only means for going on a picnic or a clambake—there were the steamboats. The *Eagle* on 1 August 1846 reported that "to Glen Cove wended we our joyful way yesterday, in the good steamer *Excelsior*—with a comfortable party of nearly three hundred ladies and men." Whitman found the trip stimulating, for he asked,

> DID you ever, sweet reader, lean over the bows of a steamboat, under swift headway, and mark the keen-cut speed with which she divides the waters—and the up-springing di-

verging jet she makes at the same time? . . . The fragrant salt-
ness of the sea-wind comes *at* you in a rough caress; and exhil-
arating consciousness of swift motion adds to the "fun"; and
that impulse, which no human mind is without, to be *taken
out of the present*, is constantly gratified. After this token
(and something more, perhaps) there is a beautiful pleasure
in swift sailing, on a large sheet of water. Then love we to
get bow-ward, where there is nothing of the boat and the
people to be seen—where, abstracted from the artificial
method of the rest, one realizes only Nature's noblest developments, the sky, the immeasurable vault of air, and the sweep
of the waters.

The party landed at Glen Cove, on the north shore of Long
Island in Nassau County, where they ate roasted clams and ham
and bread under the trees. The following summer, however, on
11 August the *Eagle* censured the growing fashion of steamboat
picnics.

THE FASHION OF GOING ON "PIC-NICS," PER STEAMBOAT.—
As our eyes yesterday morning were thrown out of our
sanctorium window upon the little strip of river (whose moving panorama is so refreshing, by the bye), we beheld the
Kosciusko steamboat, panting and blowing up to a dock nigh
the Fulton ferry. Her decks were absolutely crammed with
human beings—women, children, and men—who clustered
over every part, like bees swarming. We understood that the
boat was taking the people to West Point, on a "pleasure
excursion"! and stopped at Brooklyn to get a few more of
the same sort! In the sweltering moist air that we were "enjoying" yesterday, it must have been *very* nice indeed on
board there.

In sober truth, the new fashion of pic nicking, by way of
steamboats, has come to the pass of o'erleaping itself and
falling on the other side—the side which is *opposite* to
pleasure.

The trouble with such excursions, Whitman told his readers, was
that the boats were often uncomfortably crowded with a thousand persons rather than the rational number of three or four
hundred.

On the southeast outskirts of Brooklyn was the Camp Ground at Flatbush where the Brooklyn militia encamped for a short time each summer for "professional practice." At such times the camp ground was a popular and easily reached goal for summer excursions. The *Eagle*, 18 June 1846, told of "A Drive Out of Brooklyn" which included a visit to the militia at Flatbush. When Whitman and his party arrived at the camp ground with its thirty or forty tents, they found "an inspiring and gay spectacle" composed of "the band playing—ladies walking about, with militaires and civilians in attendance—the glitter of uniforms, the marching of sentries, and all that." From this cheerful scene, Whitman's party proceeded to the Kings County Lunatic Asylum—"What a sad spectacle indeed!" Here they saw a woman whose distrust of men was so deep-seated that she refused to shake their hands. Another poor female, "mincing and ambling," was smitten with one of the gentlemen in the party. "The cause of her derangement . . . was, unrequited love, years ago," explained Whitman. "Poor withered thing! That closely cropt grey hair—those lips and cheeks, sunk in the indentations of a toothless mouth—those peering eyes—what a burlesque on passion!"

Whitman and his party saw more distressing cases of mental illness in the iron-barred violent ward of the asylum. But if the sight of these "poor sick looking wretches" was depressing, the end of the day's drive was such as to elevate the spirits; for the party drove from the asylum to Coney Island through the refreshing scent of clover fields.

> How grand . . . the rolling scope of the ocean, whose waves dash into the sand-hills there! We drove some distance on that hard, clean, level sand, snuffing up the air with such delight as a man feels, who rarely gets away from the purlieus of the crowded city—The phantom shapes of vessels, with full-bellied sails, saw we in the distance, moving along like children of the mist. There, too, were the white plumes of many a mighty ripple—ere it threw its long hollow scoot high up the shore. Nor was the scene wanting in solemnity. How can human eyes gaze on the truest emblem of Eternity, without an awe and a thrill?

74

Perhaps around this time Whitman sensed "that instead of any special lyrical or epical or literary attempt, the sea-shore should be an invisible *influence*, a pervading gauge and tally for me, in my composition" ("Sea-Shore Fancies," *Specimen Days*).

Whitman went farther afield on Long Island than the beaches and the villages in the immediate vicinity of Brooklyn. The Long Island Railroad sponsored a "flying pic-nic" from Brooklyn to Greenport, eighty miles away on the east end of the island, and back for one dollar. On the following day, 27 June 1846, the *Eagle* printed its editor's impression of the trip. Whitman was pleased with it all: the handsomeness of the village of Greenport, from which a dozen whaleships operated; the Peconic House, "a jewel of a hotel"; and the car attached to the train in which "the obliging waiters served the passengers just as the latter might have been served in an ordinary public dining or ice-cream room." He took the same jaunt the next year. The *Eagle*, 3 September 1847, briefly reported the expedition, marvelling mostly that one could leave Brooklyn after breakfast, spend five hours at Greenport, and arrive back in Brooklyn at nine in the evening.

A few days later, leaving Brooklyn at one p.m., 9 September, Whitman made a third trip into east Long Island, this time extending it into a proper vacation of perhaps two weeks.[46] He spent several days at Riverhead, county seat of Suffolk County, and shorter periods at other villages thereabouts. The subscribers of the *Eagle* were informed of its editor's progress by three letters published as "East Long Island Correspondence." The first two letters were simply descriptive of the villages along the railroad. In the final letter Whitman told his readers of the few Indians who remained on the eastern end of the island and of their past history. He quoted a local tradition that "the natives were *as many as the spears of grass*," especially in Suffolk, where the royal tribe, the Wyandanch, ruled from Montauk Peninsula. But in the 1840s the population of Suffolk was small, and the Long Island "spears of grass," now European in origin, were thickest in Brooklyn in Kings County, where the *Wyandank* (a variant spelling which Whitman objected to) and the *Montauk* ferried

Whitman and his contemporaries from Brooklyn to Manhattan and back again. And urban Brooklyn was the real milieu of Whitman.

Though it had no theatres and its citizens were largely dependent upon New York for other types of entertainment as well, Brooklyn amused itself in ways other than by saunters in its streets. There was the occasional circus. Whitman attended the performance of Rockwell and Stone's Circus on the evening of 21 May 1846. The large crowd was especially enthusiastic over the "bull fight," a spectacle in which the bull was impersonated by a horse of "great sagacity" but who forgot his role and attacked "his assailants with his *heels*." In the fall of 1847 Sands, Lent and Company's American Circus thrilled the Brooklyn public with its equestrian feats. On 4 November the *Eagle* reported:

> The last performance of Sands and Lent's circus took place last evening, and the tent was crowded to repletion. . . . The very great success with which this exhibition has met with here would seem to imply that any meritorious exhibition of a permanent character would be well sustained in Brooklyn. Is it not about time for this city to be independent of New York, in some measure, in the way of resources for amusement?

Akin to the circus, and exciting in its way, was the wild animal exhibition which visited Brooklyn each year. The *Eagle* noted, 12 November 1846, a "Great Event" which that morning had excited big and little alike—"the grand *entree* into the city of that menagerie, which has been so anxiously expected for a week past." The menagerie made its grand entrance with a "long column of ultramarine blue box carriages," holding the wild animals, preceded by "an imposing 'triumphal car,' in all the glory and glitter of gold leaf, decorated with an infinity of gilded lions, drawn by eight stout black chargers, and containing a band of music, which made the brick walls and crowded thoroughfares melodious with a spirit stirring air from 'La Fille du Regiment.' " Whitman swore to his readers he was "bound to see the 'bear dance'—we *are*." The menagerie was in the city again the following spring. When it closed its Brooklyn booking

76

and moved on down the island, Whitman remarked, 30 April 1847, "We commend it to the attention of our Long Island friends, as a very rational and instructive source of amusement."

Another but quite different "rational and instructive source of amusement" was the lecture courses during the winter season in Brooklyn. The *Eagle* of 5 March 1846 noted:

> There are no less than three courses of lectures now in progress in this city, viz: The Institute course; Dr Baird's lectures on Europe at the Church of the Pilgrims in Henry street; and Professor Fowler's on Phrenology at Hall's Buildings.[47] From the numerous attendance which each receives, an impartial observer would imagine that there is an almost unquenchable thirst for knowledge on the part of our citizens.

The lecture course, or lyceum, was an established American institution, and its popularity was as great in Brooklyn as elsewhere. At this period in Brooklyn, "all the serious minded and many of the frivolous flocked to the lecture halls."[48] The Brooklyn Institute lectures, which had the greatest prestige, presented topics ranging from astronomy to consumption; and Whitman carefully noted the beginning of the institute's winter series each year. On 13 October 1846 the *Eagle* reported the first lecture of the season.

> The introductory lecture before the Brooklyn Institute was delivered last evening by George S. Hilliard, Esq. a legal gentleman of Boston. There was a large audience present, and seldom have we seen an assemblage so captivated by a literary performance . . . The principal aim of it was a truthful survey of the literary taste prevailing in the country, and the moral position of the United States in a governmental point of view. The lecture was a perfect chaplet of gems in brilliancy of its thoughts and its strikingly beautiful and expressive diction. . . . Notice was given that Mr Gliddon the lecturer on Egypt would commence his series on Thursday evening next.

The institute series for the winter of 1847-48 was begun by Louis Agassiz, recently emigrated from Switzerland, who found a subsistence in lecturing before becoming professor of natural history at Harvard in 1848. The *Eagle* noted on 26 November 1847 that "the customary winter entertainments of the Brooklyn Institute were commenced last evening with a lecture by Prof Agassiz upon . . . the transportation of boulders generally and the Swiss glaciers particularly." Agassiz gave his topic "a greater degree of relevancy" by alluding to the boulders on Long Island as examples of glacial transportation of the same. Whitman reported the lecture in some detail, judged it "an interesting lecture to the audience generally," and concluded by remarking that "the enunciation of the professor is sometimes a little difficult to understand, though he speaks fluently and seems to have mastered most of the difficulties of our barbarous mother tongue."

The institute sponsored attractions other than lectures. The *Eagle*, 6 November 1847, spoke of the institute in this fashion: "Being decidedly the most interesting feature of Brooklyn life, it has so insinuated itself into the affections of a large class of our citizens that its absence would create a blank much to be deplored." The article continued on to specify some of the things that made the institute so interesting a feature of Brooklyn life: the lectures, naturally, but also the annual exhibition of paintings, and the several musical concerts.[49] The article might have mentioned, but did not, the annual exhibition of flowers, fruits, and vegetables at the institute, which Whitman first reported on, at some length, in the *Eagle* on 29 September 1847. The first thing he had noticed that morning on entering the exhibit was "a cast of the goddess Flora, decorated with blossoms, and elevated in a large bower." Among the flowers that pleased him was "the toad-flower, whose speckled leaves put one irresistibly in mind of the reptile that in poesy's age bore 'a precious jewel in its head.'" Some of the plants were exotics with which he was not acquainted, "but it needed no instruction to take in the grace and superb delicacy of the sight in general—the rich bloom of the flowers, the mellow ripeness of the fine fruits, and the glossy lustre of the dark green lemon and orange trees! Beautiful indeed were they all—those children of earth and sunshine; and an eloquent plea in behalf of blending the practical and the ornamental in life!"

Also of interest to Whitman and to some of his fellow citizens was the Natural History Society of the Brooklyn Institute, which met weekly for scientific demonstrations and discussions. Accounts of these weekly meetings appeared fairly regularly in the *Eagle*, and Whitman seems to have attended some of them with varying degrees of appreciation. One meeting that he found relatively dull was reported on 18 November 1846.

> There was less than ordinary interest in the proceedings last evening of the Natural History Department of the Brooklyn Institute. The most interesting part occurred before the sitting, when a member instituted some experiments with the *gun cotton* which then began to make some *noise* in Brooklyn. The experiments did not strike us . . . as being very satisfactory. . . . When discharged from a pistol, its expulsion of the ball was very weak. The burning upon a piece of paper was more satisfactory.

A more interesting meeting of the society was reported on 10 April 1847.

> A numerous attendance of members took place last evening at the meeting of the department of natural history. The specimens were various and of striking character . . . Disgusting reptiles of various kinds were to be seen in juxtaposition with the beautiful representatives of the floral kingdom. Lizards paid devout court to flowering azalias . . . Toads looked as if they were preparing to swallow large specimens of copper ore; and large stuffed owls gazed on these strange sights . . . no doubt pondering on the purpose for which certain . . . flagging stones with antique bird feet prints upon them, were brought there. Alligators looked with longing eyes upon several beautifully arranged nests of butterflies and other entomological specimens . . . The business of the evening was equally interesting, and consisted in discussing, principally, the recently published opinion of Prof Lyell upon the fossil human bones found last year at a great depth in Alabama.[50] His opinion was that the bones were not antediluvian, and that the depth of their position was attributable to some accident. During the debate which ensued upon reading the article, most of the members coincided with the views of the distinguished geologist.

For Whitman, such meetings of the Natural History Society as he attended were steps in self-education. In "A Few Words to the Young Men of Brooklyn," in the *Eagle*, 17 December 1846, he said, "To those who are just entering upon manhood, the paths of science present pleasures of the most alluring kind."

Patriotic celebrations also furnished entertainment. The Fourth of July had not been celebrated officially in Brooklyn for several years prior to 1846. On 5 June 1846 the *Eagle* remarked, "It is probable that our Common Council this year will pluck up spirit enough to vote a small appropriation for celebrating 'Independence day,' in a becoming manner, apart from the celebration of it in the metropolis over the river. Good!" Some complained that a public celebration of the day encouraged dissipation; but, Whitman pointed out, "There will be just as much dissipation, either way. . . . The celebration may well be a manly and decent one, too—though little boys *will* fire their crackers, and some ill-advised people *will* go on a bit of a spree." The fourth was celebrated in Brooklyn on Fort Greene, but only after the businessmen of Brooklyn, abetted by pleas in the *Eagle*, had collected a private fund to supplement that voted by the common council. The fourth in 1846 was an uncomfortably wet day, reported the *Eagle* on 6 July, but the city guard, the Columbian Riflemen, Fusiliers, Union Blues, the Hibernian Benevolent Society, the city officials, and several bands assembled at the junction of Sands and Fulton streets and marched to Fort Greene. There the Reverend Mr Thayer, pastor of the Universalist Church, gave the opening prayer, which contained what Whitman believed to be "a neat little thought"—"the tears which heaven was shedding, are—let us think—the tears of joy, for so sublime an occasion." The principal address was very good, though the speaker's oratorical powers were "indifferent," and "the singing of the odes, music by the band, salutes, &c., all went off to announcement."[51] Then the procession re-formed and marched back to Fulton and Sands, where Alderman Burbank "invited the soldiers to a handsome collation at the Brooklyn Garden." In summing up the day, Whitman was pleased with it all.

> When we take into consideration the miserable weather, we
> reiterate our assertion that the day was kept *well.* Our New
> York contemporaries speak of an unusual number of intoxi-
> cated men in the streets. In Brooklyn we saw hardly any at
> all.—The mass of our citizens evidently "kept it up" with
> determined glee. Crowds were in the streets—and the rat-
> tling squibs, firing of guns, ringing of bells, and drumming of
> drums, made "glory enough for one day," of themselves.
> The crowd on Fort Greene . . . stood the rain bravely. . . .
> We know, then, we have many *not* fair-weather patriots in
> Brooklyn.

There was one contretemps: it was not until three days later that
the weather allowed the firing off of the municipal fireworks on
top of Fort Greene.

The Fourth of July of the following year fell on Sunday
and so was celebrated on Monday. The common council again
appropriated insufficient funds for the affair, and again a group
of citizens organized to ensure the success of the day. The *Eagle,*
9 June 1847, reported that this group had "appointed the following committee of three, to perfect the arrangements necessary
for raising subscriptions, and for other means requisite to celebrate the day: Gen H. B. Duryea, Gen James E. Underhill, and
Walter Whitman." The celebration on 5 July went off well enough
except for the failure of the common council to cooperate. The
Eagle said this on 6 July:

> Taken altogether, the celebration of independence day in
> Brooklyn went off pretty well. The salutes and bell-ringing
> at sunrise—repeated at noon, and again at the close of day—
> made the principal part of the *official* recognition of the great
> era. The procession at 6 o'clock, though small, was one of the
> neatest we ever saw. It marched over the route designated,
> and, in due time, arrived at the place where the military were
> to be reviewed by the common council. But no common
> council was on hand, and the procession was dismissed. . . .
> That part of the procession occupied *not* by the city digni-
> taries, was a marvel all along the route.

Whitman took the municipal government to task for its "*wretched
conduct*" which had caused "the greatest dissatisfaction to the

citizens." But despite the common council, "in the evening, thousands and thousands of people assembled on Fort Greene to see the fireworks, which went off well, and every way to the pleasure and gratification of the multitude."

"By the by, what atrocious music the hired bands always give on these public occasions!" Whitman had remarked when writing of the Fourth of July celebration in 1846. "Such a diabolical grating rub-a-dub as they kept on Saturday (not a single *tune* on the whole route!) was enough to set any body's teeth on edge!" But when it came to midnight serenading (a fairly common amusement in Brooklyn, judging from how often it was commented upon in the *Eagle*), these bands forewent the rub-a-dub and played tunes enough. The *Eagle* said on 11 July 1846:

> MUSIC AT MIDNIGHT.—A treat intended exclusively for some young ladies in Willow street last night was enjoyed by half a thousand sleepless denizens of the neighborhood. A magnificent brass band (could it have been Lothian's?) commenced their delicious music at half past one o'clock, and made the vicinity melodious for about an hour—causing all the young ladies' hearts to flutter, within hearing distance, and eliciting sundry screams from babies who were disposed to sleep but couldn't make it out for the music; besides waking up several deep-mouthed mastiffs who gave loud token of their vigilance. All these conglomerated sounds made the welkin ring in a style wondrous to hear. The band, however, had the best of it and kept up their music, until a watchman (wonderful to tell!) gave them a gentle but unwelcome hint by striking his club on the pavement, whereat they evacuated the neighborhood.

Apparently Whitman did not resent such musical intrusion into his rest. The *Eagle* on 5 November 1847, remarking on the unseasonably warm weather, mentioned that its editor had been awakened the previous night at two in the morning "from a profound slumber by the delicious strains of 'Love not,'" played by Granger's Brass Band. Whitman vowed, "If there be anything more agreeable than another it is to hear music in the stillness and repose of the night while you are half awake and struggling for dear life to understand what particular portion of the spheres has suddenly thrown you under obligations by sending their strains down to your front windows." The band serenaded the city until morning, moving from one street to another. During much of the time it was audible to Whitman, and in the next day's *Eagle* he thanked Granger's band instead of damning it.

Brooklyn had its daytime serenaders too, largely as a result of the flood of immigrants pouring into Brooklyn and New York. On 23 July 1846 the *Eagle* informed its readers that its editor had been "highly edified by a band of strapping German vocalists, and one with a violin, who performed various airs, and sang songs under our editorial window this morning." Perhaps the Germans were back again the next day, for the *Eagle* of that date had more to say on the subject.

> PUBLIC SERENADES.—There has been a great influx of musical talent into the country of late, judging by the numerous bands of serenaders who make our thoroughfares "vocal," and instrumental too.—A tolerably good German band, consisting of five persons, among whom is a female who plays the German flute, have recently commenced public business in our streets and discourse tolerably eloquent music. These peripatetic musicians manage to pick up (for a rarity) *less* "kicks than coppers," and are in a fair way to make money. The profession of street minstrelsy is getting somewhat overburdened, however.

A year later "the profession of street minstrelsy" was even more overburdened. The *Eagle* noted on 31 July 1847: "This fine morning has started out about a score of the professors of the music-grinding profession. Our city is vocal and instrumental from one end to the other. Query—which is the hardest for these able-bodied vagrants—lugging about a heavy organ in the boiling sun or digging respectably in the earth?" Whitman did not answer his question, but he knew, for he had written about them, that there were hundreds of Irishmen and Germans laboring "respectably" at the Navy Yard, at the Atlantic dock, and elsewhere in the city. They too, along with the "native" Americans, were part of the Brooklyn scene in the late 1840s—the scene which the editor of the *Brooklyn Daily Eagle* caught in his columns not only in the descriptions of his saunters about the city but also in his comments upon newsworthy happenings and upon issues, ranging from political to medical, that interested the Americans of his time.

two

THE POLITICAL AND ECONOMIC SCENE

Nationalism and the West

IN THE EAGLE of 4 June 1846 Whitman noted that John L. O'Sullivan, founder and until recently the editor of the *United States Magazine and Democratic Review* (and founder and still co-editor of the Democratic *New York Morning News*) was "about to withdraw from that active participation in political affairs which he has been distinguished for during the past five or six years" because of ill health. Whitman eulogized the *Democratic Review*, as conducted by O'Sullivan, for presenting "the plain unvarnished recognition of the first principles of democracy." He did not mention, however, that O'Sullivan had originated, the year before, a term which apotheosized American nationalism in the 1840s. Whitman seems never to have used the term in the *Eagle*, but he expressed its essence time and again in his editorials. In the *Democratic Review* in the summer of 1845, O'Sullivan had written an article supporting the annexation of Texas, and in it he had stated that it was "our manifest destiny to overspread the continent allotted by Providence for the free development of our yearly multiplying millions."[1] O'Sullivan, in the expression "manifest destiny," had given the majority of Americans of the 1840s a shibboleth.

> "Manifest Destiny"—the term used to describe the American expansionist spirit of the 1840's—was characterized by a bumptious enthusiasm and naive nationalism; its proponents

claimed that the United States had the world's best government, that its people were better off than those of any other nation, and that its imperialistic designs were sanctioned by both divine and natural law.[2]

Even the socialistic Brook Farm Phalanx saw the workings of Providence in the Mexican War. In 1846 its weekly newspaper, the *Harbinger*, said of the war: "In many and most aspects in which this plundering aggression is to be viewed it is monstrously iniquitous, but after all it seems to be completing a more universal design of Providence, of extending the power and intelligence of advanced civilized nations over the whole face of the earth."[3] But not only Americans were seduced by the concept of manifest destiny. An intelligent foreigner, and one fully aware of American deficiencies, regarded the Mexican War as a step in the unfolding of America's destiny. Ole Munch Raeder, who in 1847 and 1848 was investigating the American jury system for the Norwegian government, wrote the following to a newspaper back home:

> Anyone who is able to look beyond the immediate future must surely hope, in the interest of peace and humanity, that this Union may continue to extend its dominion over the continent so that even the stagnating population of Mexico may be aroused to new life under the influence of the Anglo-American race. Must we not see the hand of Providence in the present war, even if it did have a rather unjust beginning?[4]

If the Mexican War had had an "unjust beginning," Whitman came close to admitting it on only one occasion and immediately declared it unimportant in comparison with the fulfillment of his country's destiny. In the *Eagle* on 7 January 1848, he commented on the "Disagreement Among the Legislative Doctors."

> It is useless to deny that there is a very potent anti-war feeling in the house of representatives . . . and kept in check only by the overwhelming voice of the mass of the people (the "common people," if you please), which does not refine upon abstractions and cannot see the use of making our republic the world's laughing stock, as we should be by withdrawing our troops at once and unconditionally from Mexico.

86

> How useless is it, too, that sage grave men, and not a few editors, spend much breath and brains in arguing what way the war began, and who had the most of wrong or most of right at the commencement! . . . What *has* been done, is past; and whatever the causes were, they will have just as much weight in our future "destinies" as though those causes had been totally reversed.

This was written by a man who, as a result of this very conquest of Mexico, seriously supported the Wilmot Proviso, which demanded that slavery be prohibited in the territories to be annexed from Mexico. Unlike many advocates of the proviso, Whitman was unwilling to halt American expansion simply to block the spread of slavery.

When Whitman assumed the editorial chair of the *Eagle* in early 1846, the American people were profoundly interested in the westward extension of the United States, a matter to which the new Democratic administration in Washington was pledged. A brief item in the *Eagle* on 16 March 1846 amusingly illustrates the public concern: "The Hickman, Ky, *Standard*, says, 'A lady residing within fifty miles of this place has recently given birth to four sons within an hour. They have been named Polk, Dallas, Texas, and Oregon, and all are in a thriving condition.' " The *Eagle's* editor mused on the same date: "Twenty Seven Stars counted we on the blue ground of the American flag, flying from the staff at the Battery yesterday. How many more will be added, before many of us, now throbbing and breathing, will be laid away in our graves?" Whitman believed he knew where some of the future stars would come from. On 12 March he had written the following in the *Eagle:* "A Large and active party in Mexico are now striving to change that republic (!) into a constitutional monarchy. They had far better 'annex' themselves to the United States, as their northern provinces wish to do, and probably will do."

From its beginning, Whitman ardently supported the Mexican War. On the afternoon of 7 May 1846 the subscribers to the *Eagle* saw on page three, inserted amid advertisements, under the heading of "Postscript" in the largest type available and of "Half Past Two O'Clock," the following: "Actual

WAR ON THE TEXAS FRONTIER. MATAMOROS BLOCKADED!" The item stated briefly that four American soldiers on a fatigue party had been killed by fifty Mexicans. What was to Whitman "actual" war, was not actual war to President Polk, who was anxious to ease the consciences of some of his cabinet members by citing a positive act of aggression by the Mexicans before asking Congress to declare war. On the evening of 9 May word reached the White House from General Taylor of such an act: General Arista had crossed the Rio Grande and one of his cavalry patrols had killed some American dragoons and captured others. Polk, with his cabinet's approval, sent a war message to Congress on 11 May (10 May was Sunday), and two days later Congress declared that a state of war existed between the United States and Mexico.

Whitman asserted in the *Eagle* for 11 May that "the news of yesterday has added the last argument wanted to prove the necessity of an immediate Declaration of War by our government toward its southern neighbor." The Mexicans, he said, had refused to settle the Texas question peaceably; further, they had wantonly massacred Americans during the Texas Revolution. "Who," asked Whitman, "has read the sickening story of those brutal wholesale murders . . . without panting for the day when the prayer of that blood should be listened to—when the vengeance of a retributive God should be meted out to those who so ruthlessly and needlessly slaughter His image?"[5] The editor of the *Eagle* scorned the lukewarmness of the New York Democratic press toward the commencement of hostilities and the "contemptible anti-patriotic criticisms" of Greeley's *Tribune;*[6] these journals did not voice the "wishes of the *people*." But the *Brooklyn Daily Eagle* did: "Let our arms now be carried with a spirit which shall teach the world that, while we are not forward for a quarrel, America knows how to crush, as well as how to expand!"

Whitman's war spirit did not go unchallenged by his readers. On 21 May 1846 the *Eagle* said:

CRYING 'PEACE!'—A correspondent inquires how we reconcile our peace principles, as formerly expressed through this journal, with our present position on the Mexican War. We are not for peace, under *all* circumstances—and have never been so. We think no man with true life in his soul can whine the "peace doctrine" now; and though we would not "imitate the action of the tiger," we yet think that, being attacked, this nation should prosecute a vigorous and stern war with the enemy—carrying our arms, if need be, into the very capital of Mexico.

Indeed, the war was an opportunity for young men. Whitman noted on 25 May that Governor Silas Wright had been notified by Washington that New York's maximum quota of troops for the war was seven regiments. "There are," said Whitman, "thousands of our young men—not a few in Brooklyn—who will like no better 'fun' than an excursion to the south, on this business. To all who have no 'encumbrances,' indeed, the chance is a first rate one." Apparently Whitman had encumbrances; perhaps one was a disposition to be a spectator rather than a participator.

But even as a spectator of the hostilities on the southwestern frontier, Whitman served his government, and his party, by consistently supporting the war in his journal in opposition to the other two Brooklyn newspapers and a number in New York. Whitman was indignant at the refusal of the English editor of the *Brooklyn Advertiser* to support his adopted country in its struggle against Mexico, but he was more shocked at the anti-war views of native Americans such as Greeley and Spooner.[7] That Greeley and Spooner distrusted the motives of the United States was not important, as Whitman related in "A Fable" in the *Eagle* on 3 June 1846.

There was once a very nice old woman, who had an immense number of children. . . . she treated every body well, even strangers, whom she always welcomed, and gave them food, clothing, and so on. Immense numbers of strangers therefore came to this old woman, and she never refused to let them settle on the land she possessed—which, if unoccupied, she even *gave* to them. I am sure this was very kind, indeed; how surprising is it, therefore, that the distant places from which those strangers came were continually abusing the old woman.

But that is not what I was going to tell about.—Our old

woman was a little this side of angelic perfection; as indeed most old women are. But she had a great big heart, and though sometimes caught in the commission of foibles, she was pretty generally right. On one occasion, when she had been insulted, and her property stolen by a neighbor, she directed some of her servants to place themselves on the boundary of her lands, and resist all aggression. A series of contests occurred, in which the dame's servants were victorious. But, wonderful to relate! several of the old woman's own born children lifted up their voices in denunciation and ridicule of her! Was not this very unnatural? Even if she had been entirely in the wrong, was it the office of a son to denounce and accuse his own mother? I trow not.

The sacred loyalty of a child to a dear parent is not like the loyalty to Kings. It is sometimes a virtue to forego the latter, and slay a King who becomes a tyrant. But ingratitude to one's *mother!* O, no, no! Who ever did it, and was not sorry afterward?

The unnatural sons of the old woman in the fable were, of course, generally Whigs. Whitman made this clear in an editorial—"Points of Wish and Belief in the Two Parties Illustrated by the Leaders of the Democratic and American Reviews for February.—The Mexican War"—printed in the *Eagle* on 10 February 1847.[8] The lead article of each of the rival magazines for that month was on the war with Mexico, and each professed to speak for the majority of the American people. The *Democratic Review* candidly informed the world, said Whitman, "that the impulse of democratic freedom which built up thirty states on this continent . . . must go on spreading and conquering, and diffusing human happiness—or rather *preventing* Governments from inflicting human misery." The acquisition of vast territory from Mexico, which would erase tyranny from that territory and open it to settlement by freedom-loving Americans, was a "cause for joy" to the *Democratic Review* and the party it represented. But the Whig *American Review* appeared to dread "the spread of democratic institutions, and was all but willing to contract the American power, instead of enlarging it." It had no faith in the manifest destiny of the United States. "Said we not well," asked Whitman, "that the characteristics of democracy and whiggery were exemplified in the twain disquisitions?"

As for the foreign lands who spoke badly of the old woman who had welcomed so many of their people, Whitman was never at a loss to find points of comparison unfavorable to the former. And when the British press accused the United States of gross imperialism in its war with Mexico, he aptly compared that conquest with British actions in India and China. In the *Eagle* on 18 September 1847 Whitman noted the generally malicious tone taken toward the United States by the British press, but he especially deplored the intrigues of the British government with the undemocratic elements in Mexico. Whitman felt that such actions were not consonant with the gratitude the British should feel toward America for taking its naked and hungry off its hands. Furthermore, Britain should keep out of our affairs in reciprocation for our keeping out of hers. "When have we intrigued to stop her conquests in India, although our souls have been harrowed by the accounts day by day and year by year, of the atrocities perpetrated in that region by her ruthless soldiery?" And there was China: "Our prayers were all that we opposed to this most iniquitous war." At the present the British were intriguing in Mexico for the establishment of a monarchy, taking advantage of the Mexicans "while they are in a state of semibarbarism." The British professed to fear the entire annexation of Mexico to the United States—"a thing she does not believe, and has no reason to dread if it were so, as the only evil that could flow from it, would be to establish a peaceable liberal government, where the most horrible despotism now exists, and to induce a horde of mountain robbers to become quiet and orderly citizens and peaceable cultivators of the earth." Once acquainted with the benefits of a free government, the Mexicans would never willingly submit to a monarchy—and that, said Whitman, was "the rub" so far as the British were concerned.

In the early months of the war Whitman had enthusiastically entertained the notion of the annexation of the greater part of Mexico. In an editorial, "Annexation," on 6 June 1846 he had asserted, in support of such a possibility: "The scope of our government (like the most sublime principles of Nature) is such that it can readily fit itself, and extend itself, to almost any extent, and to interests and circumstances the most widely different." But as the war neared its close, Whitman had less confidence in the protean scope of the American form of government, though no less faith in the American destiny. On 22 November 1847 he wrote on the "Annexation of Mexico," saying that "the idea of 'annexing' the *whole* of Mexico to the United States . . . is not a sensible idea, and we do not think any body seriously entertains it." The sparsely populated northern provinces (which were certain to be annexed) were well suited for settlement by American republicans; but the other portions of Mexico were more thickly populated—"The inhabitants could not assimilate to ours; and the institutions could not work with ours." Perhaps after many years, after assimilation of democratic ideals through intercourse with the United States, those provinces might voluntarily seek annexation. Meanwhile, the Whigs should stop getting excited, for "it is as fixed as fate that a very large territory *will* be added . . . to these free and independent United States." Though Whitman firmly supported the proposed Wilmot Proviso,[9] he was not inclined to see in its defeat, as were some of its more radical advocates, the seeds of a disrupted union; his faith in the American destiny was too strong.

> That there will be some want of smoothness, some contention perhaps, in the organization of the new states, is every way probable at the beginning. But . . . our faith in the final triumph of christianity is not more clear and full than our faith in the harmonious progress and increase of the United States of North America—and their added brethern, as the latter join us from time to time. To us, nothing more proves the short-sightedness of a man than his speculating on the rupture of this union as a thing to be taken into account. Nor is it with any blind faith that we feel our *perfect* confidence in the perpetuity of the union. We feel the same confidence in it that we might feel in the strength of any thing . . . that has surmounted greater obstacles than any that *can* befall it again, and whose failures would plainly overwhelm the seceders within their own weakness, taking their very life-blood from them!

In the following year on 9 September, in the first issue of the *Brooklyn Freeman*, Whitman was to say that "we shall oppose, under all circumstances, the addition to the Union, in future, of a single inch of *slave land*, whether in the form of state or territory."[10] But as long as he was editor of the *Eagle*, he so plainly saw the hand of Providence in the acquisition of Mexican lands that he was willing to run the risk of the establishment of slavery in that new territory.

The Oregon question came to a head along with the Mexican War and gave expansionists another topic suited to expressions of manifest destiny. Since 1818 the United States and Great Britain had jointly occupied Oregon without reaching any agreement on the ultimate division of that territory. One of Polk's election commitments was to acquire Oregon, and in his inaugural address on 4 March 1846, he stated that the title to the whole of Oregon clearly belonged to the United States. Whig alarmists at once prophesied war, though cooler heads saw an equable compromise as more likely, especially since Americans would inevitably populate the southern portion of Oregon. Whitman's was one of the cooler heads. On 9 March 1846 he discussed the matter in a lengthy editorial. He saw no reason for war; it was not important that we get all of Oregon.

> When one thinks of the future greatness of this republic—how our territory is stretching in almost every direction (in way of settlement and increased prosperity we mean)—how even distant provinces of other countries are eagerly seeking to come under the wings of our eagle—how the name of "American" must, in a few years, pale the old brightness and majesty of "Roman"—he will see that the mere ownership of a few million acres more or less of Northern Oregon, does not involve our power or honor hereafter, in any degree worth serious estimation! . . . The United States in twenty-five years, or less, *must* be the most potent nation on earth! No human means can retard this great consummation . . . Shall we . . . fight for any thing short of our lives, independence, or dearest rights?

Should the United States fight or compromise on the Oregon question was a moot point in the Senate during March and early April, and Whitman followed the speeches of the senators with interest. On 16 March John C. Calhoun made an eloquent speech in favor of peace and compromise, a speech which so delighted Whitman that he referred to it and quoted from it for days. On 21 March he made a remark on Calhoun's speech which later caused one of his readers to ask how he reconciled his former peace principles with his belligerency toward Mexico.

> Further reflection has only convinced us more firmly of the sense and patriotism of Mr Calhoun's late Oregon speech. . . . No: let us not go to war. . . . The world has tried *that* agent of redressing wrongs and grievances long enough, and the result—do we not see it all around us? Why are these bitter prejudices between nations? Why do men of the same flesh and blood hate one another? Why are the lines in geography permitted to be moral divisions as well as physical?
>
> It may be utopian—it may be a chimera—but it is at least a beautiful chimera, this of universal brotherhood and peace! And the world were better did it believe it practicable.

But meanwhile many of the Whigs were denying that the United States had a valid claim to any of Oregon, and Whitman could not stomach this lack, as it seemed to him, of proper patriotism. On 16 March the *Eagle*, under the heading of "Pretty Patriots!" had this to say:

> We consider ourselves not of those affectionate bigots who exalt with zeal, every custom, claim and attribute of the native land, above all other lands on the face of the earth . . . We love our country with a deep enthusiasm—and yet we own our country's faults. . . . it runs into errors and excesses many a time and oft. Also—we see divers evil customs that a long and dreary time of trial and perseverance alone can purge us from.
>
> But we have never yet learned, like many of our whig neighbors, to take up the cudgels in behalf of a foreign nation, when the dispute lies between that nation and our own. The whig organs in New York, Washington, and Albany . . . and the prominent whigs, are striving day after day to advance the interests of Britain—to show how superior is the British Oregon claim to ours. . . . and, indeed, never lose an occasion to put bars in the path of their own government when difficulties arise between it and a distant ruler—particularly if that ruler is in England, a spot for which a large part of the whig faction have a special reverence for.

94

Had hostilities resulted from the Oregon dispute, it seems a safe conjecture that the editor of the *Eagle* would have taken up his pen in support of his native land as strongly as he did in the case of the Mexican War.

Fortunately, war was not necessary. The British offered to divide Oregon along the forty-ninth parallel, and the treaty incorporating that settlement was signed on 15 June 1846. The *Eagle*, 19 June, remarked that the flag had been run up on the staff of the Eagle Building in celebration of the ratification of the Oregon treaty. "We hope our 'Fifty-four Forty' friends will not grumble at this. We, too, would have marched up to that line—if we could have gone there. But what is decreed, is decreed." And it was decreed, though Whitman did not know it, that the southwest and California, rather than Oregon, were spectacularly to illustrate the operation of manifest destiny in the 1840s.

Nationalism and the Old World

THE AMERICANS of the 1840s were sensitive to what they regarded as a blind prejudice against American institutions and mores on the part of most Europeans, especially the British. Whitman's generation esteemed Alexis de Tocqueville's *Democracy in America* but deplored such accounts as those given by three English travelers in particular. Frances Trollope's *Domestic Manners of the Americans* had appeared in the early 1830s, but the Americans of the 1840s vividly remembered that Mrs Trollope had condemned things American from spitting to politics in order to illustrate the superiority of the rule of the few over the rule of the many. Captain Frederick Marryat's *Diary in America* (1839) was still generally considered a libel on the American national character. Charles Dickens' patronizing *American Notes* and uncomplimentary *Martin Chuzzlewit* had appeared in the early 1840s and were still unpleasantly familiar to Americans. It was so seldom that British visitors were sympathetic to American political institutions that when Whitman reviewed Sarah Mytton Maury's *American Statesmen*, he scarcely touched on its defects: "There is a genuine American feeling here, and generally throughout the work, in the midst of much evidently over-wrought."[11] But Mrs Maury was a rare exception, and Whitman was but adding his voice to the general chorus of the American press when he wrote an editorial, "Minor Moralities," for the *Eagle* of 25 September 1846.

> Foreigners, travelling among us, have frequently thought proper to attack the American people for their lack of what may be called the minor moralities of life. Thus we see some horrified at the practice of spitting—some indignant at the scarcity of towels—others denouncing rapid mastication— and so on. In this way we have "all our faults observed, set in a note book," and spread before the European reader as a conclusive argument against democratic institutions. And Boz writes about the pigs in Broadway, and Mrs Trollope writes about the pigs of Cincinnati. . . . But . . . let us imagine any civilized kingdom of Europe changed to a republic . . . the masses elevated to the same grade with the nobility, and the nobility depressed to the masses. Let us suppose France, for instance. Who would not be shocked at the stupidity, the indecency, the total absence of all polish, which would then prevail? In the distant provinces of France . . . the masses do not read or write; they are but little removed from the more sagacious brutes. And not dissimilar would be the result of the same rule applied to England, Germany, or Spain. And shall a person come among us, and from the . . . aggregate body of the American people, take out here and there a few violators of trivial etiquette, as a sample of America? The faults of the people here are exceptions to the general rule. In Europe, refinement is the exception.

Whitman had never been to Europe, but he was as confident of the general degeneracy of the European masses as he was of the unjustness of the portrait drawn of the American masses by European visitors.

This American trait of prejudice against the Old World seemed to Ole Munch Raeder to be distinctive, as he explained in a letter to the Christiana *Den Norske Rigstidende* in 1847.

> That which has annoyed me most in my association with the Americans is their prejudice against Europe, which they re-

gard as hopelessly lost in slavery and wretchedness. Three-fourths of the people in the East and ninety-nine hundredths of the people in the West are fully convinced that the other side of the Atlantic is nothing but a heap of medieval feudal states, which, indeed, show some slight indication of a reform here and there, but have not made much political progress and have not enough vitality to rise from the abyss of misery and corruption into which they have fallen as the result of centuries of ignorance and despotism; their doom is inevitable. If one tries to dispute any portion of this creed of theirs, they simply point to the foreigners [immigrants] . . . They simply cannot see . . . that a monarchical form of government can be combined with any liberty.[12]

Most of Europe was "but a heap of medieval feudal states" to Whitman, and he was alert to pick from the foreign news brought by the transatlantic steamers those events which revealed the corruption of Old World institutions: the deceit of Louis Philippe, sordid royal weddings in Spain, the dismemberment of the free city of Cracow by the Holy Alliance. Writing of this last event on 19 December 1846, Whitman exclaimed: "Listen, men of the New World! but for one hour to the tale of oppression . . . to the hellish wrongs of the coroneted few on the continent of Europe toward the masses—which those masses tamely bear." Whitman often spoke in the *Eagle* of the existence of a sentimental attachment between the United States and England similar to that between a son and his mother (though this attachment was more ideal than real). Too, despite the anti-democratic doctrine of many British writers, the English, unlike the continental Europeans, said Whitman on 10 February 1847, had "that sturdy spirit of progress and independence, which is the *greatest* treasure a people can possess." But the British had not kept pace with the political and social progress made in America, and Whitman commented caustically upon their oppression of the Irish and their imperialism in China and India. Numerically, more critical comments were made in the *Eagle* on the British than all the continental nations combined. This was partially the result of both the times, which brought England and the United States into diplomatic collision, and the habit of the British to write books and articles which depreciated American aspirations and institutions in a language only too available to the sensitive inhabitants of the United States.

"In books are the staunchest exposers of wrong and the readiest inducements to right," Whitman remarked in the *Eagle* on 26 November 1847 in an article entitled "The World of Books." One might expect that Whitman, the devoted republican, used his frequent book reviews to expose, when possible, the evils of monarchical rule and the unwholesomeness of anti-democratic foreign literature.[13] The contrary was the case. For example, Whitman reviewed, sometimes merely noticed, 100 works of fiction (excluding works for juveniles) in the *Eagle* without an allusion to unwholesome foreign influences, though the great majority of books reviewed were written by Europeans. In only one review of fiction did Whitman illustrate, by contrast with Old World ills and evils, the virtues of republican government—but he thought this work of fiction a "democratic book." On 31 May 1847 he reviewed Eugene Sue's *Martin the Foundling*.

> Perhaps no work has yet been written, of what are called novels, which more fully exhibits the potency of the romancer, *to do good*, in a certain way than this! It cuts into the very heart—the sore, gangrened, suffering, guilty heart— of that immense social evil which has accumulated for long and artificial ages over the states of Europe; exposes the monstrous effect of undue distribution of wealth, by unnatural means, which prevails in the monarchies there . . . Little credence have we in that cant of modesty . . . which is shocked at *the truths* themselves . . . Would they rather the guilt and pain should go on growing farther and stronger *under the surface?*.....We like this book well and hope it will be read widely. It is a democratic book.

For further remarks critical of European society, one must go to Whitman's reviews of historical and biographical works.

Whitman noticed in the *Eagle* twenty-two historical works, fourteen dealing with Old World history and the remainder with American. But Whitman did not make full use of his opportunity to castigate European corruption. For example, his review on 23

November 1846 of Carlyle's *French Revolution* was mostly occupied with the need for an international copyright. In only two of these particular reviews were there any references to monarchical evils. Whitman reviewed Henry Hallam's *Constitutional History of England* on 27 March 1847, and found it to be a book with good principles and wholesome examples. He especially liked its accounts of the sixteenth and seventeenth centuries, for "then it was that the buds swelled which have since burst into the bloom of a better freedom for man and mind—the precursor, haply, of a still higher and wider freedom in the future."

Perhaps the longest of the reviews in the *Eagle* of a single publication was that of Lamartine's *History of the Girondists* on 10 August 1847. Whitman quoted a passage from the work which expressed some commiseration for Louis XVI and his queen, suggesting that they were not vicious, merely susceptible to bad advice. Whitman partially agreed with Lamartine,

> But the great faults of Louis and Marie Antoinette were . . . that they lifted themselves in their blasphemous and insane pride, so high above humanity as to have no sympathy for the horrors and sorrows that were spread over France, and which entered into the every day life of so many millions of people whose flesh and blood were just as divine as the king's or queen's.

The overthrow of that despotism, added Whitman, was "a glorious work, for which whole hecatombs of royal carcasses were a cheap price indeed!"[14] Later in the review he quoted a passage from the history describing the corrupt conditions in France immediately prior to the revolution. This description, he felt, should confirm the readers of the *Eagle* in their love for democratic institutions.

> Such are the workings of an unfree government—such but a few of the manifold mischievous results of an unholy power, of monopolies, of hereditary riches and privileges. They bear a mighty lesson, those results do! And as what comes to pass on the human physical structure, after long years of unwholesome influences, is the best teachings of health, so the consequences of constraint are the best argument for liberty.

The consequences of constraint were not to be seen just in the past history of the European nations; if at all, those consequences were greater than ever. One in particular of the fourteen biographical and autobiographical works noticed in the *Eagle* aroused Whitman to remark on contemporary despotism in Europe. That book was Hazlitt's *Napoleon*, reviewed 15 March 1847.[15] He said little of the book itself, which he liked, and much of the need to reconsider, free of Tory bigotry, the French Revolution. He then spoke of the excesses of the revolution and, as in his review of Lamartine, excused them as sufficiently provoked by aristocratic abuses. He dreaded violence, "bloodshed, and a maddened people,"

> But we would rather at this moment over every kingdom on the continent of Europe, that the *people* should rise and enact the same prodigious destruction as those of the French Revolution, could they thus root out the kingcraft and priest-craft which are annually dwindling down humanity there to a lower and lower average—an appalling prospect ahead, for any one who *thinks* ahead. Moreover, when it is observed how deeply the fangs of that kingcraft are fixed—and how through-and-through the virus of that priestcraft is infused—it will make one come nigh to think that only some great retching of the social and political structure can achieve the blessed consummation.

The spring of the year following that in which Whitman reviewed Hazlitt's *Napoleon* was one of revolutions in Europe. Ole Munch Raeder, writing from Boston in May 1848, told how everyone flocked to the newspaper offices for the latest news on the revolutions whenever a steamship arrived in the harbor or news came that one had docked in New York.[16] Whitman was then in New Orleans, working for the *Daily Crescent*, and none of his identifiable pieces in that paper commented on the upheavals in Europe. But Ole Raeder probably was speaking for Whitman as for many other Americans when he wrote his Norwegian compatriots in the spring of 1848 that "the most surprising of all, to the Yankee mind, is that *all* of the European nations have not got rid of their kings."[17]

100

Government and the Party

WHITMAN had a triumvirate of national heroes to whom he often alluded with reverence in the *Eagle:* Washington, Jefferson, and Andrew Jackson. In an editorial on 15 March 1847, commemorating Jackson's birthday, Whitman placed Jackson at the head of these heroes. Washington was a man of "honor and august virtue"; Jefferson "was in democracy and politics somewhat as that Corsican 'child of destiny' amid the thrones of Europe"; but Jackson was a "truly sublime being" who breasted "with a great will, such waves of aroused interest, of seeming public opinion, as try mortal courage to their utmost endurance!" However, it was Jefferson, with his maxim that the best government is that which governs least, who most influenced Whitman's idea of the role of government in a democracy.

To Whitman the welfare state was an incongruity in view of American potentialities, and it was his hope that democracy would prevent such a state's coming into being. He had this to say on the matter in the *Eagle* on 26 July 1847:

> In plain truth, "the people expect too much of the government." . . . *Men* must be "masters unto themselves," and not look to presidents and legislative bodies for aid. In this wide and naturally rich country, the best government indeed is "that which governs least."
>
> One point . . . ought to be put before the eyes of the people every day; and that is, that although government can do little positive *good* to the people, it may do an *immense deal of harm*. . . . Democracy would prevent all this harm. . . . It would have no one's right infringed upon and that, after all, is pretty much the sum and substance of the prerogatives of government. . . . While mere politicians, in their narrow minds, are sweating and fuming with their complicated statutes, this one single rule, rationally construed and applied, is enough to form the starting point of all that is necessary in government: *to make no more laws than those useful for preventing a man or a body of men from infringing on the rights of other men.*

Though Whitman wrote often in the *Eagle* on the proper functions of a democratic government, the idea expressed in the editorial just quoted is basic to all his statements on the subject.[18] When the chance occurred, he applied his Jeffersonian principles to current legislative matters. A seduction bill was introduced into the state legislature at Albany, and Whitman at once, on 18 and 27 March 1846, decried the attempt to "legislate men into virtue." He protested vigorously several times in the winter of 1846-47 when the New York legislature submitted to local-option vote a "No License" law (no distilled liquor to be sold by the drink or in quantities less than five gallons). When the New Jersey legislature passed a bill making it illegal to race a horse for money or before an assembly of twenty or more people, Whitman reported it without comment but under the heading of "Questionable Policy."

At times Whitman found it possible to cite Jacksonian as well as Jeffersonian principles. In the summer of 1847 a number of the western states sent delegates to a convention at Chicago to discuss ways of getting federal appropriations for harbor and waterway improvements. On 8 July Whitman reported that the convention had begun, and he wondered "why don't the rich and populous states of the west *themselves* go to work, and effect the necessary result?" He added, "For our own part we confess to a liking for General Jackson's principles on the subject," thinking, no doubt, of Jackson's Maysville Veto. On 15 July Whitman wrote on "The Anti-Democratic Doctrines of the Chicago Convention."

> It seems to us . . . the great error of that convention . . . is this: it assumes that the general government is the *protector* of, and *improver* for, the people. Strictly, and in a democratic view, this is by no means the case. Monarchies may be viewed in that light, but not such governments as ours. Keeping within its true scope (which it has already travelled too far out of), what we call our government has rightfully and really the most meager code of duties, and the simplest array of prerogatives, of any on earth. It is the mere agent, not the principal.

One of the last pieces Whitman wrote before leaving the *Eagle* was concerned with the American mania for passing laws.

Under the head of "More Legislative Doctoring," Whitman remarked on 4 January 1848 that the state legislature had convened that date and would remain in session for about one hundred days.

> It is not, as yet, known upon what subjects the legislative doctors will try their hands. That they *must* give physic, however, seems to be a settled necessity, in their minds. Whether well or ill, we have to take it—and pay for it too.....
> Will the day ever arrive when people will see the folly of this excessive legislation?

Though Whitman was in many ways a party hack during most of his stay on the *Eagle*, his editorials show beneath their conventional journalistic rhetoric a genuine liberal idealism more identified with the Democrats of the time than with the Whigs, and more particularly identified with the so-called Young Democracy or Young America—terms constantly appearing in newspapers and magazines as epithets for those, chiefly young, members of the Democratic Party who supported "pure" Jeffersonian and Jacksonian principles and also expansionism, real or ideal. Shortly after becoming editor of the *Eagle*, on 21 March 1846 Whitman wrote "Some Plain Paragraphs, For Plain People," in which he pointed out the opposing principles of the two major parties. He expressed surprise that the Whigs in some years were victorious at the polls. Both parties, he admitted, contained the same sort of human beings: demagogues, "ignorant, ill-bred, passionate men," and men with good qualities.

> But if the inquirer after truth will reflect a moment . . . he will see in this as in all civilized countries, two great currents running counter to one another. . . . In each modern nation there is a class who wish to deal liberally with humanity, to treat it in confidence, and give it a chance of expanding, through the measured freedom of its own nature and impulses. Also, there is a class, who look upon men as things *to be governed*—as having evil ways which cannot be checked better than by law; a class who point to the past, and hate innovation, and think that the nineteenth century may learn from the ninth, and a generation of light can be taught by a generation of darkness.

There was, of course, the problem of conservatives amid the Democrats, and liberals amid the Whigs, but "it sometimes happens that an individual whom nature intends for one class gets entangled in the other." There was Greeley: "Who that has an intimate knowledge of the editor of the N. Y. *Tribune*, ever supposed that he was intended to sacrifice himself in behalf of high duties and paper money? The whole other principles and course of the man are at war with him, as he befogs himself in the darkness upon those two subjects."

But not many months passed before Whitman found his party following a course which eventually he could not abide. In August 1846 Polk asked Congress to appropriate two million dollars for the purchase of lands taken from Mexico. David Wilmot, a Democratic representative from Pennsylvania, introduced a resolution into the House which attached to the proposed appropriation a proviso that slavery be outlawed in the territories acquired—a resolution passed after much argument, but refused by the Senate. However, "every Northern legislature [including that of New York] but one, whether Whig or Democrat, passed resolutions approving it, and acclaiming Wilmot as a great statesman."[19] The proviso appealed to Whitman, though he did not oppose the successful prosecution of the Mexican War because of the proviso's failure to pass Congress. Coincident with his vision of an expanded United States as a result of the war, on 21 December 1846 he called on his party for support of the proviso.

> If there are any States to be formed out of territory lately annexed, or to be annexed, by any means to the United States, let the Democratic members of Congress (and Whigs too, if they like) plant themselves quietly, without bluster, but fixedly and without compromise, on the requirements that *Slavery be prohibited in them forever.* We wish we could have a universal straightforward setting down of feet on this thing, in the Democratic Party. *We must.*

But Polk refused to take Wilmot's proviso seriously. To him it was a sectional intrigue and he damned it officially. As a result, factions developed in the Democratic Party, and it was necessary for Whitman to choose sides. He chose that faction which had received the epithet of Barnburner and which opposed a group that had gotten the invidious label of Old Hunker.[20] Whitman, though he surely knew better, refused at the time to admit such distinctions in the party. State elections were held in New York on odd years, and on 16 September 1847 Whitman announced the coming election of Democratic delegates to district conventions, who in their turn would choose delegates for the state convention, who in turn would select the candidates for state offices. He admitted that divisions existed in the party within the state, but

> We confess to our ignorance of who are "Barnburners" or who are "Old Hunkers," as applied to democrats; and we are glad to acknowledge that we are intensely ignorant of the causes whence arose those euphonious appellations. We recognize no clique or faction; our duty is to work for the good of *Democratic principles*, which cannot divide themselves into quarreling bands; which are harmonious for the welfare of *all;* and to the advancement and universal spread of which, we ever have been and ever will be devoted.

Whitman was being, at the least, rhetorically naive when he professed no knowledge of the names applied to the principal factions of the Democratic Party in New York State. He was equally so when on 30 October he struggled to keep faction out of Kings County.

> If disputes and angry bickerings have pervaded other counties in the state, they have, thank heaven! not yet pervaded ours. . . . *We* do not recognize the distinctions of "old hunker" or "barnburner." *We* know only the name of *democratic republican*—a time-honored appellation, which comes to us from the era of Jefferson, and has been handed down through Madison, Jackson, and Van Buren.

On election day Whitman still stubbornly refused to publicly admit that his party and his political ideals—now reduced to the dimensions of David Wilmot's proviso—did not agree. He wrote the following plea on 2 November 1847:

> Friends of the Wilmot proviso! we earnestly hope that *you*, of all men, will not abstain from voting the regular ticket,

105

> presented at the head of your paper. Is not Mr Hungerford
> [candidate for Congress] a fast friend of the principle of the
> proviso, as recorded by his votes in congress last winter? We
> are surprised that any of the advocates of that principle can
> . . . refuse to support a ticket *made up principally of men
> who are, by their past action, committed in behalf of the
> intent and scope of that proviso.*

The regular Democratic ticket lost throughout the state, including Brooklyn. The Whigs, who had adopted a free-soil plank,
won the election.

Less than a year later Whitman was in the new and short-
lived Free-Soil Party. But he reluctantly gave up the Democratic
Party. On 3 November, the day after the 1847 elections, in an
editorial titled "Some Reflections on the Past, and For the
Future," Whitman blamed the Democratic defeat on lack of
radicalism and hoped that more liberal doctrines would prevail
in the party.

> As a fact without reasonable question, we would mention that
> our party has not been of late, sufficiently bold, open, and
> radical in its avowals of sentiment. . . . The heartier then,
> our party's avowal of high radical doctrines—and the farther
> it goes for freedom—the more sternly it rebukes and puts
> aside conservatism . . . the more likely to succeed. But all
> conservative influence is pestilential to our party. It may suc-
> ceed for a day or a year—but fate itself is not more fixed and
> immutable than that the more liberal doctrines will gradually
> become paramount. . . . And it is to this progressive spirit
> that we look for the ultimate attainment of the perfectest
> possible form of government—that will be where there is the
> *least* possible *government*, when the barbarism of restrictions
> on trade shall have passed away—when . . . the plague spot
> of slavery, with all its taint to freemen's principles and pros-
> perity, shall be allowed to spread *no further;* and when the
> good old democratic party—the party of the sainted Jefferson
> and Jackson—the party, which, with whatever errors of men,
> has been the perpetrator of all that is really good and noble
> and true in our institutions . . . shall be existing and flourish-
> ing over the grave of this fleeting whigism, and all its passing
> brood. . . . Conservatism . . . must leave the field—and the
> democracy unite on its boldest and noblest and most radical
> doctrines.

106

But conservatism was not ready to leave the field in the regular Democratic Party, and Whitman was without a job or a party before the end of January 1848. In the following September, after his jaunt with his brother Jeff to New Orleans, he was able, as editor of the free-soil *Brooklyn Freeman* and as a member from the seventh ward of the Free Soil General Committee for Brooklyn, to speak of President Polk—whom he had loyally supported in the *Eagle*—as "What Sort of Man Has New-York Made President?" Such was the head of a paragraph in the first issue of the *Freeman;* and the paragraph explained why Whitman, who had voted for Polk in 1844, had turned against the Democratic President: "The Chief Magistrate of this nation intimates that he would veto any law establishing freedom instead of slavery, nearer to the equator than a certain line. The state of New-York, by the most incessant and self-sacrificing efforts of the Democratic party—the Van Burenites most of all—gave the votes which made this man President. God forgive us!"[21]

And Jefferson was no longer the precursor of the incumbent President. The lead editorial of this first issue of the *Freeman* was "Jefferson on the Non-Extension and Abolition of Slavery." In this article Whitman disregarded the manifold national problems which concerned Jefferson and conveniently labelled him "in the literal sense of the word, an *abolitionist*." Indeed earlier in the *Eagle*, Whitman had invoked the founding fathers in support of the Wilmot Proviso. On 22 April 1847 he had asked the citizens of Brooklyn "whether the mighty power of this republic . . . shall be used to root deeper and spread wider an institution which Washington, Jefferson, Madison, and all the old fathers of our freedom, anxiously, and avowedly from the bottoms of their hearts, sought the extinction of, and considered inconsistent with the other institutions of the land." It was not until the 1860s that Whitman found a new and an effective symbol of "democratic" integrity in President Lincoln.

Mayor Stryker and the Common Council

THE MAYOR and the Common Council (as the board of aldermen was called) of Brooklyn were elected to office annually. When

Whitman came to work for the *Eagle*, the incumbent mayor, Thomas G. Talmadge, and perhaps half of the council were Democrats. Whitman at once prepared for the impending city election, which was scheduled for April. In "Some Hints to the Mayoriality [his more common spelling of the word] Convention," 14 March 1846, he pleaded for moderation in the exercise of political favoritism. "We who are immersed in the vortex of politics are too apt to imagine that our own little circle is 'the world,'" he explained. "But in reality the great strength and numerical potency of the ballot-box . . . comes from the quiet business man, the mechanics and the farmers of the land. . . . It is far better to satisfy the calm common sense of these men than to please the brawlers of a party." Whether the political or the lay group of Democrats was the more satisfied Whitman did not say when he reported on 20 March that Talmadge (whose name he consistently misspelled) had been renominated for mayor: "Mr *Talmage*, is one of those efficient, business, unimpeachable men, who just fits the office of the mayoralty—fits it, in our opinion better than any man who could have been selected, taking all things into consideration." [22] As for the Democratic nominees for the common council, they were "all worthy and estimable men— known to their friends, and the city at large, as possessed of sterling integrity and intelligence."

Talmadge had two opponents: the Nativist and Whig candidates. Whitman discussed "The Opposition Candidates for the Mayorality" in the lead editorial of the *Eagle* on 25 March. He had thought the Nativists' party dead; as for their candidate: "His name is Pinckney—an obscure lawyer, an abolitionist, and a whig of the rankest rabidest kind." The Whig candidate was Francis B. Stryker, a journeyman carpenter, and erstwhile tax collector and sheriff. [23] Stryker, according to Whitman, had no qualifications for the office he sought and was the sort of man to be ruled by an unscrupulous clique. "His good character," admitted Whitman, "is a thing of course; we could not expect any less. [24] But a Mayor must have something more than this."

From Whitman's later remarks in the *Eagle*, it appears that the Brooklyn Whigs had picked Stryker because of his appeal to the city's large population of workingmen. Whitman's efforts to belittle this aspect of the Whig campaign shows the increasing importance of the common man's vote. The following editorial, "Funny Struggle," appeared in the *Eagle* on 28 March:

> It is every way amusing to see what efforts the principal whig organ in this city makes to push its candidate for the Mayoralty into the position of "a plain man of the people." Mr Stryker forsooth is "*not* a great financier," and "*not* able to make a rhetorical speech," and so on. But Mr Stryker has "lived with the masses, and attracts them to himself, as the magnet attracts steel." . . .
>
> As to the spasms of the whigs hereabout, in the way of identifying themselves and their men with *the real people*— it is little but cool brazen impudence! Nine out of ten of that perfumed, finical, dainty faction will not touch a sturdy workingman's hand, large and dark with honest labor, at all, on any terms. . . . Stryker is a mere instrument in the hands of certain selfish whigs in Brooklyn. . . . And in order to gain his election they have prepared more than one "cunningly devised fable" . . . and lastly this laughable proposition that *we* are the aristocrats and *they* the friends of the masses!

Despite Whitman's repeated appeals in the *Eagle* to the citizens of Brooklyn to support the genuine people's ticket, Stryker the journeyman carpenter was elected mayor by a substantial majority and the Whigs secured half of the eighteen seats on the common council.

On 27 March the *Eagle* had censured the conduct of the common council prior to the April elections in an editorial, "Municipal Short-Comings." Whitman first made it clear that Mayor Talmadge was not to be blamed for any of the shortcomings of the board of aldermen, since his powers were limited by the city charter. But the common council itself—

> Who that has regularly attended the debates in the legislative branch of our Brooklyn government will deny that the *useful* and *sensible* bear but the tithe of a proportion to the flippant, the verbose, and the personal? The *real business* of the corporation is transacted in a few minutes; the folly and vulgarity of the corporation take up many weary and tiresome

hours. . . . The coarse sneer, the retort, the imputation of falsehood, and all the long train of dock-loafer vulgarity ought to condemn every one who indulges in them, to a hopeless obscurity forever.

And who was to blame for this ill-placed vulgarity? The "Whig blackguards in the Common Council," as Whitman explained in an article of that title on 7 April, who lacked "all good manners, good sense, and common decency." A new Whig leader, however, elected to the council in April 1846, was to become the black-guard *par excellence* for the *Eagle's* editor, and Mayor Stryker was to be labelled the new alderman's catspaw.

State elections were held in early November 1846. It appears that a Mr Van Brant was granted a license on or about 30 October to operate an omnibus from the Fulton ferry to East Brooklyn. Soon after the election it was rumored that he had voted the Democratic ticket, and about eight days after the election his license was revoked.[25] Whitman sprang to arms. The *Eagle* for 28 November contained a "New Text Book For Mayor Stryker" in which the mayor was likened to a jealous monarch because of the revocation of Van Brant's license; and his so-called prime minister, a Mr Fowler newly elected to the common council,[26] was defined as "a convenient mouthpiece; and a fit instrument to do all the dirty work of the Whig party in the board." On 1 December the *Eagle* carried an editorial—"That Omnibus Monopoly"—which illustrates Whitman's dexterity in conventional journalistic rhetoric as well as the malignancy of contemporary political exchanges.

It may be as well to observe, in recurring to this subject again, that, as far as our opinions . . . are concerned, we do not involve the *persons* interested in the granting or withholding of the license; it is the *principle*—it is the *wrong* which has been done. Have we to stand on the etiquette of the old rusty courts of Europe? In memorializing OUR SERVANTS, are we, the common people, to weigh nice phrases and observe the humble attitude of Austrian or Russian suppliants at the feet of the Emperor or Czar? Is every little word [in a petition to the mayor and aldermen, Van Brant had complained that his license had been "capriciously" revoked], that may be twisted into an offence at the high and mighty dignity of the Mayor,

("Upon what meat doth this, our Caesar, feed,
That he is grown so great?")

to be a reason for depriving us of our plainest *rights?* O, a very dignified and high-mannered gentleman is Mr Fowler himself in the Common Council—blackguarding night after night, with his filthy tongue and vile phrases, the character of some of our worthiest citizens. . . . Your clown when he accidentally gets a chance of claiming the *position* of a gentleman is the touchiest fellow in the world!

Van Brant's license was restored to him, and on 6 December Whitman admonished, "Well we advise Messrs S. and F. never to let us catch them cutting up such a caper again!"

The two Whig gentlemen did not cut precisely that caper again, but their behavior continued to evoke harsh criticism in the columns of the *Eagle*. On 7 January 1847 the paper indignantly spoke of Fowler's gratuitous attacks in the meeting of the council the night before several of his fellow aldermen (mostly Democrats). Fowler had "out-Heroded Herod." The motive for his disgraceful conduct, as Whitman professed to see it, was "probably . . . nothing but his own envious, jealous, and disappointed nature—full of twopenny venom and baffled ambition." It was the mayor's duty to prevent such spectacles, but he "sat meekly in his chair" through it all. The *Eagle* hoped the mayor had "not yet become *quite* such a catspaw in the hands of a clique, as to make him powerless to quash these scenes." During the next few months Whitman continued to inveigh against the ill-natured antics of Fowler and against the inefficient way in which Stryker presided over the sessions of the council.[27]

Fowler shortly passed from the scene, as Whitman had predicted he would, for the Whigs chose another candidate to represent the fourth ward. But Stryker remained as candidate for reelection to the mayor's office. On 10 April, a few days before the 1847 election, Whitman remarked to his readers: "It is well known that since Mr Stryker has been mayor of Brooklyn, he has been managed by two or three persons. . . . If the present mayor can't act for himself, what on earth is the reason for his wishing to be a candidate again?" Regardless, Stryker was re-elected on 13 April and his party gained a majority in the common council.

Though as a whole the old common council had more amiable qualities than had Alderman Fowler, it had not taken its duties seriously enough to please the *Eagle*. For example, Whitman reported on 16 March 1847 that on the previous evening the common council's "six hours' session was productive of little else than drowsiness to all present and was for the most part frittered away in frivolous discussions about trivialities." The new council seemed an improvement over the old when Whitman reported on "The New City Government" on 4 May 1847. "As to Mr Stryker," he said, "we never thought him at all fit for the office of mayor—and don't think so now." Yet the new Whig council had one merit at least—brevity in transacting business. "If the whigs behave well in their offices we shall treat them with consideration," promised Whitman. "If not—if they don't keep the streets clean, the lamps lighted, and observe a proper economy in outlays—also, giving us Fort Greene park—they needn't expect any mercy." But the new common council, like the old, did not keep the streets clean, or the lamps lit, or want to give the citizens Fort Greene for a park, or do many other things that Whitman thought they should. Whitman's entire tenure at the *Eagle*, before and after the election of 1847, was marked by his constant prodding of the city government to do efficiently its duties.

As seen earlier, the common council in both 1846 and 1847 was reluctant to appropriate more than a token sum for the celebration of the Fourth of July. In both years Whitman began campaigning early in the *Eagle* for a sufficient appropriation, and in both years was left to lament the niggardliness and lack of patriotism of the aldermen. Another project was his urging of the council to purchase the Revolutionary War site of Fort Greene for a city park. Whitman anticipated, correctly, the time when the area about Fort Greene would be a congested region of brick and masonry, and already that section of the city needed "lungs," as he frequently expressed it. In the *Eagle* (as an ex-

112

ample of his many editorials on this topic) for 11 June 1846 he wrote:

> There, too, the mechanics and artificers of our city, most do congregate. There you will see row upon row of their neat plain wooden houses, with unpretensive appearance—and without the ornamental attractions (except the plentiful children thereabout, may be called so) which are characteristic of the Heights. We have a desire that *these*, and the generations after them, should have such a place of recreation as Washington Park [Fort Greene's proposed name as a park], where, of hot summer evenings, and Sundays, they can spend a few grateful hours in the enjoyment of wholesome rest and fresh air.

Despite the bill the legislature at Albany passed on 27 April 1847 for the fencing of Washington Park on Fort Greene, it was not until after Whitman left the *Eagle* that the common council provided for tax assessments to pay for the park.

Whitman's most persistent grumble against the city government was over dirty streets and street lamps that did not burn. Beginning in the fall of 1846 and continuing until he left the *Eagle*, time after time he called on the common council and the city lamp inspector to do something about the street lamps, which burned only fitfully or not at all on the whale oil that fueled them. On 21 September 1846 he warned, "The ground of this complaint must be removed, or there will be difficulty somewhere." The ground of the complaint was not removed, and in almost every issue of the *Eagle* Whitman commented sarcastically on the poor state of the Brooklyn lamps.[28] On 4 December he asserted that though the city had contracted for "Pure Winter pressed sperm oil," it had received only summer or fall oil; and on 8 December he was indignant because the council, the night before, had ordered nearly $600 paid to the contractor who furnished the oil. The lamps continued their flickering career for the following year, causing the citizens of Brooklyn considerable inconvenience when the moon did not shine. And on 7 September 1847 Whitman was outraged by the raise in salary given the city lamp inspector: "As a payer of taxes for what we don't get an equivalent,[29] we should just like to know what the common coun-

cil means, by increasing the salary of the present lamp inspector
$150 [to a total of $750]." Three day later he pointed out that
dark streets were precisely "what burglars and rowdies desire."
He asked, "Will the increase of salary sharpen the inspector's
vision to discover and remove the evils we complain of? *Nous
Verrons*."[30] But the inspector's vision was not sharpened nor,
apparently, did Mayor Stryker and the council heed the *Eagle's*
scoldings. Whitman vacated his editorial post in January 1848,
still expostulating at the "Egyptian darkness" that fell over
Brooklyn almost every night.

Whitman was no more successful in prodding the street
inspectors than he was in prodding James Van Dyke, the lamp
inspector. Mrs Trollope and Mr Dickens had made the dirty
streets of the American cities notorious, but they had not incited
any pronounced movement toward cleaning them. Pigs were still
there rooting about the garbage, and so was plain dirt (or mud
when it rained). On 18 March 1846, in "Clean the Streets,"
Whitman described the filthy condition of the local thoroughfares
and recommended that the street inspectors institute immediate
work with "broom, shovel, and dirt cart." He warned: "We shall
keep our eye (and nose, too) open from this time forth—and if
the officers don't carry out ideas of this sort, we shall lash them
soundly every few days." In the months that followed, Whitman
was sometimes pleased but more often displeased by the way the
street inspectors carried out their duties. During the summer of
1846 the streets generally were clean enough to suit the *Eagle's*
editor, largely because of the frequent rains which washed Brooklyn's dirt into the East River. But in the fall and winter the streets
became uncomfortably untidy again. Whitman wrote on 24
March 1847:

> Our invocation to the city government—pursued in the strain
> of thirty similar articles written within the past year—in the
> behalf of clean streets, and suggesting the addition of more
> force to that effect—is taken by one of the whig papers of
> Brooklyn, as a deep-laid political plot . . . which is meant to
> blow up Brooklyn whiggery. Ridiculous! We want the streets
> of Brooklyn cleaned of all rubbish; leaving only the whig or-
> gans and whiggery, which are quite enough, in all conscience.

114

Whitman, who placed the final blame for the "shameful condition" of the streets on Mayor Stryker, continued his invocations to the city government, noting on 13 May that the accumulation of dirt in Prince street, where he and his family resided, was the result of that street's not being cleaned in nearly a year. In the summer and fall months that followed, the *Eagle* noticed only the rain as an active agent in the cleaning of the streets; and on 30 December, about two weeks before he vacated his editorial chair, Whitman noted that "not in the memory of 'the oldest inhabitant' have the Brooklyn streets been so abominably dirty as at the present writing," despite his unremitting crusade for cleaner streets.

Street obstructions, some resulting from the slowness with which various repairs were made, were also a subject for complaint by Whitman. On 28 September 1847 he observed that the city government was dilatory in all things, including street repairs. "Some four weeks have now been used in patching that little bit of Fulton street (hardly four rods in length) just at . . . the very part of all Brooklyn which is used most as a thoroughfare for vehicles. . . . The work should have taken no more than four or five days." The repaving of "that little bit of Fulton street" was not done until two months later. On 2 December Whitman remarked that this repaving, "which should have been completed in a few days, *consumed* months." The fault was with "the executive power of the city," just as it was in the case of the slowness with which a public cistern was being built in Prince street. The cistern was needed (Whitman frequently recommended the building of more public cisterns for use in firefighting), but it probably would remain unfinished all winter, since the city saw fit often to employ but one man on its construction. Meanwhile, "not an evening passes without alarm and danger being created in the neighborhood, through some unadvised driver getting in the toils there, or some stranger half breaking his bones." On 10 January 1848, probably only a few days before S. G. Arnold became the new editor of the *Eagle*, Whitman complained that "those open mouths yet remain to the public cistern in Prince street."

Another sort of street obstruction was also inveighed against by the *Eagle*. On 26 May 1846 Whitman remarked on the increasing habit of moving houses through the public thoroughfares. "Generally speaking," he said, "the privilege saves but a few dollars to some wealthy man, who is desirous of putting up a larger structure on his property." And since the practice interfered with the passage of traffic, Whitman believed that the common council, in the public interest, should not grant house-moving privileges to any person. The council did not follow Whitman's suggestion; in the fall of 1846 the *Eagle* illustrated the justice of its complaints by following the passage of a house down Myrtle avenue. The first of the items tracing this peregrination appeared on 12 October, when the *Eagle* noted that the house had commenced its travels on the preceding day and would probably block the street for several more days. Nine days later the *Eagle* reported that it "was seen last evening, in the position of giving 'one long, lingering look behind' into the avenue . . . as if on the point of paying its respects to Stanton street." Whitman paid his last respects to the perambulating house on 6 November. "Wending our way quietly down Willoughby street last evening we were suddenly brought to a full stop at Stanton street by an immense ugly looking pile . . . completely blocking up not only the street, but the sidewalks, and extending into the lots on each side!" It was his "ancient friend *that same old house*, which has been for several weeks past on its journey down Myrtle avenue." Perhaps the house intended to make a tour of the entire city; in that case, "the present generation (including you and us, reader) will be sleeping in the grave," before it ever got opposite the *Eagle's* office.

Whitman's attempts to badger the common council into prohibiting the moving of buildings through the streets was, of course, totally unsuccessful; for Brooklyn in the late 1840s was in the process of almost doubling its population, and house-moving was but one symptom of that growth. After November 1846 Whitman seldom reverted to the subject of house-moving. The Whig mayor and the common council were more vulnerable in their failure to keep the streets cleaned and the lamps lighted; and the Democratic editor of the *Eagle* found ample copy in these municipal shortcomings to heckle the opposition party. If one judges by the *Eagle* of 1846-47, the Whigs were as hostile to efficient city government in Brooklyn as to the manifestation of national destiny in the southwest.

Banks and Currency

ECONOMIC MATTERS in the late 1840s were closely connected with politics, as they are in any era. Earlier, Whitman's idol Jackson had destroyed the Bank of the United States, whose recharter had been urged by the Whigs in the second term of his presidency. Another though lesser Democratic hero of the *Eagle's* editor was Martin Van Buren, who had secured with difficulty the passage in 1840 of the Sub-Treasury Bill, which established an independent national treasury unconnected in any way with any bank, state or national, and provided that the receiving and disbursing of government funds was to be done on a strictly specie basis. The independent treasury, however, was short-lived, for the bill which established it was repealed in the next year by Tyler's administration. But Polk, who became President in 1845, had pledged, with the approval of his party, to secure the enactment of a lower tariff and the reestablishment of an independent treasury. He redeemed both pledges in 1846.

One of the salutary effects of the Sub-Treasury Bill had been the elimination of government deposits as one of the bases on which state banks had issued excessive and inflationary amounts of paper money. The virtue of an independent treasury was stressed by Whitman on 19 March 1846 in "An Independent Treasury—How It Will Affect the Working-Men." It was the Whig doctrine "to offer a man a dollar and a half in March, instead of his dollar—but at the same time scattering so much artificial money in circulation, as to make the nominally increased wages bring but three-quarters as much as the dollar only." The banks were like those ancient frauds, the pagan temples, and their "priests sit and send forth flimsy deception, not in Delphic sayings, but in printed sheets." The best remedy for this situation was "for the government . . . to receive and pay out nothing

117

but *hard money*, to retain in its own hands the entire and un-limited control of its own funds, without the least favor or partiality in any moneyed transactions."

On 4 April, under the head of "A Truly Noble Reform," the *Eagle* triumphantly announced that the Sub-Treasury Bill had passed the House by a large majority. Workingmen and farmers, opined the paper, should particularly be pleased, since they were the ones who ultimately suffered from the fluctuations in paper money. "It may seem otherwise to the superficial observer, who in times of financial depression beholds a few score great merchants 'bursting,' and large capitalists in difficulty," Whitman stated authoritatively. "But to one who has studied the subject, it has always been plain that on the masses rest at last the deposits of the surging waves." An independent treasury would keep active "a constant vein of solid and wholesome money." The Whigs and a number of conservative Democrats connected with banking were not so pleased with the bill as was the editor of the *Eagle*, and on 8 April the latter replied to some of their criticisms. The *New York Journal of Commerce* had complained that it could not get a copy of that "Bill of Folly and Madness," so Whitman obligingly devoted half a column to the contents of the bill. He noted that the *Brooklyn Star* was predicting "one currency for the people, and another for the government." This was nonsense, said Whitman, for section twenty of the bill stated that the government would pay its creditors in gold and silver. The *Star* also professed to tremblingly anticipating an evil day of purely specie currency. Such a day, Whitman was certain, would never come, for paper money was a convenience when freed of its inflationary dangers. If the government were restrained from meddling with paper currency (and the new bill would do just that), the businessmen and financiers could settle among themselves on the safest way to regulate such currency. "Necessity, and the law of self-preservation and profit, and the sharp eyes of the Yankee people, will do less than they have ever done before, if they don't arrange forthwith all those means . . . necessary to remedy the 'evil.' "

In the weeks that followed, Whitman continued his campaign for the Sub-Treasury Bill. Typical of his editorials on the subject was "Money That Is *Not* Money," on 10 April. He spoke of the alarm of the New York bankers and of "Wall street, the mart of paper money dealings." The Whig papers daily predicted that the banks would fail if the bill passed. "They talk as though nothing supported artificial money except acts of legislatures," said Whitman, and "they are nearer right than they would be willing to admit if pinned down in a corner." He thought that one desirable effect of an independent treasury would be the elimination of less stable banks through failure; and he asked, "Working men! will you that the government lends its potential credit to bolster up what without such credit would fall to the ground?" The government soon withdrew its "potential credit" from the banks, for the Sub-Treasury Bill was passed by the Senate and signed by President Polk on 6 August 1846, and the independent treasury system was established, which lasted until the enactment of the Federal Reserve Act in 1913.

In an editorial already noted— "An Independent Treasury —How It Will Affect the Working-Men"—Whitman suggested that "when the next bloated bank gets too tall for its roof, and tears away the old edifice to make room for a bigger, we suggest as most appropriate for its copy, some of the temples dedicated to Mercury, *the god of thieves*." Bankers were "selfish . . . purse-proud, and full of all corruptions." Whitman reminded his readers that he was, of course, referring only to the majority of banks; for there were exceptions—"several banks conducted on fair and honorable principles so far as it is possible for them to do so." A brief paragraph on 27 March 1845, titled "Banking," seemed to substantiate the justice of Whitman's distrust of most banks. Its first sentence read: "In Maine there are 30 banks, of these 28 are worthless; three at three per cent discount, and one at 8 per cent discount, and four good ones." The rest of the paragraph gave similar statistics on the banks of New Hampshire, Vermont, Rhode Island, Massachusetts, and Connecticut. Of the seventy-two banks in these five states, only nineteen were good and the rest were worthless or doubtful, usually the former. Whitman did not give the source for these figures, but they were not greatly exaggerated. Banks were chartered by the individual states, but they were of widely varying stability. Even among the soundest banks, chiefly eastern, credit extensions were greater than legal reserves. Individual bank-note currency was so motley and so prolific that it was easily counterfeited. In addition, the values of the bank notes were fluctuating. Probably much of Whitman's concern with paper money and the general weakness of the banks was motivated by his desire to see the Sub-Treasury Bill passed, for after August 1846 he seldom referred to either of the topics in his paper.

However, Whitman did wish to protect his subscribers against worthless or depreciated paper money issued by unstable or insolvent banks. The lead article for 6 March 1846, "Shaving and Shinplasters," objected to the frequent practice of New York and Brooklyn employers "of purchasing uncurrent money from Brokers, and paying it out to laborers and mechanics for their wages." When the worker bought necessities with these notes, they were not accepted at face value but were discounted by the storekeepers. This was unjust to the workers, but their employers apparently believed that "in the hands of the poor, bad money is just as useful as good." The merchant who accepted these uncurrent shinplasters might be the loser if the notes became worthless before he could get rid of them.

> But that the workman is frequently the loser, it is impossible to deny. Notes of Banks in an unsafe or insolvent condition, which are liable to break at any moment, and in which the community has but little or no confidence, are purchased at a discount, and paid out in the manner we have stated. If the man to whom they are paid happens to keep them over night, he is apt to find next morning that the Bank which issued them has failed—and then the laborer's wages and the comfort of his family are sacrificed, to enable his employer to profit by the shaving operation.

Even if it was the storekeeper and not the workman who had the notes in his possession when they became worthless, it was still the workingman who suffered. The merchant could get his money back by increasing the price of his goods. As a result, the losses resulting from this circulation of debased currency *"fall chiefly, if not exclusively, upon the laboring classes."* This evil could be eliminated if "our mechanics and laborers insisted on receiving their wages in *cash*."

In the same editorial Whitman remarked on the habit of "associations of knaves and swindlers" in New York of buying up worthless charters of "exploded" banks in other states, making themselves various officers of these firms, circulating their worthless notes and discounting them until a large number are in circulation, and then "suddenly disappear, and leave the holders of the miserable stuff to suffer for their credulity." Just such a bogus firm was passing its bank notes at that very time among the inhabitants of New York and Brooklyn, and in parts of New Jersey as well. For several months Whitman warned his readers against this company, known as the Bank of Georgia Lumber Company, until the anticipated denouement closed the matter.

On 3 March 1846 the *Eagle* printed a query from a reader who asked if such a bank as the Georgia Lumber Company existed in Maine and if the Wall street broker Peck was the same Peck who signed the notes of that bank as president. Whitman replied: "We understand that some persons are making great efforts to get the bills of that concern into circulation in this neighborhood. We think we have banks and bank paper enough of our own, and always view with suspicion all attempts to make foreign Bank notes part of our New York currency. . . . We have had enough of shinplasters in this neighborhood." Next day the *Eagle* quoted from a letter which had appeared in the *Newark Daily Advertiser* relative to a flood of three-dollar bills issued by the Bank of Georgia Lumber Company. According to the *Advertiser's* correspondent, the bank, which professed to be chartered by the state of Maine, was completely unauthorized to do business in that state. From this date on, Whitman persistently warned his readers against accepting the bank notes of the Georgia Lumber Company. Typical of his warnings is the following from the *Eagle* of 11 March:

> BANK OF THE GEORGIA LUMBER COMPANY AGAIN.—The managers of this fictitious Bank are still making great efforts to force its worthless money into circulation. We once more tell them and the community generally that any man who

121

passes the bills of this concern . . . is liable to be imprisoned
in the State prison for a term of seven years. We know that
some citizens who claim to be very pious, respectable and
exemplary citizens are engaged in this infamous attempt to
swindle the public. . . . Mechanics and laborers! have nothing
to do with the vile trash, and if any scoundrel attempts to
pass it, to you, make a complaint against him at the Police
Office. That is the only way to break up the concern, and
protect the public.

The notes of this firm were still in circulation on 25 April when
Whitman again warned his subscribers against them, saying they
were "not good for any thing except tinder." Ironically, the first
page of the *Eagle* for 25 April carried, as it had for the past
month, a small advertisement (signed by D. R. Peck, 11 Wall St.,
New York) asking for Georgia Lumber notes at three-fourths
percent discount. Of course, Van Anden, not Whitman, was responsible for the sale of advertising space in the paper. Three
months passed before this worthless currency ceased menacing
the public. On 15 July the *Eagle* briefly noted that "this shin-
plaster concern has stopped." Its New York agent had disap-
peared the day before.[31]

Some banks were trustworthy, and one such was the Brooklyn Savings Bank, whose new home Whitman visited on 10 August 1847 and duly reported in the next day's *Eagle*. He admired
its inside stucco work, but he especially liked its function as a
repository for the savings of "the prudent poor."[32] He speculated
sentimentally on the private histories of the depositors, many of
whom were workingwomen whose savings were devoted to the
"holiest objects," the relief and sustenance of parents, husbands,
invalids, and children. Indeed, "there might be seen, if they were
unveiled, stout young hearts, made prematurely wise in the way
of gain—but whose purpose sanctifies the chilling precocity for
wealth." Whitman commended "to those of our readers who have
no great plenty of this world's goods, the practice of putting by
a weekly trifle for time of need." The savings bank formed the
most convenient means of exercising this praiseworthy prudence.
Whitman saw in the Brooklyn Savings Bank a type of institution
which provided—in contrast to those too frequent banks that

were either doubtfully stable or plainly fraudulent—a partial shelter for the masses from the disastrous fluctuations of paper money.

The Tariff

HENRY CLAY finally got part of his American system into law when the tariff of 1842 was enacted. Though this tariff was protective in character, Tyler had agreed to it because of the need for increased governmental revenue. Polk redeemed his campaign pledge to reduce the tariff when in 1846 the Walker Tariff (so-called after Polk's secretary of the treasury, who was active in its passage) superseded that of 1842. The Walker Tariff was lower than the tariff of 1842 but, as events proved, it produced more revenue than its predecessor. The new tariff had been opposed vigorously by not only the Whigs but also many northern and eastern Democrats. Their cry had been that a lower tariff would result in ruin for the manufacturers and in financial depression for the country in general. On the contrary, the manufacturers and the nation as a whole became more prosperous than ever, and an even lower tariff was enacted in 1857.[33]

The *Eagle* under Whitman's editorship consistently proclaimed, as it pointed out on 2 November 1847, "its enmity to high tariffs, and its friendship for the lowest possible ones (even amounting to none at all)." Protection was "full as great a humbug, and as silly as Millerism." Whitman basically was a free-trade man, as he often asserted, and in part this stand was the result of his enduring dislike of excessive and restrictive legislation rather than of a fanatic faith in the inherent blessings of free trade. On 20 March 1846 he noted with "almost devotional joy" the impending repeal of the British corn laws and the probable sharp reduction by the English of their high tariff on other articles of trade. The result would be near to free trade, but

> We are of course not so wild as to think that free trade is directly going to shower down on England . . . every blessing under the sun—and cause the people to become rich, well fed, well clothed, and happy. . . . It is as the removal of the

corsets, the tight neckcloth, the pinching boot to the human body. It conveys no *positive* advantage.—It but lifts up and carries off a disadvantage. The after doings . . . may be foolish, unjust, and unfortunate—but the perpetual capacity remains with that nation which is not hampered by restrictive laws, of quickly coming back to a wholesome condition again.

The corn laws were repealed shortly by the British, who also abandoned protection on a large number of other commodities. This encouraged Polk and his administration to push successfully the Walker Tariff.

Whitman was quick to deride the industrialists' gloomy prophecies of a financial collapse and their efforts to align the workingmen and the farmers on their side of the tariff question. Whitman remarked on 7 March 1846 that "the despair of the Massachusetts cotton lords and their satellites, at the prospect of the speedy reduction of the tariff to a revenue standard, is becoming ludicrous in the extreme." He laughed at their attempts to appeal to the mechanic, the laborer, and the farmer in behalf "of American industry—and 20 per cent dividends." The industrialists were not satisfied with the tremendous wealth they had amassed by taxing the people; the workingmen and farmers, who really produced the country's wealth, "must still be subjected to onerous and unnecessary taxation, that Abbott Lawrence, Nathan Appleton, and their associates, may revel in luxury."[34] During the following months Whitman saw to it that the large laboring population of Brooklyn remembered the interests of the protectionists were opposed to theirs. As he said on 3 September 1846, "Has any one of our laboring fellow citizens such thin perceptions—does he imagine in his most abstracted dreams—that all this hubbub made by the pale-fingered richly-housed Whig manufacturers, and their organs, is for *him*, the laborer?"

The Walker Tariff went into effect on 1 December 1846. In the months (and years) that followed, the protectionists were as vocal as ever in demanding a high tariff despite the general prosperity. Whitman enjoyed being satirical at their expense by citing current industrial expansion, as on 11 March 1847 when he asked, "Why don't they, in view of such facts as the following

. . . explode with grief and wounded sympathy?" The fact that followed was an exchange item that $40,000 worth of stock, of a $100,000 total, had been subscribed to "at once" for a new cotton mill at Wickford, Rhode Island. On 21 April 1847 Whitman quoted part of a letter from Henry Clay to the "young whigs" of Auburn, New York, in which he regretted the loss of the election of 1844 because it had eventuated in the destruction of "the *protective policy*, under which we had made such rapid and encouraging advances." Clay's lament was best answered, said Whitman, by "the present condition of American commerce and the country. Never were our traders doing a better and sounder and more profitable business." The few months that had passed since the new tariff had gone into effect had convinced Whitman of the correctness of his belief that trade best regulated itself when freed of legislative restrictions.

Wage Earners and Immigrants

THE BULK of the voters in Brooklyn in the late 1840s was composed of mechanics and laborers. As has been seen, both Whigs and Democrats courted their votes. An increasingly important element of these workingmen were the immigrants, particularly the Irish. They, too, were wooed by both the Whigs and the Democrats, though damned by the Nativists. The great potato famine of 1845-47 in Ireland (and to a lesser degree on the continent) caused the already steady stream of Irish to America to increase to a torrent.[35] Though the most recently arrived Irish could not legally vote, many of their earlier arrived compatriots could, and the day would come when they themselves and their numerous progeny could. Meanwhile, they were welcomed by construction contractors and industrialists, who had lost many native workers to the operations of O'Sullivan's manifest destiny. And the Irish, and all the other emigrating nationalities, were welcomed by Walter Whitman.

"Come along, all hands, and welcome!" he hailed the peoples of Europe in the spring of 1846.[36] It was no wonder that the impoverished Irish came, after their centuries of oppression by English landlords, said Whitman on 22 May 1846 in his summary of "Foreign News" brought to New York by the steamship *Brittania*. In view of the increasing starvation of the Irish, "shall we not welcome them? Shall they starve in their pent up and misgoverned island, while we have millions on millions of unoccupied and fertile acres, created by the same God who rules over them and us—and destined for the use of all his creatures who need it?" But not just the poorer and less literate sort emigrated from the Old World. On 1 June 1846 the *Eagle*, after recollecting a time when immigration was much less, reported that "among the many thousands that arrived in our ports last week, we noticed in the streets of Brooklyn, on Saturday, a large number of apparently highly respectable people whom we should judge had not sought a home in this new world, from destitution of the comforts and necessaries of life. We bid them welcome to our shores!" Five days later Whitman marvelled that 8,289 immigrants had arrived during the past week in New York alone. "Curious to know where this immense accession to our population bestows itself, we took a stroll yesterday afternoon through Washington street, New York . . . and truly we saw fifty scenes which would have delighted Rembrandt himself." Extending from the Battery, the street was lined by "the most squalid habitations, each one being fitted out in the lower story as a low groggery." Here teemed the new arrivals from Europe, "in all manner of costume, and speaking all manner of dialects, from the ancient Erse and Teutonic, to the modern low Dutch." The immigrant had become so notable a part of the local scene that on 13 July 1847 the *Eagle* was constrained to give its readers a few definitions: "An *emigrant* is one who *migrates* or removes, bag and baggage, out of a country—an *immigrant* is one who *migrates* into a country. The same person who was an *emigrant* at the beginning of his journey or voyage, is an *immigrant* at the end of it."

As a newspaperman, Whitman was mostly concerned with the immigrants from Ireland: they formed the largest element among the newcomers and so had the greatest effect on the social and political life of Brooklyn. That the Irish contributed considerably to the rowdier life of the city cannot be doubted after reading the police-court news in the "City Intelligence" column of the *Eagle;* and that they were lacking in the rudiments of education was natural in view of their usual peasant origin. But Whitman championed the "warm-hearted" Irish, as he often described them, and viewed their weaknesses with tolerance. He had no sympathy with the prejudices of the Nativists (and he generally identified the Whigs as latent Nativists).[37] On 3 April 1846, dealing with a laborers' strike, Whitman envisioned a "flippant whig gentleman" saying of the Irish, "They are a low ignorant set, and have no business here, at all!" Then Whitman framed this reply:

> Ah, Mr Native, or Mr Whig, you are true to your instincts, we see. The Irish laborers are ignorant in book lore we grant —and perhaps uncouth in manners. But they are *men* like us, and have wants and appetites, affection for their offspring, and anger for all kinds of tyranny, and if they don't get work or food, they will starve to death. . . . Shall we suppose, because we came here a few years before them, that they have therefore no claim on the limitless . . . capacities of America for human happiness, not to say subsistence? Away with such miserly and monstrous doctrine! Let us (for not *all* even of us democrats are free from a taint of this "foreign" prejudice), let us lift our minds out from the silly disposition to find fault with the foreigner, because he is not perfection and is derelict in some things. . . . The petty confines of the Old World are crowded to suffocation. . . . And shall *we* . . . not encourage . . . the drawing off from superannuated Europe of its poor?

On 30 September Whitman referred to a letter from a Philadelphian to the *Boston Evening Traveller* which gave some of the causes of the destructive rioting two years before in Philadelphia between Nativists and the Catholic Irish. One of the causes, said the letter, was "the introduction of a foreign population, unaccustomed to liberty regulated by law. The notion of liberty formed by these men is *to do as they please*." This was unjust, Whitman thought, as the Nativists had begun the riots, not the Irish. Further, the Irish had brought a "wealth of sinewy arms, stout hearts, and an energetic will" to the development of America's potentialities; and certainly there was more than enough room for them. Nor was it amiss to recall the contributions the Irish had made to the Revolutionary War and to the War of 1812; and Whitman proceeded to list the heroes of both wars who had been Irish either by birth or by ancestry (the Scotch-Irish also were included in the list, which allowed Whitman to bring in Andrew Jackson). "It is rather too bad, then," he concluded, "that a class of men who did their devoir in the very outset of our national existence . . . should still be subjected to these flings from people who ought to know and do better!"

Most of Whitman's remarks about the Irish in the *Eagle* were related to the Irish relief movement, in which both the government and private citizens were participants.[38] An almost complete index (and summary) of the *Eagle's* support of the relief appears in the issue of 7 July 1847. The Whig *Advertiser*, referring to the Irish relief movement in Brooklyn, had said, "The first meeting was held, but not a word did the *Eagle* say to help the cause. The third passed and it remained silent." Whitman indignantly quoted the *Advertiser* and then said, "As early as the commencement of October last, we, in common with most other papers, seized the opportunity, on the receipt of the various arrivals of foreign news, to call the attention of our readers to the then approaching famine in Ireland," and after the fall elections, "we took frequent and warm interest in the relief movement." He then cited the specific issues of the *Eagle* in which editorials had appeared supporting Irish relief and pointed out that the *Eagle*, "with other Brooklyn papers," had received a note of thanks for its efforts from the first meeting for relief. The political importance of the Irish was shown by Whitman's assertion that the *Advertiser* had endeavored to fasten "a partisan cast" on the relief movement: "It flourished in its editorials about the whigs giving more than the democrats—and endeavored to prove that the democratic administration was 'against' relief—and so on." Of course, on this and many other occasions, Whitman averred that the English editor of the *Advertiser* congenitally "hated" the idea of Irish independence. Meanwhile, he sent files of the *Eagle* to Lees and on 9 July reported that the *Advertiser* agreed the articles by him on Irish relief had actually appeared but "were what printers call 'close,' that is the lines were not spaced apart!"

This was an outrageous quibble, cried Whitman; and again he accused the *Advertiser* of opposing Irish independence and of blackguarding O'Connell, the Irish patriot, and quoted supporting passages from that paper. "*These* make us regard the Brooklyn *Advertiser* as the 'enemy of Ireland and Irishmen,'" he declared. "We appeal to any true-hearted Irishman whether we are right or wrong."

Several hundred of these true-hearted Irishmen were involved in a labor dispute which furnished the most sensational local news in the spring of 1846. Toward the end of March the laborers employed by the construction firm of Voorhis, Stranahan and Company, which was building the Atlantic dock and basin in South Brooklyn, went on strike for higher wages. The number of workmen on strike varied in stories in the *Eagle* from three hundred to six hundred, but it seemed to include all the laborers on the project, who in turn were apparently all Irish. The strike, which involved some violence, lasted until May and was followed closely by the *Eagle*. Ordinarily, Whitman had little to say about workingmen except as they were affected by paper money, the tariff, and sometimes, slavery (see "American Workingmen, Versus Slavery," 1 September 1847). But in his pieces on the strike at the Atlantic dock, he offered some opinions on labor unions for the first and last time in the *Eagle*.

Whitman mentioned the strike for the first time on 25 March, merely remarking that the strikers "say they are determined to prevent others from working at the old rates of 70 cents per day." The next day he printed a long editorial titled "Illy Paid Labor in Brooklyn." It began with this sentence: "There is hardly anything on earth, of its sort, that arouses our sympathies more readily than the cause of a laborer, or a band of laborers, struggling for a competence . . . and standing out against the exactions of grinding 'bosses' and speculators." Then Whitman reported he had been informed that two evenings before, a large group of Brooklyn laborers had met to organize a "benevolent association" for the caring of its sick and the burying of its dead, and for the regulating of wages. At the meeting letters had been read from three contractors who agreed to meet the demand of the workers for a daily wage of seven shillings (eighty-seven and a half cents).[39] Voorhis, Stranahan and Company, however, had sent word it would not make any terms except those that suited it. The *Eagle* had no desire to meddle in the matter, but

> It thinks that organized associations, to "regulate" the prices of labor, are the most fallacious things in the world. There is not, to our knowledge, one single instance of their having met with permanent success. They are, moreover, when proceeding beyond a certain limit, contrary to the dictates of that clear, high, immutable truth, the freer and the more without restrictions of any kind you leave trade and prices to regulate themselves, the better for all parties.

Clearly labor unions were of the same breed as morals legislation and tariff laws so far as the free-trade Jeffersonian editor of the *Eagle* was concerned. But Whitman's sympathy for the workers, as workers, remained. He referred to their miserable pay for a working day which lasted from sunrise to dark, to their brief dinner period, the penalty they received (one-quarter of their day's wage) if they were only three minutes late to morning roll call. "And many of these men have families of children to feed, and clothe, and *educate*—and potatoes are a dollar a bushel, and flour and beef unusually high!" he said. "Not four dollars a week —and the plentiful crop of children most poor men get, *living* on such a sum for seven days! Let our philanthropists not go to oppressed England and starving Ireland for samples of scanty comfort; if these things are so, we have enough ground for our indignation in our very midst."

On 2 April the *Eagle* announced that a good reason existed for the slowness with which the dirt heaps in the city were being removed, since "the new Laborers' Association forbid the acceptance of the established prices by a portion of the men, *unless all are set at work*." Whitman regretted that the laborers were going "to the very excess of injustice which they complained of in their own former employers." But Whitman had been misinformed. The next day the *Eagle* carried an editorial captioned "Oppress Not the Hireling!"

> Several of the members of the new Laborers' Association called upon us yesterday—and from the statement they made,

130

we are constrained to believe that we have not done that Association . . . justice. It did *not* prevent men from going to work at the prices demanded, unless all were set to work; our information . . . must have been incorrect. . . . On the contrary, its members will gladly receive work . . . in any quantity, or from whoever will give it.

While upon this matter, we may as well improve the occasion to say a few words on the payment of labor in this country, and about the treatment of the lower grades of honest laborers. 87½ cents per day is all that Brooklyn laborers ask—and we do say . . . that the man, or set of men, who refuse to give that price, show a most heartless meanness, and that if the curse of ill gotten profits does not attach to their wealth, it will not be because it is undeserved! Just a little over $5 a week! and that with children to support!

Whitman followed these remarks with an extended defense of immigrants in general and the Irish in particular. This defense was, he said, "the outpourings of honest heart-impulses."

Voorhis, Stranahan and Company remained adamant to the demands of the strikers; and on 15 April the *Eagle* reported that a party of Germans, hired to replace the striking Irish, had been set upon by the latter, armed with clubs and stones, and driven from the dock area. Two days later Whitman complained that the ringleaders of the Irish, whose names were known, had not been brought to justice. On 20 April the *Eagle* reported that three nights earlier a large shanty, erected at the Atlantic dock by Voorhis and Stranahan for their German workers, had been burned by the Irish; and since that night "a military corps" had been on guard there.[40] Also, the company intended that very morning to put a larger number of Germans to work on dock and basin. The sheriff and "the whole police force of the city" had already gone to the dock to guard the Germans and were to be followed soon by General Underhill and several of the city's militia companies. The next afternoon, as described on 22 April, Whitman had visited "the scene of military operations at the Atlantic Dock." Two hundred Germans were working inside the lines on the dredging machines in the basin. A large crowd of men, women, and children were "gaping in wondering astonishment at the scene." Whitman supposed that by special press favor "(for the other loafers were kept at a respectable distance,) we were passed through the guard, and proceeded over the draw-bridge towards the barracks." The strikers, who usually hung in force about the dock, were nowhere to be seen. They were at that moment assembled, with two or three thousand persons "from Brooklyn and New York," upon Bergen Hill. There the Reverend N. O'Donnell of St Paul's Catholic Church appealed to them to disperse, but a deputation from the New York Laborers' Union persuaded them to go to a hall, where the said deputation made "inflammatory speeches." [41]

Despite the thrashings in the streets of occasional Germans by occasional Irishmen, the environs of the Atlantic dock remained quiet, and the militia returned to their civilian duties on 23 April. On the same day officers were roaming the city, rather unsuccessfully, with warrants for about twenty of the Irish ring-leaders. Whitman fancied the storm was over. But it was not. At dusk that day, as the *Eagle* reported on 24 April, a party of the German workers, going to the South ferry to return to their homes in New York, were attacked by a group of Irish. In the melee that followed the Germans were worsted and fled. Deputy Sheriff John Swertcope appeared on the scene and called upon several citizens (one of whom had the interesting name of Dr Moriarty) to help him stop the fray. The deputy and his allies managed to arrest two of the leading rioters, but their Irish compatriots rescued them. This battle, however, was the end of violence in the strike. A grand jury immediately indicted a large number of the Irishmen involved in the rioting, and the Germans were no longer molested. By 6 May Whitman was able to announce that "a large number of the disaffected workmen have resumed operations, while many of the remainder have sought employment from other sources."

On 11 May Whitman visited the Atlantic dock where he saw the Germans and the Irish working peacefully side by side. Those of the Irish who had come back to the employ of Voorhis, Stranahan and Company had been forced to accept that company's wage rate. The *Eagle* for 22 August, writing of the five hundred men employed at the dock, stated that half the force was

German and the other half Irish, and that the company intended to keep that ratio as a safeguard against future strikes. "The wages given at the present time are 80 cents per day to those who labor in the bank—mostly Irishmen; and 85 to the dredgemen . . . who are all Germans." The standard summer wage before the strike had been eighty cents, so the Irish gained nothing by their walkout.

After his "Oppress Not the Hireling!" of 3 April, Whitman never again in connection with the strike spoke of the Brooklyn Laborers' Benevolent Society with any sympathy or accused employers of "heartless meanness" for not paying their "honest laborers" eighty-seven and a half cents a day. Perhaps the physical violence of the striking Irish was enough to alienate the *Eagle's* editor. But it was the theory behind the violence that was most repugnant: that the workingmen had the right to "regulate" the price of their labor. As has been seen, Whitman believed an organization devoted to that goal was a contradiction of the "immutable truth" that the less interference in trade and prices (including that of labor) the better for all concerned. His contention, he must have felt, had been validated by the course and the result of the Atlantic dock strike.

Irish laborers were not the only persons resentful of the low wages they received. The *Eagle* for 19 August 1846 cited the *New York News* as saying the sewing girls of that city planned to hold a mass meeting to show their employers "that they have some 'independence' left, and that they will not be dealt with so shamefully for the future." Whitman commented on the "extortion" practiced toward the sewing girls and added,

> Old gossips may prate about virtue and morality, but if any one will watch the movements of these patient and gentle N. Y. sewing girls from day to day, and tell why they prefer the crust of bread and pallet of straw to silks and satins, luxury and fine living, they will be wise indeed. No wonder the pest houses and brothels in that city are increasing in number every day: no wonder that so many are seeking refuge from poverty and distress in those places, while such unrighteous treatment is dealt out to them. Something should be done, and done quickly, to remedy the evil.

When Whitman again reverted to the subject of underpaid working women on 9 November, he explained that "when we see how the continued, persevering, incessant, honest efforts at reforming any old abuse, by means of newspaper writing, at last succeed . . . we are inclined to think that in this subject of poor pay for females' work, good results would sooner or later follow from the faithful adherence of the press to the advocacy of 'the rights of women' in the matter."

On 20 November Whitman remarked on the inconsistency of public opinion that sympathized with the workingman whose wages were lowered below a reasonable figure but did not sympathize with the workingwoman in the same position. All working-women received "miserably poor" pay. Some people suggested that they should go into service; but, said Whitman, "the supply of servants is already profuse, and . . . is a more unpleasant life to an American girl, than any other which could be mentioned."[42] In the few articles he wrote in the *Eagle* on this topic, Whitman did not suggest any concrete means by which women might secure adequate wages. "The only remedy we know of," he said on 29 January 1847 ("The Sewing Women of Brooklyn and New York"), "is to be found in the operation of an awakened public opinion."

A third class of Brooklyn workers were the boys, largely apprentices and junior clerks. The *Eagle* almost never referred to any abuses in their employment, preferring to give them good advice on self-education and physical exercise. Occasionally Whitman pontifically lectured the apprentices on their conduct toward their masters. "Be careful how you allow yourself to indulge in a spirit of secret fault finding with your employer," he advised on 29 July 1846.[43] There were few masters without faults, and the faithful apprentice who overlooked his master's faults was sure to be at last handsomely rewarded. And if one unhappily had a cruel master, "even him you can bring to your feet by gentleness." While Whitman seemingly admitted that some masters were cruel, he must have felt that no great abuses existed in the apprentice system, as at no time did he lecture those who employed apprentices.[44]

Those who were employers of junior clerks, however, were criticized by Whitman on a few occasions. On 3 June 1846 the *Eagle* briefly noted it had received a letter, "apparently from a clerk in a dry goods store," urging that stores be closed at eight in the evening. The arguments of the correspondent were sound, but his communication had been much too long to be printed. No more was said on the topic until 4 September when, in an editorial titled "Junior Clerks," Whitman quoted the *Boston Bee* as saying that clerks should meet and take measures to improve their condition. This reminded Whitman that two weeks earlier a young man, who had just been discharged by his New York employer, had called at his office. His salary had been fifty dollars a year, and his "employer came over to Brooklyn—where, we believe, he resides—and outlaid just forty times the amt. of the young man's annual wages in a pew or pews in one of our fashionable churches." Most of the junior clerks in America, said Whitman, worked like "dray-horses" and many received no money; and those who were paid in money ($50 to $150) were expected to board and neatly clothe themselves with that sum. Whitman lectured their employers:

> They appear to forget that young fellows have stomachs which possess a marvelous affinity to bread and beef—have generally a great deal of spirit and ambition—are susceptible to kindness and generosity . . . like to enjoy . . . some of the numerous pleasures God has vouchsafed in this goodly world —like to have a few leisure hours now and then, and a few extra dimes in their pockets, for contingencies. All these things are seldom realized by those who employ clerks: it is a mere strife, with them, to get the utmost possible service, for the lowest possible payment. Then, too, how rarely the employer enters with any thing like friendly interest into the personal hopes, aims, and schemes of those who work for him!

Personally, Whitman concluded, he thought "the clerk market over stocked—and should never, except under peculiar circumstances, advise a boy to 'go into a store.'" But even so, junior clerks were as much flesh and blood as their employers. And in the following year he was pleased to note in the *Eagle* on 4 December that the dry goods stores of the city had agreed to close during the winter at eight o'clock instead of the customary nine, except on Saturday when there was no limit. It would be a good practice, he thought, if all retail stores did the same so their clerks might have "the use of their evenings." Clerks, especially junior clerks (or boys), were "compelled to be less independent than mechanics," and their wages were inadequate. "It is irksome, at any time," declared Whitman, "for young people to be confined from morning till night in a sedentary way." One may be certain the peripatetic editor of the *Eagle* wrote from the heart when he penned that line.

"There is a complete 'coast guard' all around the island of leisurely cit[izen]s who are in quest of seaside pleasure," wrote Whitman in a brief item unobtrusively tucked away in a corner of the second page of the *Eagle* on 23 August 1847. "The toiling million, however, are forced by poverty to remain amid the bustle, din, heat, smoke, and turmoil of the city.—Alas, there is too much difference in men's condition." This sentiment was rarely so explicitly expressed in the *Eagle* during Whitman's tenure and was probably a semi-humorous reference to the plight of editors of daily papers. The poverty of the toiling million was most often alluded to in connection with Whitman's favorite projects of an independent treasury and a low tariff. The young editor of the *Eagle* understood the plight of the underpaid worker. But he was confronted in the late 1840s with too many things more engrossing and demanding than the poverty of the working class to devote much time to crusading against it.[45] The difference in men's conditions could not compete for the interest of a successful young journalist with manifest destiny, the Mexican War, Oregon, the Wilmot Proviso, the tariff, the sub-treasury, the Irish, the Brooklyn boom, politics, or even, as will be seen, with the movement to abolish capital punishment.

three

THE SOCIAL SCENE

The Humanitarian Impulse

ONE of the notable currents in the society of the American republic from its beginning was that of humanitarian reform. For example, in the early days of the republic Dr Benjamin Rush supported educational and prison reform, humane care of the insane, and peace and temperance movements. Later reformers, especially in the 1830s and 1840s, shared Dr Rush's philanthropic catholicity.[1] William Lloyd Garrison, rather typically, was not only an abolitionist but also a worker for world peace and a delegate to the first World's Temperance Convention, held in London in 1846. Humanitarian reform was not just an American phenomenon; it was mainly the result of the European Enlightenment and the Romantic movement. Yet in the 1840s the American masses were intelligently aware of the arguments and objectives of contemporary reform, whereas in Europe and even in England they were generally only half-conscious of the tenets and aims of humanitarianism except as they directly affected their individual members. This contrast between the Old and New Worlds may have been the result of the greater literacy of the Americans and the abundance of cheap newspapers available to them. So thought Alexander Mackay, a British barrister who toured the United States in 1846 and 1847. He was pleased to note that "on the great majority of questions of a social and political import, which arise, every citizen is found to entertain an intelligent opinion. He may be wrong in his views, but he can always offer you reasons for them. In this, how favourably does he contrast with the unreasoning and ignorant multitudes in other lands!"[2]

The United States, with its democratic institutions, its religious tolerance, and its ample *Lebensraum*, was a propitious spot for the cultivation of utopias—political, religious, and social. It lured from the Old World such reformers and utopians as Robert Owen, Harriet Martineau, and Frances Wright; but it had a thriving native stock as well.

> The American reformer was the product of evangelical religion, which presented to every person the necessity for positive action to save his own soul, and dynamic frontier democracy, which was rooted deep in a belief in the worth of the individual. . . . Education, temperance, universal peace, prison reform, the rights of women, the evils of slavery, the dangers of Catholicism, all were legitimate fields for his efforts.[3]

Whitman, like most of his fellow editors, commented on the earnest laborers in these various vineyards of reform and occasionally joined forces with them, though never so fanatically and indiscriminately as Horace Greeley. He offered an explanation for his not being the complete reformer when he told Horace Traubel in 1888, "I was in early life very bigoted in my anti-slavery, anti-capital-punishment and so on, so on, but I have always had a latent toleration for the people who choose the reactionary course."[4]

Though Whitman may have been obstinately attached in his *Eagle* days to the anti-hanging cause, he was not inclined to radical theories of reform. Under the heading "Quixotic Labors" he said of a notorious arch-reformer in the *Eagle* on 6 June 1846:

> We notice that Robert Owen, the philanthropist and human reformer, has arrived again in this republic. . . . Very well. We surely don't think R. O. will do any harm; in all probability, too, he will do no good.
>
> At the time of the "World's Convention," got up in Clinton Hall, New York, we attended the debates of that singular gathering; and were somewhat in doubt whether to laugh at the whole thing as a humbug, or commend it inasmuch as it

contained the germs of a bold though fruitless inquiry into the wrongs and evils of the world.[5] The first day was certainly occupied with a greater quantity of bickering . . . about unimportant forms, than we ever remember of having seen in any deliberative assembly before. Assuredly such men (in this connection we except Mr Owen; his demeanor was patient and dignified) are the last ones to come forward as reformers of the world . . .

Of Mr Owen we may add that he seems to be an honest and enthusiastic old man, and to believe what he would have others believe. But the present system of society has . . . little to fear from his hardest blows. There is truth in Mr O's speeches and addresses, two or three of which we have listened to with much pleasure; and yet it is utterly chimerical . . . to attempt remodelling the world on an unalloyed basis of purity and perfection. God did not see fit to do so, and we hardly expect the thing will be accomplished by Mr Robert Owen.

On his return to the United States in 1846, Owen set about his routine of organizing meetings before which he expounded his dream of a socialistic utopia and urged his hearers, as Whitman reported on 23 June, to promote "a complete social and political revolution." "Ah, Mr Owen!" Whitman reproved, "when God has ordained that evil shall exist, do you think that *you* can banish it altogether?"

Common sense said that in a dualistic world evil was fundamental and could not be eradicated entirely; but, as Whitman and his romantic generation knew, it could be alleviated. "How sweet is the remembrance of a kind act!" rhapsodized the *Eagle* on 28 March 1846, in a style worthy of an era which admired the writings of Mrs Lydia H. Sigourney. "As we rest on our pillows, or rise in the morning, it gives us delight. We have performed a good deed to a poor man; we have made the widow's heart to rejoice; we have dried the orphan's tears. Sweet, oh! how sweet the thought!" And in a muddled way one might dally with the idea of a utopia, being careful to locate it very tentatively and vaguely in what amounted to almost another dimension of time. So dallied the *Eagle* on 14 August 1846, as it editorialized on the word "Philanthropy."

One of the most beautiful words which our language has borrowed from the Greek, is . . . *Philanthropy*, signifying the "Love of Man." It has a musical sound; and the very utterance of it begets pleasant thoughts, and inspires prophecies of good. . . . A vision, however, far off, of the relation existing between all men, as members of one great family; the duty and pleasure of loving and helping, one the other; the dwelling together of the nations in peace, as being of the same flesh and blood and bone, and bound together by the ties of a common brotherhood . . . these are the thoughts and feelings which must have lived somewhere, in some hearts in the olden time; and which, struggling for utterance, gave birth to this beautiful and musical speech. . . . Let us rejoice in its existence, and seek to give [it] divine second birth in action.

But Whitman knew that the heaven of the philanthropists was indeed far off, and he never asked the impossible when he appealed to the humanitarianism of his Brooklyn readers. Most of the reforms he advocated in the *Eagle* were sensible, and none was unique. They ranged from anti-capital-punishment to anti-swill-milk; and Whitman's remarks upon them illuminate the social scene of the 1840s.

Crime and Punishment

MUCH OF the "human interest" in the newspapers of the 1840s was provided by stories covering police-court proceedings. Benjamin Day, who established the first successful penny newspaper, the *New York Sun*, in 1833, appears to have been the first to capitalize on this sort of sensationalism when he hired George W. Wisner, a veteran reporter of the happenings at London's Bow street police station, to cover the New York police courts. Wisner "relied largely on police reports and the coarse humor of the police courts for the interesting matter in his columns"; and in doing so, he created the American police reporter, whose merits consisted in his "being facile with his pen, and sufficiently indifferent (after the fashion of the press generally, of that day) to the feelings of the poor creatures left to its mercy."[6] Whitman, who was

140

police reporter as well as editor of the *Eagle,* frequently wrote in the accepted Wisner tradition when he prepared his daily report on what he had seen and heard during his morning visit to the Brooklyn police court. Ordinarily the court was a busy place each morning and its usual business is illustrated by the following item in the *Eagle* on 9 July 1847:

> STATISTICS OF IMMORALITY.—Seventeen warrants were issued yesterday at the police office; of which nine were for assault and battery; five for disorderly conduct, drunkenness, and breach of the peace; and three for petit larceny.

On the previous day the police court had dealt with thirty cases, twenty-six of which had been for assault and battery. This daily procession of persons brutalized by drink and by an unwholesome environment might have elicited some reformatory and humanitarian comments from the editor of the *Eagle* as he recorded its exhibitions of folly and tragedy; but it did not. "Andrew Ryan, an aged subject of Alcohol Rex, and who has subsisted from the time whereof the memory of man runneth not to the contrary, at the public expense in sundry jails, alms and watchhouses, was last night taken in charge by a watchman," Whitman reported on 27 February 1847. "When brought up to the police office he formed the most perfect specimen of perpetual motion ever seen in these demesnes, being afflicted with a shaking that would have done credit to a western ague. He was convicted of being a 'vagrom man,' and dealt with accordingly." Such was the flippant tone which characterized the *Eagle's* accounts of routine police business.

Brooklyn prided itself on being freer from the more sordid and violent crimes than was the metropolis across the East River, but it had more important law-enforcement problems than the simple restraint of drunks, bullies, vagrants, and wife-beaters. During Whitman's two years with the *Eagle* Brooklyn was plagued by burglaries, which received due notice, along with advice on precautions to be taken, in the "Local Intelligence" column of the paper.[7] "Burglarious demonstrations," as Whitman sometimes styled them, steadily increased during 1846. Few arrests were made. The Brooklyn police, who worked on a fee basis, complained of being insufficiently paid. On 2 November the *Eagle* demanded that they be adequately paid unless the city officials were resigned to seeing the number of burglaries increase. "Something should instantly be done in this matter," Whitman announced, "or Brooklyn will get a bad reputation, as an unsafe dwelling place." The burglaries increased, as Whitman had predicted, especially in the suburbs where an efficient watch was particularly lacking. On 9 November the *Eagle* suggested that the suburban residents of the city protect themselves with "a brace of patent revolvers . . . together with a good watch dog." For a watch dog he advised "a cowardly 'cur of low degree' " whose craven howls would wake the householder and frighten off the housebreaker. Perhaps some citizens followed this advice, but on 30 May 1847 the *Eagle* made this melancholy report: "The old saw of 'thick as leaves in Vallambrosa' is no longer expressive enough, and it is accordingly to be changed to 'thick as burglaries in Brooklyn.' For some time past we have regularly recorded at least one burglary per night." Again Whitman urged that the police be paid more.

Earlier, on 5 May the *Eagle* had reported an assault by a footpad on a respectable citizen walking home from the South ferry. On that occasion, after damning the miserable street lights, Whitman placed most of the blame for the crime on the city's inefficient police system: "It suggests itself to us . . . whether there should not be *good* watchmen, *paid a good price;* a man can't take a mere pittance, and work as though he had reasonable wages." And he commended the matter to the attention of his fellow citizens and the city fathers. On 7 June Whitman indignantly predicted that the city would go on being inadequately protected against "midnight outrages." The common council added twelve men to the watch in the sixth ward, the favorite theatre of operations for burglars, where as many as five burglaries a night occurred despite the increased police force. But the aldermen had decided they could not raise sufficient funds to increase the watch in the rest of the city or to raise its pay. "Far cheaper would it be," declared Whitman, "for every householder to pay directly the equivalent of his valuables for ample protection than to wait until he is robbed of them, and his life jeopardized." Sometime after this date the common council did take a step to decrease the number of burglaries in the city, but soon recanted, as an item from the *Eagle* of 28 September shows:

> INTERESTING TO THOSE WHO ARREST BURGLARS.—The resolution which offers a standing reward of $25 for the apprehension and conviction of every burglar in this city was repealed last evening, at the instance of Ald. Smith. This is a great pity, and we fear that Mr S. will see his mistake ere long.

But no dramatic denouement marked the withdrawal of the reward; the closing months of Whitman's editorship saw burglaries decline, perhaps because of the cold weather, until the *Eagle* had nothing more sensational to report in that line except the purloining of silver spoons by Negro servants.

The Brooklyn juveniles engaged in their share of petty thievery, but only once did Whitman suggest that something might be done about it.[8] In the *Eagle* of 21 July 1847 he suggested that the police keep their eyes upon the "too frequently disreputable" junk shops. "The lures which they hold out to the young and thoughtless to perpetrate petty crimes no doubt tend in time greatly to swell the number of the desperate rascals who infest large cities."

Whitman commented more frequently on the bands of boys who roamed the streets on Sundays and at night. From time to time, as on 13 June 1846, he hoped "that the numerous gangs of boys and other disorderly persons will be induced to forget their usual Sabbath amusements in the way of pitching coppers, fighting dogs, &c." The fifteen Sunday officers, he warned, had orders to arrest all who behaved disgracefully on the Sabbath. The watch also was instructed to stop the vandalism of the gangs of boys who so often made "night hideous." But the watch was no more successful in this than in apprehending burglars. On 4 September 1846 Whitman reported that a gang of boys had dragged the putrifying carcass of a cow through a street in South Brooklyn, stopping before various houses to give their occupants "a good smell." The same gang was in the habit of turning in false fire alarms as "thick as leaves in Vallambrosa." Whitman did not know if the gang was too formidable for the police, but he did know "the officers are stated to be remarkably scarce whenever the b'hoys choose to cut up their pranks." There was a large number of similar gangs in Brooklyn, and it was "about time a commencement was made somewhere to stop their pernicious proceedings."

Apparently the watch did not make a commencement. On 31 July 1847 the *Eagle* warned: "The young gentlemen who alarmed the neighborhood of Myrtle avenue on Thursday evening by their noise had better be more careful in future, or they may wake up the watchmen." And on 2 August, in "Rowdyism in Brooklyn," Whitman blamed the ineffectual police for the continued rowdyism. "Perambulating wretches" not only made the "night hideous with their unearthly voices and obscene songs" but engaged in "more tangible outrages." Houses were despoiled of their railings, ironwork was wrenched from stoops, and the awnings of stores were beaten to the ground. The Brooklyn police were useless: "In the first place there are not half enough of them, and, in the second place, what we have are not good for anything." One could walk through the city late at night and never catch a glimpse of the watch. "The watch system of Brooklyn invites rowdyism to do its prettiest; and the invitation is accepted, too."[9]

Sometimes the police were able to apprehend a juvenile delinquent, as Whitman reported on 27 May 1847. On the evening before, he had glanced out of his editorial window at the foot of Fulton street and seen an officer arrest a "little boy about knee high, who had been guilty of the mortal offence of stealing *one apple* from an old woman's stand opposite our office." The numerous spectators objected, but the officer led the boy off, holding a hand over his mouth to suppress his cries. "After some time ineffectually spent in finding a police magistrate, the highhanded young culprit was taken before the mayor, who promptly and properly discharged him. This is rather a diminutive business, but we suppose the officer made two or three dollars out of it."

Murder and suicide were as rare in Brooklyn as drunkenness and rowdyism were common. Whitman professed to dislike the reporting of sordid crimes of violence, and fortunately he had no murders and only one sensational attempted suicide to

144

cover on the local scene.[10] But enough violence occurred else-where in the nation to provide the citizens of Brooklyn with the melodramatic reading which attracted a large audience then as now. Whitman had hardly taken the helm of the *Eagle* when he told his readers on 16 March 1846 that the family of a Mr Van Ness of Fleming, New York, had been butchered by a person dis-guised as a Negro. During the next few days, the *Eagle* reiterated the gory details—the bloody bodies of Van Ness, his pregnant wife, and their infant child; Van Ness' mother-in-law running after the murderer with her "intestines protruding" (or her "bowels gushed out"), and the hired man Van Arsdale, severely stabbed but successfully fighting off the assassin with a broom-stick. The murderer was captured quickly and was found to be William Freeman, a young Negro who had just been released from Auburn State Prison after serving five years for stealing a horse from the late Mr Van Ness.

The exchange papers provided other murders, but with fewer victims. And on 20 March, under the exclamatory heading of "Another Bloody Affair!" Whitman declared, "We are quite sick of reading the numerous murders that happen of late!" On this occasion Edward H. Rulloff, "a school teacher, and part doctor," had slain his wife and child only to have unusually high water near Ithaca, New York, disinter the box in which he had hidden the evidence of his crime. A very common heading in the *Eagle* during Whitman's tenure was "More Bloody Work," and the story that followed expressed revulsion for murder but, none-theless, let the honest mechanics of Brooklyn know that brains had been spilled by hoe, shovel, or axe.

A more sophisticated type of murder was reported by the *Eagle* on 4 December 1846. Under the "New York &c." column Whitman said, "Loving not loathing, we present the sad case (ah, how many like it there have been, and are yet to be, in the American Gomorrah!) of a young girl, as reported in the N. Y. prints." A seventeen-year-old girl, deserted by her lover, had died from medicines taken to produce a miscarriage. Perhaps the no-torious Madame Restell, who blatantly advertised her "Preventa-tive Powders" at five dollars a package in many of the New York newspapers, had been the indirect assassin of the young girl; but

145

Whitman said nothing of her then. In the fall of 1847 Madame Restell was brought before a New York court on the charge of performing illegal operations. Whitman followed the trial with interest, describing her as the "child-murderess" and wondering if she would escape again (as she had in 1841 under similar circumstances) because of her wealth. On 11 November the *Eagle* deplored that the "she-wolf . . . was yesterday pronounced *guilty* of a misdemeanor (!) by the jury." Madame Restell's inadequate sentence was one year in Sing Sing, but her conviction was later reversed while Whitman was in New Orleans and occupied with other matters.

Whitman had little to say in the *Eagle* about what characterized the criminal type. But he did indicate on 25 May 1846 what he fancied was the antithesis of a murderer. A man known as Babe had appeared on the Long Island shore amid the wreckage of a schooner, and the absence of his shipmates led the authorities to prosecute him for piracy. Babe was sentenced to death but was soon pardoned, which Whitman noted with pleasure on 25 May. "We went into that interesting establishment [the Tombs], some time ago, to take a look at the prisoners," said Whitman. "Babe seemed to feel jolly enough; he was fat and ruddy, and laughed like a real good fellow. Indeed, it struck us, when we heard his loud clear laugh, that he could not have committed such bloody deeds—for a man with a clear ringing laugh is never an ingrained villain."

An ingrained idleness, in Whitman's opinion, characterized many of the lesser lawbreakers such as vagrants and habitual tipplers. The jail sentences meted out by the Brooklyn police court were served in Kings County Jail where, as Whitman often noted, the inmates were assured of food, shelter, and leisure— particularly in the winter. On 18 June 1847 the *Eagle* reported that the county board of supervisors had appointed a committee to investigate possible sites for a workhouse. Whitman added the following:

> The county has quite long enough been to the expense of supporting in idleness and comparative comfort those who disturb the peace of the city; and it is settled that many worthless and dissolute persons have been tempted to infringe the laws for

the sole purpose of securing an asylum. A workhouse would put an end to this abuse, and be a great stroke of economy . . . by the prevention of law-breaking. For some time past the number of able-bodied prisoners and paupers have been unusually low; but . . . there is ground to believe that it will soon reach its accustomed amount. The millenium has not yet arrived, nor is human nature a whit better than it always has been.

Meanwhile, the county officials should provide their prisoners with some sort of work. Noting on 10 July that a vagrant had been sentenced to jail at hard labor for fifteen days, Whitman was moved to say:

Curiosity is alive to know what is done in prison, which is entered upon the police records as being so "hard." We never happened to see the convicts doing anything harder than masticating wholesome victuals, lolling on comfortable straw mattresses and staring stone walls out of countenance. This would be "hard" enough to a man of active habits but to such lazzaroni as the city is infested with, it proves a perfect asylum. . . . It is a wonder to us that the supervisors have not long since attached some little reality to these hitherto fictitious sentences.

When autumn came Whitman was convinced that the Kings County Jail was a haven for the cold months for Brooklyn's petty criminals. He reported on 14 October that Patrick Hickie, arrested for stealing some silver spoons, had been furnished with "comfortable winter quarters" for the next six months. To Whitman, Hickie was a representative of the numerous class of "thieving beggars" who had nothing to lose in stealing. If not detected, the thief was rewarded by the value of his loot. "While on the other hand, if detected, his condition would be improved by the occupancy of a shelter during the winter months without care, labor or trouble, and enabled to emerge like a chrysalis on the approach of warm weather into a renewed state of existence." A few days later the county determined on the construction of a cesspool in the jail yard. It was with satisfaction that Whitman wrote on 30 October: "There are at the present time only about fifty five prisoners confined in the jail of this county, some fifteen of whom are furnished with constant and agreeable employment in digging upon the sewer recently commenced. A few more able bodied gents wanted immediately."

Whitman's only objection to the Kings County Jail was its failure to enforce "hard labor" sentences. But he was aware of other undesirable conditions in other prisons, especially in New York (the Tombs) and the two state penitentiaries. On 1 August 1846 Whitman remarked that "with all our boasted improvement on the past, we have *not* much bettered the condition or reformatory influence of our places for criminals." He then referred to a publication recently issued by the New York Prison Association describing the conditions in the Tombs, where as many as 10,000 persons were confined in a year. While Whitman professed dismay at the profane manner in which the male prisoners of the Tombs spent their Sundays, he was primarily indignant at the intermingling of hardened criminals with children, lunatics, paupers, and other comparative innocents. The state prisons, on the other hand, were criticized in a number of articles in the *Eagle* for their severe disciplinary measures which degraded both the punisher and the punished.

The so-called Auburn System came into being when it became evident that the practice at Auburn Penitentiary of confining prisoners in individual cells day and night resulted in an excessive amount of sickness and even insanity. In 1823 workshops were built inside the walls of Auburn where the prisoners worked together in the day and were returned to their cells at night. Not only was the general health of the prisoners improved, but the prison was also able to show a profit above its upkeep in the sale of the products made in its shops. This development in penology operated efficiently because of severe discipline, which included walking to and from the cells in lock step and absolute silence. The slightest infraction of a rule was punished, ordinarily by flogging. When the Mount Pleasant Prison was built in 1826 at Ossining, it was organized on the Auburn pattern. Whitman, who spoke out against the flogging of seamen and school children, spoke out as loudly against the flogging of criminals.

A prisoner at Auburn named Plumb had been flogged to death for feigning insanity; and Whitman rose in righteous anger in an editorial in the *Eagle* on 10 March 1846 titled "The Officers of Our State Prisons." "At the risk of arousing a ready cry about 'mawkish sympathy' from that worst part of the conservative faction, which is composed of unbelievers in the good of humanity," he began, "we would make a few suggestions about the officers in our State prisons." The death of Plumb, not the first of its sort, showed that the rulers of Auburn were "persons of hardened and morose natures, disposed to judge harshly and punish severely—the last men in the world . . . for the position they hold." Whitman reminded his readers it was now generally agreed that the insane responded best to mild government; certainly the criminal, still possessed of his faculties, should be more tractable when ruled with kindness. "O," he exclaimed, "it is a disgrace to this wide and noble country—it is an insult to the very soul of our constitution, which assumes the rule of reason, not might— that a man should be scourged to death—that others should be daily tortured and lacerated—for *any* crimes they might commit!" Especially was this so in view of the pettiness of the faults for which flogging was the punishment. Plumb, so it was claimed, had assumed madness. "Others are tied up naked, and lashed until the blood runs down their backs, because they have spoken to a fellow convict, have fallen into a fit of anger, or some other equally *heinous* offence!" Whitman concluded his article with a call for reformation based, as so many of the reforms of the time were, upon Christian ethics. "We call upon those who have any faith in human goodness—any abhorrence of brutal cruelty —any honor for Him who, amid the agonies of the crucifixion, turned his dying sight upon a felon, with words of promise and bliss—to *act* reform upon this subject!" A typical comment appeared in the *Eagle*, 30 June 1846. Whitman said he did not wish to have the prisons made pleasant places, but there were few matters "more worthy the attention of philanthropists" than that of prison management. "Still does the lash hold its livid rule in our prisons . . . Still is the remnant, (little enough in some!) of humanity left in the wretched convicts there, crushed out of them —systematically, as it seems!"

There was one state prison official of whom Whitman approved—Mrs Eliza W. Farnham, matron of the women's division of Sing Sing (as Mount Pleasant Prison already was being called, after the village of Ossining, where it was located). Whitman first mentioned Mrs Farnham on 1 May 1846 when he commented on a letter she had written to a New York paper which had "some refreshing testimony in behalf of mildness among prisoners." The doctrine of human depravity, said Whitman, had been so long held that it was difficult to promote humane treatment of criminals. "In this connection, the world, at present, sees orthodoxy arrayed against the precepts of Christ"; apparently only the good deserved "love and sympathy." Mrs Farnham's letter showed the good effect on felons of "that forbearance which is due to them on account of their unhappy early training, their neglected moral nature, and perhaps many extenuating circumstances connected with their very guilt." Whitman quoted from the letter two anecdotes illustrating his and Mrs Farnham's sentiments, one of which concerned a Negro girl who was put to work in the flower garden at Sing Sing and was found later "bathed in tears" because the flowers had recalled her past innocence. On 31 July 1846 the *Eagle* received a similar letter from Mrs Farnham, which Whitman published under the heading "Prison Reform.....A Noble Effort, Well Promulged by a Noble Woman."

But the *New York Sun* did not think at all well of Mrs Farnham's theories; on 2 September 1846 the *Eagle* attacked the *Sun* for its "sentiments averse to prison reform, and to ameliorating the old rigidity of law." The *Sun* advocated that sanguinary revenge so contrary to the spirit of Christ. "Of all the cant and stuff we hear in this artificial world," declared the editor of the *Eagle*, "the worst and weakest . . . is that cant which calls humanity for the sons and daughters of vice 'mawkish sympathy.' " Then he concluded with a paragraph on the reform which received more notice in his paper than any other—the abolition of the death sentence. Instead of the murderer's being himself murdered by society, let him be imprisoned for life. "Let the assassin's heart be gnawed by remorse . . . There let the long seasons of his weary time roll heavily on, till his iron soul is conquered, and the deep fountains which sleep even in the wickedest bosom are touched. Perpetual imprisonment? Good God! is not that enough? Why we are almost shocked at our own inhumanity, when we write an argument for so cruel a doom in any case."

The New York State Society for the Abolition of Capital Punishment, its office in New York, was active in lobbying at Albany and in organizing local societies over the state. In addition it published a monthly, the *Spirit of the Age*, which Whitman recommended to his readers from time to time.[11] Brooklyn had a local anti-hanging society, but it seems to have functioned only fitfully. On the evening of 13 March 1846 Whitman and about one hundred other persons attended, despite a downpour, a meeting called by the society at the Brooklyn Institute lecture room. None of the officers of the society appeared and the meeting resulted in a few impromptu speeches on the evils of capital punishment. The later meetings of the society were equally unsatisfactory. On 20 November the *Eagle* noted that a hanging was scheduled for that day in the yard of the Tombs and that, ironically, the same day had been set aside by the State Society for the Abolition of Capital Punishment for statewide propagandizing by means of lectures, debates, and newspaper editorials. "What is our Brooklyn Society doing, by the bye?" asked Whitman. "We hope it will not be discouraged by a few malapropos occurrences at its meetings of last spring . . . let no petty difficulties stand in the way!" But the society was discouraged, for on 8 January 1847 Whitman commented on the hostility of the legislature toward the anti-capital-punishment movement and then wondered what had happened to the Anti-Hanging Society of Brooklyn. After this date the *Eagle* never again mentioned the society.

But Whitman by himself was a kind of society for the abolition of capital punishment. In his many comments in the *Eagle* on the death penalty, he gave several reasons for his opposition to it. Though the modern world chose to practice only those Christian precepts which were "practical," legal murder was as clearly contrary to the laws of Christ as was wanton murder. But regardless of the moral aspect of the matter, the execution of a convicted murderer was patently illogical; hanging was "teaching the pricelessness of human life, by destroying it" (as Whitman

noted on 16 March 1846 when he again recorded another in-
stance of capital punishment). It did not seem to the editor of the
Eagle that the "hanging plan" deterred anyone from taking another's life. On 7 May he observed that the lower house of the
state legislature had refused to pass a bill allowing the people
to vote for or against capital punishment.

> During the month of March, and the first week of April, we
> have the record of *over forty atrocious murders*, with fifty-
> one suicides (there were doubtless more, of both, but these
> we collect from a cursory examination of the prints), two of
> the former being most horrible fratricides—one case in which
> a man absolutely *tore* the quivering body of his child to pieces,
> and then slaughtered his wife—two parricides—and more
> than half the rest attended with circumstances of peculiar
> cruelty. Does the fear of hanging, then, deter from the com-
> mission of murder?

A particularly vicious result, as Whitman saw it, of the "hanging
plan" was that many murderers escaped punishment of any sort
because some jurors were unwilling to compromise their consciences by sentencing a fellow human to death. Whenever an
accused murderer was acquitted, the readers of the *Eagle* were
sure to be told that again a jury had allowed a villain to go free
rather than condemn him to the mandatory death sentence. If a
jury did find a murderer guilty, in many states (though not in
New York) his hanging was a public spectacle—sometimes the
scaffold was hidden by a canvas covering—which excited the
baser nature of the spectators to such a degree that often the
event had the air and the accompanying vices of a carnival. Public
executions also, by some mental chemistry which Whitman never
clearly explained, impelled some spectators to kill either themselves or another person. On 16 July 1846 he described two
recent hangings of a very unpleasant sort, which were, he said,
"rich with inferences." He cited four cases in which witnesses of
these two executions either murdered someone on the day they
watched said hangings, or else hung themselves on the same day
or within a day or two. Even private executions had a bad effect
on the public, as the *Eagle* noted on 20 August 1846.

> The law of this state forbids public executions; but it cannot forbid newspapers from publishing accounts of the executions —which amounts to the same thing—only "a great deal more so." Indeed the detailed narratives of hanging, which newspapers give, circulate more widely, and are dwelt on more elaborately: the moral effect of a hanging spectacle is therefore just as much diffused by print, as though it were presented actually to the eyes of people.

Whitman continued, declaring that the *Eagle*, too, "must be in the fashion, and give the *latest* execution—that of Wyatt." He described Wyatt's swoons, his last speech, and ended the article with this ironic sentence: "And then the proper officer cut the rope, and the platform fell, the man fought the air a while—and then all was still: for the 'great moral lesson' had been achieved."

Whitman did not depend solely upon his own pen in his campaign for prison reform and the abolition of capital punishment. From time to time the page-one literary section carried a sentimental poem or sketch in which a prisoner solicited the sympathy of the reader by dying or by revealing a heart of gold. Notable Europeans were summoned to Whitman's banner. On 13 January 1847 the *Eagle* printed a long story of the career of the celebrated English prison reformer, the late Mrs Elizabeth Fry. On 28 March 1846 three-quarters of a column was given to Dickens' remarks on capital punishment, which ended with the comment that if he, Dickens, were on a jury trying a murderer, he would rather find him mad than hang him. On 24 December 1846 a brief item read: " 'As I grow older,' said Goethe, 'I become more lenient to the sins of frail humanity. The man who loudly denounces, I always suspect. . . . The hypocrite always strives to divert attention from his own wickedness, by denouncing unsparingly that of others. He thinks he shall seem good in exact ratio as he makes others seem bad.' " But there was one sin for which Whitman felt no leniency. He noted on 1 February 1847 that a slave, one Cato, had been sentenced to hang in South Carolina "for a most horrible outrage committed on a white female." For once he was not indignant: "If there be any wisdom in capital punishment in any case, it is in such a case as this.

Mere murder is white-robed innocence to deeds of this sort." Perhaps for Whitman this was the exception which proved the rule.

Fires and Firemen

THE BROOKLYN firemen, as well as the Brooklyn police, were kept busy during Whitman's stay on the *Eagle*. The midnight bell so often tolled for fires deliberately set that on 11 June 1846 (according to an advertisement in the *Eagle*) Mayor Stryker and the common council proclaimed a reward of one thousand dollars would be given for the arrest and conviction of the incendiary who recently had caused a destructive blaze or of any arsonist who in the future should set a house afire at night. Apparently the council withdrew the offer, for on 27 February 1847 Whitman asked that body to provide such a reward. "The crime of midnight incendiarism would seem to be alarmingly upon the increase in this city. The last three fires are reported to have been caused by incendiarism. . . . There can be little or no doubt . . . that there is either a systematic gang of ruffians who employ this means of gratifying their propensity for plunder, or else the conflagrations alluded to have been caused by motives of revenge." It behooved the common council to offer a large reward, as an inducement to the local police officers, for the arrest of these "abandoned and midnight villains." Much might be done in that way to "prevent a repetition of events so terrible even in anticipation to every inhabitant of a densely populated city." Whitman emphasized his appeal by printing in an adjoining column, under the heading "A City Fire," the description of an extensive fire he had witnessed "a season since" in New York.[12] The picture he drew of the scene was vividly realistic, confirming his prefatory statement about public fires: "Alarming as they are, too, there is a kind of hideous pleasure about them."

The fire companies that fought the Brooklyn conflagrations were composed of volunteers—about thirty to a company. According to the *Eagle* of 14 December 1847, Brooklyn had fifteen engine companies, one hose company, and four hook-and-ladder companies. The romantic fireman appealed to Whitman.

154

Engine Company No. 5 turned out with its machine, apparently a new one being shown off, on 23 March 1846 (according to the next day's *Eagle*): "And a dashy, bright, saucy, strong limbed set of 'boys,' they were . . . We don't know when we have seen a better show of firemen than this company with its friends, as they passed by our office yesterday." Whitman often spoke of the Brooklyn firemen as being "a brave set of fellows"; but on 9 January 1847, after describing the "Ball of the Brooklyn Firemen, for the benefit of their deceased brothers' widows and orphans," he made some comments which showed that not everyone idealized the volunteers.

> It is too common among supercilious people to look on the Firemen as turbulent noisy folk, "b-oys" for a row and "muss," only: this does the great body of them a prodigious injustice. A few are to be found, no doubt, whose conduct makes them open to such a charge . . . But as a *class*, the Firemen of Brooklyn have mostly generous traits—are swift to do their duty—and can be commended as men without whom the public safety would hardly be preserved a week!

On 21 August, however, the *Eagle* reported that a false alarm on the previous evening had ended in a free-for-all between certain of the engine companies, who had engaged in a post-alarm race, a pastime which included bumping machines in the hope of disabling that of a rival company. At one time five engines were tangled together; but of them all, "the conduct of no. 5's party was unbefitting either sensible men, or decent citizens." The latter company had taken the long way home for the pleasure of running into the engine of No. 3 as often as possible, and "the disturbance created immense confusion," which was quelled only by the mayor himself at the head of the police. The volunteers of Company No. 5 had fallen in Whitman's estimation.[13]

> The greatest evil of the fire department . . . arises from the volunteers—a word, in that connection, which is equivalent to rowdyism, and everything contrary to manliness and good order. A lot of half grown boys, ambitious of all the vices and petty excesses that they see maturer persons commit, attach themselves to the fire machines, meet at the engine houses, and early get habituated to all the precocious wicked-

155

ness of cities. These youths are first at a fire, and quickest at all cowardly mischief; for, true to an old rule, they have little of the courage of men, though bold enough, when they go in gangs. We call upon the city government to put in force the laws which forbid these fellows from attaching themselves to the city engines, and disturbing the public peace, as they almost invariably do when they turn out.

The rowdyism among the firemen did not, however, prevent them from energetically and efficiently subduing blazes. On the evening of 29 September 1847, between seven and eight o'clock, a business building burned near the foot of Fulton street. The prompt arrival of the fire companies confined the fire to the building in which it originated, at the cost of two injured volunteers. The fire—but not the spirits of the firemen—was extinguished shortly after eleven o'clock. Company No. 7 chose to go home by way of Fulton street, though its way lay in the opposite direction. The result was that No. 7 "commenced the practice of that beautiful sport which occasions most of the difficulty in the department, viz: 'running into' No. 5." The residents along the street were startled from their sleep by "fearful oaths and imprecations . . . frightful and revolting." No. 5 finally cut the dragrope to No. 7's engine and a battle royal ensued in which the men of Company 7 were "handsomely threshed" and forced to abandon their machine. The mayor arrived too late to do anything except tow, with assistance, the abandoned engine to its house in Front street. "It is a pity," said Whitman, "that with the gallantry and enthusiasm which they possess and the brave bearing which they exhibit in moments of real and critical danger, our firemen should so sully their reputation as good members of society by engaging in scenes of the lowest rowdyism."

The firemen were chastened, perhaps, after this escapade, for the *Eagle* did not complain again of their conduct. And, after all, they had their complaints too. For one thing, Brooklyn lacked sufficient public cisterns in some parts of the city, and the *Eagle* was continually demanding that the common council build more lest the predominantly wooden city suffer a holocaust. Too, the firemen were harassed by false alarms. This, Whitman thought,

156

resulted from the key to the fire-bell tower being hung in a nearby public house where anyone could take it. But worst of all, the fire bell was always being "mis-rung." On 21 October 1847 the *Eagle* noted that in the morning the bell had rung for a fire in the fifth district when it should have been rung for the fourth— much to the confusion of the firemen. "We have repeatedly called attention to the mis-management of the alarm bell, which is getting to be a worse nuisance than ever." Though the Brooklyn firemen were hampered by lack of water, false or faulty alarms, and a rowdy element, they performed an indispensable public service without pay. Whitman paid tribute to them in the *Eagle* on 30 October 1847 when he reprinted from *DeBow's Commercial Review* an article on firemen which lauded their heroism, courage, and chivalry, and described them as "brave sentinels and soldiers of peace." The Brooklyn firemen were not precisely soldiers of peace, but the editor of the *Eagle*, saunterer and spectator *par excellence*, admired them as men of action and of physical daring.

Temperance

THE TEMPERANCE MOVEMENT in America became a force to reckon with when in 1833 the United States Temperance Union (which became the American Temperance Union in 1836) was organized. Later, especially in the early 1840s, other national anti-liquor societies developed, such as the Sons of Temperance and the Washingtonians. At first the temperance movement had attacked only distilled liquors, allowing abstainers the delights of wines and malt brews. But in the late 1830s a radical faction arose in the ranks of the temperance reformers and demanded total abstinence in all things alcoholic, which drove wine, beer, ale, and hard cider beyond the pale of respectable temperance. Soon "total abstinence" became the shibboleth of the temperance societies, and the word "temperance" acquired a gratuitous meaning which has persisted into the twentieth century. A further development of the temperance movement was the campaign for prohibition in the 1840s which, for a number of reasons, seems an illogical phenomenon for that individualistic era. As Carl Russell Fish has said of this early prohibition movement: "Such a program seems to fly directly into the face of the individualism of the period and that conception of governmental functions which was being reenforced by the *laissez faire* doctrine of the only group of British thinkers whose influence reached America."[14] Nonetheless, the prohibition movement got enough support in the state of New York for the legislature to pass a bill in 1845, calling for a statewide vote—with the exception of New York City—on the question of local option, or "license or no license" for pubs. The measure was put before the electorate, and the voters of 856 New York towns went to the polls in May 1846; 528, including Brooklyn, voted "no license."[15] The measure was not totally prohibitory, since it concerned only distilled liquors which, wherever local option was approved, were not to be sold by the drink or in quantities of less than five gallons.

Whitman (as noted in an earlier chapter) opposed "no licensing" because it was contrary to his conviction that legislation should be kept to the barest essential minimum and that morality could not be legislated. He consistently spoke out in the *Eagle* against the principle of "no license." On 20 May 1846 the *Eagle* announced that the citizens of Brooklyn had voted against the liquor traffic and supposed that New York would, as it had for other Brooklyn vices, "act as a sort of sink to carry off our surplus tippling and intemperance." But Whitman feared an effect of the "no license" would be "that many persons, who are precluded from buying in smaller quantities, will send home their five gallons at a time; and if the consumption be augmented by the increased supply, the monster which has been ostensibly checked may grow more hideous in the midst of the family circle." Three days later, admitting the unpopularity of his sentiments, Whitman presented another argument against the new law. Most intelligent opinion, he said, agreed on the evils of spirituous liquors; but no such agreement existed on the propriety of regulating temperance by legal force. "There is . . . a powerful instinct in the masses of this country, *averse to restrictions on commerce*. . . . We do not think they will be willing to see liquor venders arrested, fined, and imprisoned for one of the plainest rights of trade . . . and they should not."

Whitman believed the results of the liquor law amply substantiated his contention that the law was vicious and contrary to the ideals of democratic government. In "Prohibition of Liquor-Vending" in the *Eagle* for 17 October 1847 he noted a Virginia paper had reported that John B. Gough, the well-known reformed drunkard and temperance crusader, had been invited to spend the winter in that state lecturing, and it had been suggested that Virginia enact a license law similar to New York's. It was commendable, said Whitman, to invite Gough to lecture on temperance.[16]

> But if the people of Virginia knew what miserable effects follow the New License law in this State, they would hardly be emulous of walking in that part of our footsteps. We doubt . . . whether it has prevented one case of drunkenness . . . whether it has given the noble cause of Temperance . . . the least additional impetus. But no one can doubt—for the evidences are on every side—that it has . . . arrayed neighbor against neighbor—encouraged that worst of meanness, "informing" . . . In the very few places where the command of a "No License" majority has been obeyed by the ordinary tavernkeepers, liquor is sold clandestinely, and in places of a much more irresponsible character—the same quantity is being drunken, but in a method of hypocrisy . . . which trebles the fault. Is it too much to say that no man, disposed to drink, has been baffled by the New Law?

The new law, Whitman continued, muddled up one's notions of right and wrong: good laws should be impartial, which the license law was not. On Staten Island there were four adjoining townships, "all in a row": in the first and third, selling liquor by the drink was legal; in the second and fourth it was not. "It is a poisonous thing for the popular conscience that such confusion is created: besides, it invites comparisons. You can never satisfy a man why a privilege should be withheld from him which is granted to his neighbor over the way. All the sophistry in the world will never satisfy him." Whitman concluded his editorial by condemning the narrow fanaticism of certain temperance advocates.

> It is justly claimed for this age that among the many true re-forms that have found ardent advocates—and *success*—Temperance in its beautiful simplicity stands conspicuous. . . . We, too, admire this beneficent progress—this baffling of appetite, and the redemption of so many men from intemperate cravings which degrade their nature. . . . But we cannot go to that extreme which loses sight of other, and as great, Truths. For it must not be forgotten that there *are* other great truths in the world.

There were, Whitman reminded his readers, many customs "far far meaner and wickeder than drinking a glass of brandy; and if it be acknowledged that it is the province of the statute book . . . to destroy them . . . we shall open a work so interminable and immense that a finite mind cannot scan it—whose hopeless end is lost in obscurity, and whose success it would be folly to expect!" The plain truth was that "the best government is that which governs least."

Though he detested the prohibition movement, Whitman was a constant advocate of temperance *per se* and a firm believer that its cause could be effectively promoted only through persuasion. The intemperate individual had to be convinced personally that tippling was ruinous; and the *Eagle* endeavored to provide the proper arguments. The literary section on page one was an instrument in this effort. From time to time it carried temperance tales by such popular literary figures as Mrs Lydia H. Sigourney, temperance poems by such poets as Eliza Cook, and from 16 to 30 November 1846, an abridged and revised version of Whitman's early temperance novel *Franklin Evans*.[17] News items, often taken from exchange papers, also served as temperance propaganda. Frequent headings appeared in the *Eagle*, like "Intemperance and Parricide," "How Rum Can Change a Young Man Into a Brutal Scoundrel," and were followed by reports of drunken sons killing their aged fathers with axes and crowbars, and of besotted brutes knocking down inoffensive little boys in the street for the sport of it. Sometimes, as on 25 October 1847, such an item would be preceded by a personal appeal from the

Eagle's editor: "Here is another frightful evidence of rum-drinking, in 'common life.' Will not some of our younger men, in Brooklyn, take warning?"

"Moral suasion," as the period called it, was the most Whitman could engage in as a Jeffersonian Democrat. "The duty of the promulger of all moral reforms," he asserted in the *Eagle* on 22 December 1846 in connection with the "no license" bill, "is very simple—being nothing more than to advocate and illustrate, the more enthusiastically the better, his doctrine—and carefully abstain from identifying it or himself with any of the cliques or the passing notions of the time." Whitman's conviction was that temperance could not and should not be legislated; and he informed his subscribers, without equivocation, that such was his belief. Further, he showed them that tippling had not submitted to legislation in the state of New York. Whitman was not a teetotaler, but certainly he was temperate in the basic and better sense of the word and so illustrated—to his own satisfaction—his doctrine that temperance was enforced by common sense and not by coercion. So far as the temperance cliques were concerned, Whitman did not identify himself with any of them. Apparently he was not a member of any formal temperance society, and he rejected the idea of prohibition. Problems like intemperance had to be solved, finally, by the individual, for (as Whitman said 13 March 1847) "in his moral and mental capacity, man is the sovereign of his individual self."

Slavery

WHITMAN's anti-slavery feelings, as mirrored in the *Eagle*, mainly expressed themselves in editorials advocating the adoption of the Wilmot Proviso. The practical basis on which Whitman erected his attitude toward the inflammable slavery question was expressed in the *Eagle* on 22 April 1847:

> With the present slave States, of course, no human being any where out from themselves has the least shadow of a right to interfere; but in new land, added to our surface by the national arms, and by the action of our government, and where

slavery does not exist, it is certainly of momentous importance . . . whether that land shall be slave land or not.

In view of this statement, repeated in many other *Eagle* editorials,
Whitman could not be and indeed was not an abolitionist. He
disapproved of slavery and thought it an anachronistic institution in a republic; but he believed its dissolution would come
about by gradual emancipation which, as he sometimes pointed
out, had been the wish of Washington and Jefferson. The love of
"impartial" liberty would increase with each generation so that
finally the contradiction between slavery and the Declaration of
Independence would become evident to all—and then slavery
in the United States would end.

The fanaticism of the abolitionists had worked against the
dissolution of the "peculiar institution." On 7 November 1846
the *Eagle* approvingly noted that the Louisiana legislature had
enacted a law which permitted municipal councils to grant the
manumission of slaves. "We have often thought," said Whitman,
"that if the ultraism and officiousness of the Abolitionists had *not*
been, the slave states at the south would have advanced much
farther in the 'cause of freedom' to their slaves . . . The abominable fanaticism of the Abolitionists has aroused the other side
of the feeling—and thus retarded the very consummation desired
by the A. faction." As an example of what the slave states might
do on their own initiative, the *Eagle* on 23 February 1847 cited
the passage in one house of the Delaware legislature of a bill for
abolishing slavery in that state. Two or three of the slave states,
Whitman declared, already would have been free states had it
not been for an "angry-voiced and silly set" composed of "a few
foolish and red-hot fanatics—the 'abolitionists.' " He concluded,
"We have wondrous faith in the quiet progress of wholesome
principles in this country."

Though Whitman wrote no angry editorials on slavery as
it existed in the South, his stern demands that the institution be
excluded from the new southwestern territories were based mainly
on two points, which constituted a criticism of that institution in
the southern states themselves. As he said in "American Workingmen, Versus Slavery" on 1 September 1847, slavery was in-

consistent with the other and democratic institutions of America, and it competed unfairly with free workingmen and brought "the dignity of labor down to the level of slavery, which, God knows! is low enough." Whitman hoped that the majority of the white southerners (themselves not owners of slaves) would finally recognize these truths and abolish Negro servitude.

Other than this, Whitman had little to say in the *Eagle* about slavery. He deplored the inhumanity of the slave trade still being carried on, often by American vessels, between Africa and Brazil and wrote indignantly of its horrors. But he temperately avoided drawing a moral from news stories of incidents involving slaves—the contrary of his practice when he printed an account of a hanging. On 8 April 1846, under the heading "A Beautiful and Most Instructive 'Moral Lesson,'" the *Eagle* described the execution in New Orleans of a female slave for "cruelty to her mistress." The moral lesson was the barbarity of public hangings, not the evils of slavery. The slave's master had conceived a "licentious passion" for her and had made her mistress of his house. She had taken advantage of her position and abused her owner's wife. The abolitionists were fond of insisting upon the immorality attendant upon slavery. But the nearest Whitman came to any such criticism was to say, "If any one deserved severity, it seems to us to have been the *husband*, not the miserable, ignorant, contemptible negress." On 11 July 1846 the *Eagle* reported that an old Negress and a Negro boy and girl (all slaves) had been sentenced at Alexandria, Louisiana, for poisoning an overseer. The Negress was to be hung; the boy was sentenced to wear a five-pound collar about his neck for a year; the girl received the same punishment with the addition of twenty-five lashes a month for a year. The punishment of the boy and girl would have been condemned as barbarous by an abolitionist, but Whitman made no criticism at all, even implied.

Whitman envisioned the Negro as a free man, but it is possible that he did not envision him as a citizen exercising the suffrage and living in social equality with the White American. The slave was not romanticized in the *Eagle*. On the few occasions that he was mentioned, he was ordinarily pictured as ignorant and uncivilized. The *Eagle* on 18 March 1847 gave the heading "Can This Be In The Nineteenth Century?" to an account taken from a Mobile paper of four Negro slaves who exhumed the body of a white man for the sake of its fingers, toes, and tongue, valued as charms ensuring success in gambling. On 24 March Whitman noted without comment that the culprits had been sentenced to receive lashes ranging from thirty-nine to fifty. How were the ignorant and relatively primitive Negroes, once they were manumitted by an enlightened South, to be adjusted to freedom in a society governed by white mores? Whitman never said.[18]

The free Negroes of Brooklyn were never the subject of any humanitarian passages in the *Eagle*. They usually were depicted (ordinarily their only mention was in the police news) as if they were performing in an eternal minstrel show.[19] They had their own public school, which Whitman described as being equal to "the better sort of those devoted to their more fortunate brethren."[20] But Whitman had nothing to say in the *Eagle* about Negro education as such. And the only reference to Negro suffrage appeared on 5 November 1846: "There were 1148 votes cast in Brooklyn in favor of Negro Suffrage—and 4310 votes against the same. Majority against, 3162." The editor added no comment.

As seen earlier, Whitman became an active worker in the Free-Soil Party by September 1848, when he began editing the *Brooklyn Freeman*. In the first issue of the *Freeman* he praised Jefferson as an "abolitionist"—the very epithet which, in the *Eagle*, he had applied only to a class of reformers he despised. It does not seem enough to say that this change in Whitman from a temperate critic of slavery to one so fanatic that he could glory in the term "abolitionist" was simply the result of his espousal of the Wilmot Proviso. There must have been something more, and a clue to this something more may lie in the report in the *Eagle* of 10 December 1847 on a lecture at the Brooklyn Institute entitled "The Worth of Liberty."

> Mr Giles's lecture on this topic, at the Institute, last night, was one of the most powerfully written and warmly delivered speeches we ever heard. Rarely have the divine proportions of liberty been praised by more eloquent lips: rarely, if ever, has the accursed nature of tyranny and slavery . . . been pourtrayed in words more effective and clear, or in a manner

> more enthusiastic! The lecturer's picture of a slave, the *thing* without the feelings of a man—*not* a husband, *not* a parent, *not* a wife, *not* a patriot—and impossible to be either, in its proper sense—was burningly fearful and true.

Undoubtedly the lecture was concerned with liberty in its broadest application and not exclusively with its relation to American slavery, for Giles invoked those many persons who had suffered exile and death for the sake of that "divinest possession of our race, LIBERTY." But Whitman's concluding remarks seem to allude to the South's peculiar institution: "For ourselves and . . . all who love freedom and hate oppression, we would thank Mr Giles for this not merely intellectual treat, but for his noble promulgation of some of the best principles in the spirit of christianity, and that lie at the foundation of our republican government and the rights of all human beings."[21] Whitman's response to this lecture—he very seldom expressed such unqualified approval of a lecture—suggests that his tolerance of slavery as a matter to be dealt with by the states in which it existed may have been disintegrated gradually by the persuasive (to one who had much of the reformer in himself) arguments of the abolitionists. However it came about, the Whitman of the *Freeman* no longer possessed unimpaired, as had the Whitman of the *Eagle*, a "wondrous faith in the quiet progress of wholesome principles in this country."

Other Humanitarian Matters

FROM time to time during Whitman's editorship the *Eagle* discussed subjects for reform or philanthropy other than prisons, hanging, liquor, and slavery. Homeless children, the poor, the insane, the blind, the equine, and women were some of these subjects; and since these were matters of interest to the humanitarians of the 1840s, it was inevitable that Whitman should write of them. But relatively little space was given to these topics in the *Eagle*. And the abused horse received as much notice, if not more, as his hapless two-legged fellow creatures.

The busy commercial streets of Brooklyn were filled with horse-drawn vehicles, and Whitman had only to look out of his editorial window to see brute man maltreating the noble horse. Not uncommon in the *Eagle* were items such as the following, which appeared on 1 July 1847: "We just see (twenty-minutes to 1 o'clock) a two-legged brute off against one of the stage houses in Fulton street, beating his horse ferociously in the face, nose, and ears, with a stout whip handle. Infamous!" In his first editorial in the *Eagle* on this subject, 11 March 1846, Whitman suggested to the overloaders and beaters of horses that they go to the "brown skinned savage" of the desert and from him learn how splendidly the horse responds to gentle treatment. "We confess to a real affection for a fine horse! So strong—so harmonious in limb, shape, and sinew—so graceful in movement—with an eye of such thoughtful and almost speaking brightness . . . No man with a man's heart can be brutal to such a creature!" On 31 March the *Eagle* carried an editorial on "Overworking the Horse." Whitman had crossed the East River on the Fulton ferry the day before and had seen a team mercilessly beaten and strained because it could not, without the aid of several men pushing at the wagon wheels, pull its load up the incline from the ferry to the floating wharf.

> It may seem to many persons that the evil we are mentioning is too small a one to call for elaborate newspaper comment; but we consider not so; The merciful man hath consideration for his beast, saith the Scripture; and the implied injunction is repeated in a variety of places. Who that has any spirit in him, does not love a horse? Civilization itself is bounden to that animal for much of its blessings; and without him, a large part of our comforts and enjoyments would be completely taken from us.

Without the horse, there would have been no omnibus to carry Whitman up Broadway or out to Greenwood Cemetery. But, even so, his liking for the horse appeared genuine and his indignation sincere and not perfunctory when he denounced, as he did on 22 July 1846, "a wretch of a fellow" who struck "a much nobler brute over the head and eyes with a heavy leather strap, with an iron buckle attached—opposite our office this morning. The execrable creature!"

166

Whether or not the ill-treated horses outnumbered the impoverished humans in Brooklyn, I cannot say. The latter received much less attention in the *Eagle*. Whenever the local society for aid to the poor conducted a campaign for contributions—usually in December and January—Whitman obligingly lent the columns of the *Eagle* to its notices and sometimes inserted brief appeals of his own, occasionally supported by bits of pathetic verse. During the rest of the year he had almost nothing to say of the impoverished—of Brooklyn, that is. But he was quick to reprint stories from the New York papers which showed the destitution that, along with vice, formed the darker elements of the chiaroscuro of the Gomorrah across the river. On 23 April 1847 the *Eagle* told of a penniless Irish immigrant couple found near death on a doorstep in New York. The father held a dying child in his arms, while the mother held one already dead. "And this," concluded Whitman, "is a specimen of the pictures almost daily presented in that city!"

But Brooklyn had its poor too, as Whitman recognized in an editorial titled "The Poor in Brooklyn," 29 January 1847. "The numbers of those who apply at the office of the Superintendents of the Poor, for assistance during this inclement season will average one hundred daily." Most were women, some of whom had been on the relief rolls for years. Some were gainfully employed but bent upon fraud. Still others had fallen from comfort to the extremes of poverty and were reduced to the humiliation of asking for alms (and Whitman described such a one in the fashion calculated to draw the tears of the sentimental). The superintendents of the poor, said Whitman, were good and conscientious men, but they were often hampered in their distribution of relief by the limitation of their funds; in order to let all share, they frequently had to give little where more was necessary.

So it appeared that in Brooklyn as well as in New York the poor were inadequately succored. But this deficiency could be remedied if private charity were not blinded to its proper scope. In the *Eagle* on 10 April 1846 "pharisaic philanthropists" were attacked in a wrathful editorial titled "The Charity By Which 1000 Miles Gets Much Cash, and Home None." The editorial had been engendered by a story in one of the New York morning papers telling of the response to its report, a few days before, of "the want of money of a negro man at Washington to redeem his wife." A New York gentleman promptly contributed one hundred dollars, anonymously, and other sums, declined as not needed, were offered by various individuals. Then it was discovered the Negro did not need the money, and the contributions remained in the hands of the editor of the New York paper, who reported that "he don't know what to do with it." Whitman knew what he could do with it.

> We might suggest whether the garrets and cellars of New York could not answer the doubt—whether the ragged foul-tongued children in the streets, are not fit objects of improvement: but we know with what disdain *such* fields of benevolence would be viewed, by those whose voracious tenderness takes in not only Virginia and the circle of the slave states, but the interminable range of all the Indies, not to mention every kingdom where the Papal religion is paramount.

The same gentleman, said Whitman, who had rushed to the aid of "the oppressed African" would have referred a sick and helpless widow with starving children to the officers of the alms house. These were the "pharisaic philanthropists" who "go into paroxysms of distress for the slave at the south, or the untutored savage of distant tropical islands," and expend great effort and money for their help and salvation. But these same nobly charitable persons "give no day, nor hour, nor cent, to the scores of sick, sinful, and starving ones to be found in any of our great American cities."

Whitman particularly approved of the charitable acts of one person in Brooklyn—Mrs Andrew Oakes, wife of the Kings County coroner. Brooklyn, like New York, had waifs in its streets; and Mrs Oakes, as she had been doing gratuitously since 1842, took them into her home until their parents or relatives were found or until they were placed in an orphanage. Mrs Oakes' self-imposed duties were surely not easy, for the *Eagle* reported on 5 May 1846 that she had had the care of twenty children since the first of the month. On 13 June the *Eagle* said Mrs Oakes had taken care of ninety-six children since 29 March, and hoped the common council, which planned to establish a "depot for lost children," would make her the matron of that depot and pay her at least two hundred dollars a year. The common council voted on 28 June, according to the next day's *Eagle*, to continue her house as "the city receptacle for lost children" and to pay her a hundred dollars a year and fifty for past services. This salary appeared to Whitman to be inadequate in view of the valuable services Mrs Oakes rendered to the city, and he described good work done at the New York "receptacle"—which "we had occasion once or twice . . . to visit . . . in search of a young runaway" —where the matron was well paid. But apparently Mrs Oakes' salary remained only a hundred.

Mr Oakes, a cabinetmaker, died about a month later, and shortly after his death Whitman suggested the next coroner be a physician, as was the practice in other large cities. The *Advertiser* promptly accused Whitman of blackening the character of the deceased Mr Oakes and of wounding the feelings of his survivors. Whitman replied to these allegations on 17 August. He told how he had known Mr Oakes when he, Whitman, had been a schoolboy, and how kind Mr Oakes had been to everyone, grown person and child.

> And this leads us to note one of the finest traits of the deceased Coroner—his willingness, with his wife, gratuitously to afford food, shelter and a resting place to lost children, found in the streets. Here, now, is a specimen of real acting out that sublime suggestion of Christ, "Inasmuch as ye did it to the *least* of these, ye did it to ME," which puts to scorn all the vaunted charities of organized associations, for aiding whose distant and indirect good by little gifts of money, many men take such glory complacently to themselves! A perpetual benison, say we, on the memory of a man who could do a deed like this!

In 1846 and 1847 Miss Dorothea Dix was in the midst of her strenuous campaign for the improvement of the care of the insane. Whitman on a few occasions reprinted brief paragraphs from exchange papers praising her work, but he had very little himself to say about the insane; perhaps because Kings County had an apparently well run asylum for the insane (to which Whitman's brother Jesse was to be committed in 1864) and no local need existed to prompt any crusading in Miss Dix's field. But Whitman did remind his readers of the existence of the institution and of the good it did. The *Eagle* of 3 June 1846 printed a very long article by an unidentified correspondent, sympathetically describing the inmates of the Kings County Asylum and their surroundings. Whitman briefly visited the asylum during an excursion in the countryside around Brooklyn later in the month, but he had nothing new to add to the earlier account in the *Eagle*.[22] Other than one or two other perfunctory remarks, only one editorial comment was made in the *Eagle* on the care of the mentally ill. In the spring of 1846 a bill was introduced into the senate at Albany to establish an asylum in the western part of the state where none existed. The unhumanitarian sentiments of several senators led Whitman to write an editorial which appeared on 2 May in the *Eagle*.[23] One senator had stated that since the state had done so long without an asylum in its western section he could see no reason for establishing one now. Another senator opposed the bill because the $30,000 appropriation it entailed would load posterity with debt. Such quibbles were perfect nonsense to Whitman, who was convinced that proper care at the proper time would rehabilitate a majority of the insane. "Doubtless a very large proportion—more than half, we imagine—could have been easily and effectually cured, and restored to reason, if means had been taken in time; if there were a well conducted Asylum in that part of the country." Hospitals were accepted institutions. "Are the ailments of the mind," asked Whitman, "less deserving of compassion than a broken leg or fever?"

The *Eagle* showed a brief interest in the blind in the summer of 1846 after Whitman made a visit to the New York City Institution for the Blind, reported on 9 June. Whitman's account of this visit was written in the popular sentimental key: as he stood in the asylum's chapel and looked at the assembly of children whose sightlessness had pitifully narrowed their scope, tears sprang in his eyes. The next day's *Eagle* reported, this time without pathos, a musical concert given the evening before at the Brooklyn Institute by some of the pupils from the blind asylum. Whitman particularly liked the young ladies who sang, as they "for the most part possessed very sweet voices." The ten-piece band played with precision but lacked "energy and expression; and this fault was quite evident in all the performances of the evening." This fault, Whitman theorized, was "probably traceable to the defective physical constitution under which the blind must necessarily labor from the little exercise which they are enabled to take."

In the following month Whitman crossed to New York to take in the semi-annual exhibition of the Institution for the Blind. According to the *Eagle* of 17 July, the sight there was the most pitiful its young editor had seen: "There are over a hundred mute entreating faces—and all so pale, so wilted, so meek." A long account of the exhibition appeared in the next day's *Eagle*. The pupils of the institution were taught box making, knitting, willow work, and mat and carpet weaving. Whitman admired the skill of the blind children, but the greatest wonder of the exhibition was that "the great forte and passion of the blind seems to be *music*." This time he praised the band's performance (he had discovered, by the way, that the students were given gymnastic exercises). He was especially enthusiastic over the talent on the pianoforte shown by two young boys. Struck by the natural ability of the blind in music, Whitman wondered "that its cultivation is not made more of a feature than it is even now—not only as a source of recreation but as a professional matter." Bands of which no locomotion was required could recruit their members from the ranks of the blind without any lessening of organizational efficiency. It was surely better for the blind to follow their natural talents than for them to be limited to such purely mechanical crafts as weaving and box-making.

The rights of women, as that phrase was understood by the militant feminists of the 1840s, received less notice in the *Eagle* than did the pupils of the New York Institution for the Blind. Whitman did not approve of discriminatory wages for working women and applauded the Wisconsin constitution for giving women the right to hold property after marriage.[24] On 9 November 1846 when he reviewed Margaret Fuller's *Papers on Literature and Art*, Whitman defended the capacity and the right of the female mind to create higher forms of literature than sentimental novels or verse. But it is doubtful that he thought, as did Miss Fuller, all occupations should be open to women or that the suffrage should be extended to them; and certainly he could not approve of the abolition of marriage, as advocated by Frances Wright. Woman, as woman, generally was idealized in the *Eagle* in the sentimental fashion despised by many feminists because it often exalted woman as the all-enduring wife.[25]

The lead editorial in the *Eagle* on 17 March 1846, "The Wrongs of Women," provides a compendium of the sentiments which often appeared in that paper. It had been germinated by an account in the Rochester papers of the cold-blooded desertion of a sick wife by her husband, which resulted in her death from not only illness but from grief as well. "No *true* man," asserted Whitman, "can ever be without a deeply seated impulse of love and reverence for woman . . . With all its failings, its flippancy, its affectation, and its fickleness—the female character is surpassingly beautiful!" The crowning glory of woman, indeed of mankind, was "motherly love." A class of shallow puppies made a practice of seizing on some of the trivial weaknesses of women and using them as arguments to ridicule the sex. "How dare they speak . . . against the class of which their own, and every hearer's mother, form part?" The conduct of the brute in Rochester assumed a blacker hue when one remembered that "a wife is almost invariably true to her husband through all kinds of disaster, disgrace, and poverty." Had not Whitman seen "dirty looking criminals" before the Brooklyn police court, forsaken by all but their wives? "We should never forget," he admonished his male readers, "that the nature of woman, in itself, is always beautifully pure, affectionate, and true—and where those qualities appear not on the surface, they are but hidden by the artificial forms of life, or kept back by the distorted bent of the world's example."

"Political Women," a brief editorial on 8 September 1846, well illustrates Whitman's liberal yet moderate stand on many of the topics that agitated the reformers and their conservative opponents in the 1840s. "Some wretch of a fellow," it began, "sends us the following—why, we know not." Then followed several lines from Eugene Sue damning all women in politics as being sterile, mannish, deluded—all resembling old maids. "We publish the above," explained Whitman, "to say that *it ain't so.* Women may take an interest in politics—particularly in this country, without compromising their 'position' *as* women—unless they are so intemperate as to violate the rules of decorum which apply alike to both sexes. It is not improper for a female to have a mind of her own (nor an absolute miracle either) and to express it." But Whitman confessed "to a fondness for seeing, in all the developments of thought and action, in woman, an infusion of mildness and of that spirit which 'falleth as the gentle dew from heaven.' " In other reforms, as in the matter of women's rights, that were discussed in the *Eagle*, Whitman usually supported the moderate view and rejected the extreme. Perhaps it was his "latent toleration for the people who choose the reactionary course" that preserved him from fanaticism.[26]

Churches and Religion

BROOKLYN, as "the city of churches," supported a variety of Christian sects, among which were the Dutch Reformed, Congregational, Episcopalian, Presbyterian, Baptist, Methodist, Unitarian, Universalist, and Roman Catholic.[27] As editor of a paper read daily by persons of varying beliefs, Whitman naturally had to show no denominational preference. He was successful because, for one thing, he was not a member of any church. Such bias as Whitman showed in his remarks on religion in the *Eagle* was directed toward intolerance, controversy, "hell and damnation" preaching, and what he called the "prostitution of the religious sentiment."

The comments in the *Eagle* on religion were confined generally to book reviews and to reports on Monday of the church services of the previous day. Whitman's reviews of religious works, of which there were forty-five, are of little interest, for they usually lack any enthusiasm or even interest. Most of them simply displayed his determination to be disinterested or, when the nature of the book permitted, his approval of private or family devotions. On one occasion, however, he showed his dislike for religious controversy. Reviewing on 14 June 1847 the

Reverend Alonzo B. Chapin's *Puritanism and Genuine Protestantism*, he said: "It is a controversial work; and we have not read it. The world . . . would be far better *bettered*, if the strife was to do *best* 'the will of the Father,' rather than to dispute which was the most authentic 'religion.' "[28]

The reports in the *Eagle* of Sunday church services became a fairly regular feature in the late spring of 1846. The *Eagle* stated on 11 May:

> We shall, next Sunday, glean the materials for reporting the sermons of two or three of our Brooklyn preachers, with accounts of their style, &c., which cannot fail of being interesting to our readers—and these we shall continue every week. Of course our sketches will be of such a nature as to be entirely unexceptionable and pleasing to all parties.

By far the greater number of the church notices which followed were "communicated" to the *Eagle;* but occasionally Whitman himself would attend one of the Brooklyn churches and the next day regale his readers with a temperate description of the church's architecture, choir, and preacher. His taste in church architecture and ornament inclined to the simple and plain.[29] He preferred in choirs the female voice to the male, and once suggested (8 June 1846) that it would be a good innovation to have choirs exclusively composed of women. As to a preacher's speaking style, he was never really uncomplimentary, but on one occasion he did go so far as to describe such a style as excellent.[30] Speaking of the Reverend Mr Spear of the South Brooklyn Presbyterian Church on 15 June 1846, Whitman said, "His voice is excellent . . . He has neither the twang of the old-fashioned Presbyterian clergyman, nor the ungraceful abruptness of too many of the contemporary orators from the sacred desk." So far as the contents of the sermons he heard were concerned, Whitman contented himself with a brief summary without comments, as befitted an editor pledged to please all parties. But once he expressed approval of the tenor of a young Episcopal clergyman's sermon. On 22 November 1846 he attended "the neat little secluded country church of St. Luke's," where he heard the Reverend Mr

Cox, a guest speaker from western New York. He was impressed by Cox's sermon: "There was none of the rant and denunciation which are too apt to characterize the trinitarian sermons of the day; nor was there the remotest approximation to the usual introduction of the more repulsive features of religion, one of which is to *frighten* hearers by means of dire anathemas into a proper observance of their duties."

Though a number of sermons were reported—"by communication"—in the *Eagle* whose narrow and fanatic sentiments must have been distasteful to Whitman, only one so angered him that he disregarded his rule of editorial impartiality. The outbreak that resulted had had its groundwork laid some months earlier in a comment of 27 April 1846 on an item in the latest news from Europe. "How shameful is the following prostitution of the religious sentiment!" he had exclaimed and then, in referring to the recent great victories of the British over the Sikhs in Punjab, told how the directors of the East India Company had described the frightful carnage as having taken place *under the guidance and blessing of Divine Providence.*" Two days later he recorded a similar "prostitution" when he reported that the Archbishop of Canterbury had composed a prayer thanking the Almighty for the victories over the Sikhs, and that prayers of thanksgiving had been offered in all the Anglican churches in Britain. It is not surprising then that Whitman should be shocked into protest by a pious repetition in a local pulpit of the sentiments of the East India Company. On 27 July 1846 the *Eagle* carried a communicated account of a sermon given in a Brooklyn church by the Reverend J. H. Morrison, a missionary in Hindustan, in which he referred several times to the slaughter of the Sikhs as God's method of opening India to the spread of Christianity. The following note appeared at the end of the account:

> *Note by Ed. Eagle.*—Though not our business, or disposition, in general, to comment upon these reports, we cannot let one item of Mr Morrison's address go in our columns without our dissentient.—Instead of "the operations of the British in India," being "a means adopted by God," to spread Christianity, we think those operations a bitter *insult* to Christianity, and prompted more by the Devil than a God of love.

For several weeks after, whenever he found a particularly bloody account of the battles in the Punjab, Whitman would print it as an ironic comment on Morrison's sermon. Perhaps the most effective was the one on 18 August, taken, said Whitman, from an official account: " *'The river was full of sinking men.* For two hours, volley after volley *was poured in upon the human mass*—the stream being *literally red with blood and covered with the bodies of the slain. . . .* No Compassion was Felt, or Mercy Shown.'—And this is what the Rev Mr Morrison calls 'a means adopted by God to spread the Gospel in India'!"

Sectarian intolerance and disputation was a very obvious element in the Brooklyn scene as well as in the national scene in the 1840s. The *Eagle* on 6 April 1846, under the heading "Too True," quoted the following remarks of the late Dr William Ellery Channing: "A dark feature in the present age . . . is in the spirit of collision, contention and discord which breaks forth in religion, politics, and private affairs. . . . Christians forsaking their one Lord, gather under various standards to gain victory for their sects. . . . The age needs nothing more than peace-makers . . . to preach in life and word the gospel of human brotherhood." An item (with an obvious pun in its heading) in the *Eagle* on 25 May suggests that Whitman may have aimed Channing's remarks at certain local sectarians:

A Graceless Reprobate.—While the Rev Mr Thayer, of the Universalist Church, was conducting the services yesterday at the funeral of a little child in Tillary street, and after he had administered some words of comfort to the bereaved and afflicted parents, a well-dressed person stepped up to him and whispered in his ear the following text: "When the blind lead the blind, they both fall into the ditch."—This was done evidently with the intention of insulting the minister. The person is said to be a member of one of the Presbyterian congregations in this city. We were aware that the doctrines of the Universalist church were unpopular in certain quarters; but did not know that it is necessary to adopt such means, especially upon such an occasion, to reprove them.[31]

No doubt Whitman found the liberal doctrines of the Unitarians and the Universalists more congenial than the harsher doctrines of the orthodox (trinitarian) Protestant denominations; but he avoided taking sides.[32] Nonetheless he found it necessary to publish a letter from one of the "orthodox" relative to complaints apparently being aired about Brooklyn by the Unitarians and the Universalists. Under the heading "Complaint of the Brooklyn Unitarians—and the 'Orthodox' Defense," Whitman wrote on 2 February 1847:

> Although the Brooklyn Eagle has an immutable vermilion edict (issued by itself to itself) that no influence, fair or foul, shall ever sway it into espousing any sectarian "side," in theological affairs, it sees little reason why it should deny one of the most esteemed christians and citizens of the burgh, his courteous request for the publication of the following letter. B. E. of course, is irresponsible for aught in such communications as this—as in its sermon reports—except that nothing actually unkind to persons gets the circulation of its columns.

The unsigned letter that followed denied that the Unitarians or the Universalists in Brooklyn were persecuted; in fact, the writer declared, they were more ready for doctrinal fights than anyone else.

Judging by the absence of any remarks in the *Eagle* to the contrary, there was relatively little anti-Catholic feeling in Brooklyn. There was certainly none in the *Eagle*. There had been a time in 1842 in the *New York Aurora* when Whitman approached a sort of anti-Catholicism. Bishop John Hughes of New York had demanded that the parochial schools of that city receive a share of the public education funds—and succeeded in that demand after exerting political pressure. Whitman wrote several editorials in the *Aurora* harshly denouncing Hughes and his demand. However, it has been noted correctly that "the political philosophy motivating Whitman's attack upon Bishop Hughes was not Nativism but Jeffersonianism."[33] Whitman had been concerned to keep the state and church separate; the religious doctrine of the Roman Catholic Church did not enter the matter.

Whitman's animus toward Bishop Hughes apparently had evaporated by 1846, or perhaps Hughes had been for Whitman simply a convenient symbol of a sect which had been and still was over most of the country the object of a great deal of that religious intolerance Whitman disliked. At least on 28 May 1846 Whitman championed Bishop Hughes after a fashion.

> The *Journal of Commerce* [a New York paper] is a very sensible journal indeed upon most subjects, but it is the lot of newspapers, like humanity, not to attain utter perfection. The *Journal* never loses a fling at that target for protestant orthodoxy, the Pope, his works, or his ministers. Especially doth it delight in a sly dig at Bishop Hughes, the catholic prelate—such as the extreme silly twist given in one of its little editorials this morning.

Further, the *Journal* had printed "a long and labored vindication of the tyrant Nicholas . . . that nun-flogging and Pole-exterminating worthy!" Obviously the *Journal* thought "it is no sin to wage any kind of war which has for its object the abrogation of Romanism." Whitman admired Pope Pius IX for his reforms in the Papal States, and his comments on the Catholic religion were always tolerant and sometimes complimentary.[34] The pomp and ceremony that surrounded the exercise of Catholicism was of no significance, either way, to Whitman.[35] On 13 November 1846 the *Eagle* quoted from the *New York Commercial Advertiser* the description of the sumptuous binding of a Roman Catholic prayer book. Whitman appended this comment:

> It is too much thus, with people's piety in other things than sacred books! . . . It is the *matter*—the *meaning* inside—that is the thing, after all; forgotten as that fact may be. All the curious devices of binding (the fixed ceremonials of worship) —all the ornaments and tinsel (the graceful style, or peculiarity of church devotion)—all the preciseness of clasps and corners (the rules of outward faith)—all the gildings on the edges of the leaves (the sanctity of face and manner)—are mere dross, if the *good meaning* is not inside.

Though he did not care for the ceremonials of Catholicism, Whitman admired the stout adherence of the Catholics to their faith. Speaking on 29 June 1846 of the Irish troubles, he said:

> We are not catholic ourself, but we admire the manly and high-hearted courage which, in the face of popularity and

178

> profit—in the face of the tithe system in Ireland, the most
> infamous system of ecclesiastical extortion that we know on
> earth—yet stays true and undaunted in its allegiance to the
> ancient faith of its fathers! the faith of so many of the great
> and good of the past!

The Catholics also furnished Whitman with an example of that
rare thing in the 1840s—sectarian good will and cooperation.
On 15 August 1846, under the heading "Something We Love To
Record," the *Eagle* quoted the *Boston Journal's* story that during the funeral procession of Bishop Benedict Fenwick in Boston
the bell of the Unitarian Church on Federal street was tolled in
alternation with the bell of the Catholic Church on Franklin
street. This was done because the Catholics had tolled their bell
during the funeral procession of Dr William Ellery Channing.

> Is not this a beautiful incident? Ah how much might be done
> in this way to soften the asperities of sectarian prejudices . . .
> to commend religion to the attention and reverence of the
> unbelieving and the wicked. Such incidents . . . are like oases
> in the great wilderness of sectarian dissension and opposi-
> tion . . . Heaven grant that we may have more such, and
> more—till the whole broad earth shall become like the olden
> Paradise!

After his fashion, Whitman preached the gospel of human brotherhood that he was to express later more eloquently in *Leaves of
Grass.*

Health, Doctors, and Drugs

WHITMAN usually seized every chance to refer in the *Eagle* to the
"salubrity" (a favorite word) of Long Island and Brooklyn. On
20 May 1847 he supplied his readers with some indisputable
statistics. "When one remembers that the population of Brooklyn
is between seventy and eighty thousand, it may well appear astonishing that the deaths here number only at the rate of eighteen or
nineteen a week!" Boston was not much larger than Brooklyn;
yet its death toll was about seventy a week. New York, with five
times Brooklyn's population, had twelve times as many deaths.

179

Whitman accounted for the healthfulness of Long Island by citing its generally dry soil, its salt breezes, and the resulting "happy temperature."[36]

But, as Whitman had reminded his readers on 17 June 1846, in even the healthiest localities the hot season usually produced considerable illness. At that time of year nature took her revenge on "indiscretion, ignorance, and gluttony." Whitman thought it well to give his subscribers "a hint or two" which would promote summer health, and in doing so he stressed the three cardinal tenets of his philosophy of health—frequent bathing, temperance in eating, and abstention from medicines.[37] Common sense (bathing and a moderate diet) was better than drugs.

The death rate was particularly high among children. Whitman was impressed by a statistic which was going the rounds of the papers: only half of the 450,000 children born each year in the United States lived to be twenty-one years old. On 11 November 1846 Whitman imputed this melancholy fact to the ignorance and incapacity of parents, nurses, and servants in matters of health, and to the "poisonous habits and wretched imitations" that beset the lives of children as they approached maturity. It appalled him to reflect on "how seldom we see a perfectly healthy child, or youth!" This excessive mortality among children was not just a statistic to the editor of the *Eagle*. He reported on 30 July 1847: "We don't remember the week that so many deaths happened in Brooklyn, as are mentioned in the record of interments here for last week.—An alarmingly large proportion of deaths are those of children. The poor little creatures!" Apparently many of the children had died of dysentery, for Whitman followed his remarks with cures and dietary regimens (taken from exchange papers) for that disorder. The year before, on 4 September he had suggested a simple remedy for dysentery. He knew a case of the disorder in Brooklyn that had been stopped in its early stages by "plentiful draughts . . . of un-iced Croton water and the use once or twice, of the shower and swimming bath," and a little adjustment in diet. "Mr dosing and purging Doctor!" declaimed the healthy habitué of Gray's Bath, "there are more medicines we wot, in the simplest products of nature, than are dreamed of in your philosophy!.....We are no hydropathist; but happen to know this case—and give it for the general weal."[38]

Dysentery, however, was not the only reason for the alarming rate of child mortality in Brooklyn in the summer of 1847. The *Eagle* on 7 August stated: "We are informed by a sensible and experienced physician that the immense mortality now rife, has, among other causes, that of *swill milk*. This idea is the more plausible when one remembers that the mortality and sickness are principally among children." Whitman had been campaigning against swill milk before this date, and he was to continue the campaign. The menace of swill milk was not small. A medical man of sorts, who lived in New York when Whitman was editing the *Eagle* and who was a critical observer of the scene, said, "In the larger towns the poor are supplied with the milk of diseased cows, tied up, without air or exercise, and fed into scrofula on the hot slops from the distilleries and breweries."[39] Whitman exposed those who were selling swill milk as bargain-priced "real" milk (pure milk was six cents a quart; swill milk, four cents) and pointed out dairies which used swill as feed. But perhaps his best piece of propaganda on the subject was a repulsive description of a swill dairy. He began a long editorial in the *Eagle* on 29 June 1847 with a recommendation of "natural" milk as a wholesome food for both children and adults (not more than a pint at any meal). Swill milk, however, thinned the blood and finally caused scrofula—and was disgustingly filthy. How could anyone, he asked, put that "nauseous compound" into his own or his child's mouth?

> If the reader has ever beheld . . . the manufactories of swill milk, surely he will not need *any* arguments on the subject. There, under a low roof, in rows of small partitions which, in their larger departments, are divided from each other by little stagnant creeks, covered with a thick green and yellow slime, emitting the most repulsive odor—there are kept—mummy-fashion, almost—the blear-eyed flabby-fleshed animals (we will not call them cows) that are made to furnish the semi-poison. An endless trough runs around through all the stalls, and is kept always flowing with warm swill. Gnawed by a sense of something wanting, and never supplied, the poor

beasts are constantly sucking in the liquid, and are never
furnished with food or drink in any other form. Their teeth
are then rotten, black and nasty to an extreme—the gums
blotched with abominable sores, and their throats inflamed.
Their eyes go far beyond those of the habitual drunkard in
redness and hot swollenness. Their skins, which properly
kept, would be sleek and glossy, are covered week to week
with the accumulated filth of their narrow dens. The abominable air that surrounds one of these places—bad in winter,
and utterly intolerable in summer—is enough of itself to make
any animal, human or brute, bereft of health. Such are the
places where, and the creatures from whom, swill milk is
manufactured.

Perhaps some of Whitman's subscribers were converted to his
belief that six cents was cheap enough for pure, healthy milk.

Careless of hygiene and sanitation, ignorant of the proper
methods of checking the spread of infectious diseases, and inclined to intemperate habits in eating and drinking, the Americans of the 1840s provided the doctor and the druggist with
steady employment. How capable many of the doctors of the
time were, is a question. According to Thomas Nichols, "the
Americans, who do everything in a hurry, educate their doctors
in their usual fashion"; but worse "is the fact that there is no
standard—no real science of medicine . . . Everyone may do
what is right in his eyes."[40] Whitman had a deep-seated distrust
of doctors, based largely upon his antipathy to their habit of
prescribing drugs rather than upon a suspicion of the thoroughness of their professional education (which he never mentioned).
Correspondingly, he distrusted druggists because they dispensed
the drugs the doctors prescribed, had uncritical faith in their
drugs, and often were criminally careless. This lack of confidence
in doctor and druggist was first voiced in the *Eagle* on 16 April
1846 in an editorial titled "Is Not Medicine Itself a Frequent
Cause of Sickness?"

In looking over the pages of a new statistical work, on New
York, we observe that there are in that city 242 apothecaries'
shops—and in them 242 (or more) Druggists mix their physic
stuff, and paper their doses, and shake their potions and
lotions. . . . Why do folks take so much physic? It is now

pretty well established that not mere taking of drugs cures diseases. . . . We submit to almost any of our readers, who may be "ailing," in any way—who may have that worst curse on earth, a ruined constitution—whether he or she cannot look back through a long career of medicine-taking? The violent stimulants and narcotics which are favorites with a majority of the physicians, cannot be used without the most serious and permanent effects on the system—both in the present and in time to come! . . . How much of the fevers, aches, rheumatisms, chronic and acute complaints . . . come to us through the physic vial, and the pestle and the mortar! And the consciousness of this fact is starting up all kinds of medical humbugs—some of them possessing a few points meritorious, but none of them . . . worthy to take the place of that *universal*, that remedial role for every complaint, which nearly all of them claim to be.[41] Indeed there is much humbug in the pompous pretensions of the medical art. There are very few real *specifics* for disease in the whole catalogue of the pharmaceutist. Doctors and apothecaries pretend to know altogether too much. It will go down among those who understand very little of physiology and anatomy . . . but to all others, much of the loftiest pretensions of either the "regular" doctor, or "quack" doctor, is but a matter of sounding brass and a tinkling cymbal.

This editorial was the first shot in a brief skirmish with the medical profession and a more extended one with the pharmaceutical.[42]

The *Eagle* on 1 June 1846 contained an editorial, "Innovations in Medicine—Physic Vs. Health, &c.," which seems to have irritated some of the medical men of Brooklyn. Whitman began the editorial by referring to the recent refusal of the state legislature to charter a homeopathic institute and a hydropathic college, and to the "most terrific war waging between the old doctors and the new school" in Brooklyn and New York. He supported neither school, he claimed, but in the remarks that followed he was kinder to the new school than to the old. He said of homeopathy and hydropathy:

Their excellence is nearly altogether of a negative kind.— They may not cure, but neither do they kill—which is more than can be said of the old systems. They aid nature in carry-

ing off the disease slowly—and do not grapple with it
fiercely . . . to the detriment of the patient's poor frame,
which is left, even in victory, prostrate and almost annihilated.

Orthodox physicians, as a body, were "altogether too conservative, too great slaves of precedent, and too haughty in behalf of
their standing." Almost all diseases of a serious nature, Whitman
assured his readers, were "the result either of hereditary causes,
or a train of circumstances acting, perhaps slowly and silently,
long and long before the disease itself breaks out." To assert "that
a man—however great his book-lore, or however many college
lectures he may have heard—can, after asking a few questions
and getting a few symptoms, *cure* such a result, or even *attempt*
to cure it with any chance of success, is preposterous!" But physicians invariably acted as if they could when called to attend a
sick person; and because they knew they were expected to "do
something" for the patient, they prescribed a mysterious medicine
which left the patient more ill than before. Medical truths should
be built upon investigation, analysis, and painstaking experiment;
not upon "prejudices, fears, and vanities."

A few persons (presumably physicians) had replied "somewhat sharply" to this criticism of conventional doctors, Whitman
remarked in the *Eagle* on 4 June. And he repeated his charges
in much stronger terms: "Their pride makes them ashamed to
confess an ignorance, which none short of supernatural power
could avoid. Blindly thus, they sacrifice human life to their own
miserable vanity! This is monstrous!" On the following day Whitman reported: "One of our medical friends is 'into us' again this
morning, in a note, because we have no faith in the immaculacy
of doctors, of drugs, and of bleeding.—He accuses us of being
tinctured with the 'dangerous ultraism of the age.' " Perhaps so,
but Whitman did not deny that the old system had its merits. Indeed, he thought himself "open to the merits of *all* medical theories." Here in fact lay the major fault of the old school of medicine
(and of the new as well): it pedantically refused to recognize the
merits that lay in other systems. This unfortunate dogmatism
resulted from the burial of the minds and talents of physicians
under "the rubbish of the schools." What contemporary medical
science needed was "a comprehensive scope of thought to . . .

take in the whole bearing of things, as far as they relate to medicine, disease, and that 'fearfully and wonderfully made' mystery, the human frame."[43] After this editorial Whitman either lost interest in trying to reform the medical profession or judged it the better part of discretion to drop the subject, for he stopped his attacks—except for a few mild and incidental remarks—on orthodox medicine.[44]

Whitman of course continued his propaganda for wholesome habits and common sense in hygiene. His hydropathic bias never lessened: he frequently recommended bathing at every chance, and only slightly less often advocated the drinking of water (never iced and always in moderate amounts). He reminded his readers, too, that overeating was probably the cause of most of their ailments. Tobacco, either chewed or smoked, was not only a socially vile habit but injurious to the stomach. Fresh air (a fourth cardinal tenet in Whitman's philosophy of health) was excluded from most of the homes in Brooklyn because of the prevailing use of cast-iron stoves and coal fires, and the general habit of sleeping in closed bedrooms. Whitman reported on 31 July 1846 that he had attended a lecture the previous evening given by a Mr Gordon who had developed a theory of ventilation. Gordon's idea was "to have rooms so constructed as that a force pump may increase the pressure of the atmosphere . . . and by thus making the medium in which we exist much denser, our bodies would become more buoyant than at present, as we find the case to be when in water. Besides condensing, the apparatus is so contrived as to keep up a constant renovation of atmosphere." Whitman was impressed. It was obvious that if the householders of whole blocks would combine in such a venture, the cost would be trifling. But the audience at the lecture had been very small, and Whitman was sorry to see how little people were interested in a project conducive to good health.

The health of the ladies was not overlooked by the *Eagle*. The common sense rules of hygiene and diet applied to them too; but then they had those ailments peculiar to their sex. Whitman limited himself to condemning tight lacing, but in his book reviews he encouraged women to enlighten themselves on the subjects of female physiology and diseases. Reviewing Mary S.

185

Gove's *Lectures to Women, on Anatomy and Physiology; With
an Appendix on Water Cure* on 26 September 1846, he said, "As
respects physiological truths, the sentiment of the intelligent
world is now pretty well settled down to the conviction that the
more and wider these truths are known, the better." And he
condemned the "mistaken 'delicacy' " which encouraged ignorance of physiological facts. On 4 March 1847 Whitman reviewed
Dr Edward H. Dixon's *Woman, and her Diseases, from the Cradle
to the Grave.*

> Let any one bethink him a moment how rare is the sight of a
> well-developed, healthy, *naturally* beautiful woman: let him
> reflect how widely the customs of our artificial life, joined with
> ignorance of physiological facts are increasing the rarity . . .
> and he will hardly dispute the necessity of such publications
> as this.

In a way Whitman's remarks in this review were anticipatory of
the perfect woman of *Leaves of Grass*—a healthy organism dedicated to the supreme function of motherhood.

It was possible to discuss tight lacing with propriety, and
Whitman condemned that fashion frequently. The ill effects of
tight lacing upon the health of women was staple fare in the
lectures and writings of such medical reformers as Mrs Gove
and Dr Dixon, and Whitman repeated their warnings in occasional editorials. His most extensive essay on this topic appeared
on 11 September 1846: tight lacing permanently deformed the
natural grace of the figure, injured abdominal organs, and (in the
1840s the corset often enclosed a portion of the chest) led to
fatal consumption. These arguments were familiar to the readers
of the *Eagle;* but there was also a moral argument against tight
lacing, as Whitman had pointed out earlier on 13 April.

> There is a certain class of be-chained, be-ringed, and be-
> spangled things, called dandies, which infest our streets, to
> the annoyance of well disposed persons, and who may perhaps
> affect to be pleased with those exquisite specimens of tight
> lacing with which our eyes are often pained. But why does
> such an unnatural spectacle as that of a tight laced lady im-
> part pleasure to a dandy?—Is it because it renders her more

beautiful and graceful? Not at all. The reasons are such as we do not feel disposed at present to specify. Suffice it to say, they are such as no modest female could approve.

The young editor of the *Eagle*—contemptuous of doctors and drugs, confident of the efficacy of nature's curatives—was the father of the man who wrote ("A Sun-Bath—Nakedness," *Specimen Days*) in 1877: "Shall I tell you, reader, to what I attribute my already much-restored health? That I have been almost two years, off and on, without drugs and medicines, and daily in the open air." There on the banks of Timber Creek on the Staffords' New Jersey farm, his paralysis was lessened by the gentle physic of "Adamic" air-baths, dips in the clear creek water, fed by a spring, and "slow negligent promenades . . . in the sun." These, as he had told the subscribers to the *Eagle* in 1846, were nature's "better, safer, and more pleasant alternatives" to medicines and the fierce regimens of those slaves to precedent—the physicians. These were common sense as opposed to "the rubbish of the schools." Whitman felt—and generally correctly so—that the reforms he advocated in the *Eagle* were the dictates of common sense as opposed to the "prejudices, fears, and vanities" of those who worshiped precedent.

four

LITERATURE AND THE ARTS

Literature

BRITISHER Alexander Mackay, reviewing his travels in the United States in 1846 and 1847, expressed an opinion of the state of literature in that republic not shared by many Europeans and some Americans: "In a country of whose people it may be said that they all read, it is but natural that we should look for a national literature. For this we do not look in vain to America."[1] American literature, he continued, was young, but it was "far above mediocrity," having produced good works in all branches of writing except the drama. Whether or not the United States had a national literature had been debated by Americans for several decades, and this dispute was at its height in the 1840s. On one side of the controversy were those who believed it was nonsense to speak of a "native" literature, for the current of American literature should flow from the mainstream of European, especially English, literature, in which it had had its being. The sentiments of this group were expressed by a reviewer in 1846 who spoke of "certain coteries of would-be men of letters [who] waste their time and vex the patient spirits of long-suffering readers, by prating about our want of an independent national American literature. . . . They seem to think that American authors ought to limit themselves to American subjects, and hear none but American criticism." Actually, declared the reviewer, a national literature already had been well started and would advance "under the stimulating influences pouring in from every quarter upon the agitated intellect of the country."[2] The opposing view was typified by an unsigned article in the *Democratic Review* in 1847. The writer of the article began by citing statistics which showed the present as well as the potential greatness of the United States. "And yet," he deplored, "this great country . . . has no native literature, but is, in letters, in a state of colonial and provincial dependency upon the old world." He complained of the imitative spirit of American writers, who had no clear conception of "the idea and necessity of nationality." Indigenous American literature could be created only by "homewriters" writing on "home themes"—American scenery, events, traditions, manners, and history, illuminated by an "intense and enlightened patriotism."[3]

Whitman was in complete agreement with the writer in the *Democratic Review*, and he used the columns of the *Eagle* to promote the idea and the development of a distinctively national American literature.[4] Here in 1846 and 1847 Whitman's life-long crusade for a national literature had its beginning. His earliest pronouncement in the *Eagle* on this subject appeared on 12 May 1846 in an editorial entitled "American Literature."

> The founding of an "original American literature" is desirable only if it is to be a great, lofty and noble literature. The object is stupendous, almost holy—and no presumptuous and unskillful hand should dare attempt it. We confidently believe that such a school of intellect will some day arise (and before long, too) which will possess the requisite capacity and genius. It will arise, because there is for it a *necessity* . . . The past has had its glorious gods of intellect—its Homer, Shakespeare and Goethe. But the same subtle thought burns yet in the minds of the children of men . . . Without any irreverence, we think it not amiss to say that we of America must rival *even the literary greatness of the past. . . .* Are we not confessedly the most intellectually burrowing and feverish of all nations in the world? What people on earth have done so much in sixty years, in the various departments of mind, as we, in proportion? . . .
>
> American authors, *true ones*, must be encouraged. American publishers must bring forth the talents of their own land, and not be content with flooding the country with the waves of foreign trash that do no good in any way, except to the

> printers and binders. *The people*, however, are the ones—the intelligent body of America—who form the responsible party in the matter. Talking of an ill-supported American literature as the fault of publishers alone, is nonsense. . . . they have shrewd eyes to the profits, and once convince them that the people will buy, and they embark in "native" literature as quick as any thing else!

The American reading public was the greatest obstacle to the development of a national literature. The preference of American readers for foreign works was not just inimical to the development of American talent; it also exposed the citizens of the republic to the anti-democratic propaganda that, Whitman was convinced, permeated European writings. "He who desires to see this noble republic independent of all unwholesome foreign sway," said Whitman in another editorial (" 'Home' Literature," 11 July 1846), "must ever bear in mind the influence of European literature over us—its tolerable amount of good, and its . . . immense amount of evil." Such writers as Shakespeare, Goethe, Byron, Hume, Rousseau, and Gibbon had "glorious merits." Yet "it must not be forgotten, that many of the most literary men of England are the advocates of doctrines that in such a land as ours are the rankest and foulest poison. . . . for they laugh to scorn the idea of republican freedom and virtue." Meanwhile, "perfect cataracts of trash," from Bulwer, Ainsworth, Marryat, De Kock, and others, came to the United States from abroad. "Shall Hawthorne get a paltry *seventy-five dollars* for a two volume work—Shall real American genius shiver with neglect," Whitman asked his Brooklyn readers, "while the public run after this foreign trash?"

A distinctively national literature seemed to Whitman to be demanded by the uniqueness of American ideals and institutions. In "Independent American Literature" (10 February 1847) he spoke of the writings of the past as "treasures to us Americans more precious than the treasures of kings." But, he asked, "have *we* in this country nothing to add to the store of their manifold genius? And will we fail to remember, too, that the genius of the Old World has shaped itself to a different state of things from what exists in the new?" Though some in America worshiped the literary masters of the past and others made ridiculously inflated claims for "*writing that is merely American because it is not written abroad*," Whitman was convinced that "there is a true public opinion forming here which will ere long do equal and exact justice to all, in this matter."

One would expect to find the argument for a genuine national literature carried into Whitman's comments on the 425 books (and five pamphlets) he reviewed in the *Eagle*. But Whitman's intention as a book reviewer was to acquaint his readers with literature that was moral and instructive, regardless of its origin. In "The World of Books" (26 November 1847) he was excited to the following effusion by "looking over the long list of works" in *Harper's Illustrated Catalogue:*

> What a world there is, after all, in *books!* . . . In them are put, for safe keeping, the genius and discoveries of man, the trials and experiments of the learned, and all the mysteries of science. Beautiful thoughts of poets, and passionate writhings of the o'erstrung brain, and eloquence such as moves the massy hearts of nations, are embalmed there . . . The lives of the good and great too, incentives to courage and virtue, reside aneath their pages . . . What would be the most sacred treasure of all, Sacred Writ itself, except for the bookish art? What would become of this "intelligence of the age," that we hear so much about? In books are the best guardians of religion and of liberty, the staunchest exposers of wrong, and the readiest inducements to right. We care not much what kind of books—we mean in what department—they are, so long as confessedly not open to the charge of intentional immorality. We say that *all* books do good and have their office.

Whitman welcomed the prodigal yield of such publishing houses as Harper's; for, being an earnest pedagogue, he found matter in those sundry books for the schooling of his subscribers. He believed the people of the United States (hence, those of Brooklyn) to be a newspaper-ruled people and therefore amenable to education and improvement through the medium of newsprint. As a department in the *Eagle*, Whitman's book-review column had a share in his pedagogic plan.[5]

191

Whitman was more editor than critic in his book reviews. His usual method for noticing a book was to quote from its preface or text, or more often, simply to note its publication and perhaps its format. In that minority of reviews which contained his personal comments, however, Whitman was more critic than editor, but less a literary critic than a judge of personal and political morals and an advocate of self-improvement. He was more concerned with educating his readers than with judging authors as artists. He did not entirely neglect literary criticism in his reviews, but his response to highly divergent styles prohibits the conclusion that by 1846-47 he had developed a specific critique of literary composition. Whitman commended the polished and clear style of Douglass Jerrold and condemned the involved style of G. P. R. James. Yet he enjoyed the intricate and heavily allusive writings of Thomas Carlyle. Usually the *Eagle* took no cognizance of a book's style, and if an author's mode of composition was criticized, the didactic tone of the work in question often palliated its literary deficiencies. For example, in reviewing Joseph Alden's *Lawyer's Daughter* on 31 May 1847, Whitman said:

> We have spoken before in the highest terms of Alden's writings: they are not brilliant in the way of genius, but they are always charming for their good sense and truth to nature, always inculcate a moral, and leave no reader at the end of their perusing without a hint toward good. Such books deserve well of criticism, for they perform a wide and deep benefit in the sphere of their operation.

The didactic merit of any work was the quality which really engaged the attention of Whitman as a book reviewer with a duty to his readers. His most frequent comment upon a book was that it contained a moral lesson—which was, of course, the most frequent comment of his fellow reviewers in the 1840s. It is somewhat surprising, then, that when Whitman had the opportunity to condemn some of the trash which flooded America from across the Atlantic, he did not. His treatment of Bulwer well illustrates this inconsistency. On 2 December 1846 he reported the publication by Harper's of Bulwer's *Lucretia*, saying only, "Its author's name alone will doubtlessly give it a prodigious 'run' ";

192

and eight days later he made no comment on the eagerness of American readers to buy foreign trash when he announced 25,000 copies had been sold in the two days following its release.[6] The publication of Bulwer's *Leila* was reported on 28 December 1846 by a single sentence noting that the novel was issued by Harper's in a pocket edition. Finally, Whitman expressed an opinion when he reviewed Bulwer's *Zanoni* on 30 April 1847: "This novel is a wild and vague affair—and though there are glimpses of true fire showing through it now and then, the feeling at the end is a sort of dissatisfaction—either with the characters or the author." Whitman's dissatisfaction, despite his earlier inclusion of Bulwer with trashy European authors, apparently was with the style of the novel rather than with any unwholesomeness or trashy competition with solid American works.[7]

Whitman's fervent belief in the superiority of democracy over all other political creeds was an emphasized topic in his reviews. Only such specialized categories as religious and health publications did not contain some allusion to the preeminence of democratic government. His favorite device for illustrating that preeminence to his readers was, as has been seen in an earlier chapter, to present a sordid picture of Old World governments and institutions which contrasted strikingly with the benefits of the liberal democratic government of the United States. The *Eagle* also fostered patriotism and appreciation for democracy in the citizens of Brooklyn by bringing to their attention American history and biography, New World travels, scientific and social achievements in the United States, and American fiction.[8] Whitman's desire for a national literature was more fully expressed in his editorials than in his book reviews. Relatively few of his reviews referred to the need for an indigenous literature—possibly because he felt the moral and instructive qualities of a work were more fundamental for the education of his readers than the work's possible application to a theory of national literature in which they likely had little intelligent interest. Also, it is doubtful if Whitman himself at that time had more than a vague idea of the elements such a theory should contain. Nevertheless, it is possible to assemble a tentative critique for an original American literature from scattered comments in his reviews.

Whitman had little to say about American fiction in his reviews of a hundred adult works, and nothing at all in those of thirty-three juveniles. Melville's *Typee* and *Omoo* were given appreciative notices on 15 April and 5 May 1847, but he did not say their author was an American.[9] Reviewing William Gilmore Simms' *The Wigwam and the Cabin* on 9 March 1846, Whitman agreed that Simms was "unquestionably one of the most attractive writers of the age," but objected to "Caloya," one of the tales in the volume, because its last chapter "is rendered particularly objectionable by the introduction of a revolting drunken scene— and the tale as a whole is certainly calculated to reflect no credit on American literature, either at home or abroad." Whitman did not care to have native writers picture those American coarsities which English writers had already commented upon so eloquently, even when, as in "Caloya," the drunken characters were a Negro slave and a degenerate Indian.

Only three of Whitman's reviews of fiction suggested that American novels should have peculiarly American characteristics. Reviewing *Jack Long: Or Shot in the Eye* by Charles Wilkins Webb on 24 September 1846, he said, " 'Jack Long' we have read, and know it to be a good story, and of the right sort for an American writer to write." The novel purported to be a true story of the Texas border, and so the assumption is that American authors should write about American scenes and American subjects. Of another American novel, *The Unfortunate Maid: Embracing the Life and Adventures of Bob Norberry* by Captain P. O'Shaughnessy, reviewed on 28 June 1847, Whitman said: "A well-written, dashy, warm-hearted book, with *not* a good title— which will bar the perusal of it from many readers, who would surely be pleased with the interest of its pages, the patriotism and truth running through it, and the correctness to nature of its portraitures." This review suggests that among the characteristics proper to American fiction was realism qualified by a spirit of patriotism (and decorum). On 27 September 1847 a review of William L. Stone's *Tales and Sketches* presented Whitman's idea of a thoroughly American story. "We like these stories," he wrote, "first because they are thoroughly American in their subjects, characters, and illustrations, and sentiments; secondly because the style is clear and of a purer English than that of most of the British tale-writers themselves." Stone's tales depicted colonial life in New England and were generously infused with Indian lore and life. As such, the stories were a legitimate part of American native literature. Their good style convinced Whitman the American author might write as expertly and pleasingly as the more esteemed British author.[10]

Whitman had nothing at all to say in his reviews about a native American poetry. He was a conformist in his remarks upon verse, and with one or two exceptions, the popular poets of the time, whether American or European, received only praise in the *Eagle*.[11] Of the twenty-two poetical works reviewed by Whitman, only three received unfavorable comment, and all three were by American poets: Charles Fenno Hoffman, David Reeve Arnell, and Mrs Lydia H. Sigourney. The reason for his dislike of these particular volumes is not in the least clear, since he praised other poets whose styles and subject matter were quite similar. At no time did Whitman laud a poet for picturing the American scene or expressing American sentiments[12]—except William Cullen Bryant, and then in a sort of left-handed fashion. On 1 September 1846 he noted that Bryant had returned from one of his sojourns in Europe and deplored his lack of credit, as a poet, in America. Then he quoted a British journal, the *Foreign Quarterly Review:*

> We have been all along looking out for a pure American poet, who should be strictly national in the comprehensive sense of the term. The only man who approaches that character is William Cullen Bryant. He does not thrust the American flag in our faces, and threaten the world with the terrors of a gory peace; he exults in the issues of freedom for nobler ends and larger interests . . . The woods, prairies, mountains, tempests, and seasons, the life and the destiny of man, are the subjects in which he delights.

Though he obviously agreed with the *Quarterly Review*, it was an English journalist speaking, not Whitman. Whitman himself went on to say that as a poet Bryant "stands among the first in the world" (eight of Bryant's poems were reprinted in the *Eagle*), but he reserved his superlatives for Bryant as a newspaperman and a Democrat—"It is an honor and a pride to the Democratic party that it has such a man to conduct one of its principal newspapers—to be an expounder of its doctrines, and act as one of the warders to watch the safety of the citadel." In a long review on 12 October 1846 of a collected edition of Longfellow's poems (twenty-four issues of the *Eagle* during Whitman's editorship carried poems by Longfellow—a record neither surpassed nor even approached by any other poet), the only reference to his nationality occurred in the statement that the country did not sufficiently appreciate the poet, who was "an honor and a glory . . . to the American name." Never in the *Eagle* did Whitman call out for a poet to celebrate the "en-masse" with a "barbaric yawp."

In the matter of travel books, Whitman did speak out for the need of American writers to describe the American scene. On 1 February 1847 he said that Mrs Elizabeth F. Ellet's *Rambles About the Country* "involves several graphic descriptions of American natural scenery, and incidents of American life. We welcome every thing that truly treats of *our own land*—and we therefore welcome this!" Samuel Parker's *Journal of an Exploring Tour Beyond the Rocky Mountains,* reviewed on 12 December 1846, suggested to Whitman "that American curiosity might quite as well turn its attention to Indian traits, as to Egyptian or Druidic ruins &c.—the wrangle-ground even of our new world antiquarians." Several other travel books led Whitman to comment on the American Indian as distinctly American literary material. For example, he said of the anonymous *Altowan; or Incidents of Life and Adventure in the Rocky Mountains* on 26 September 1846, that "every book which truly contributes, as this does, to an authentic knowledge of the life, manners, and peculiarities of the Great Aboriginal Race now passing slowly but surely away, is a precious thing in American literature."

In addition to books, Whitman reviewed some thirty different periodicals in the *Eagle* from month to month, and it is here that he was more often articulate on the subject of a national literature. Too frequently there was little substance in American periodical writings, which caused Whitman to complain of the *Columbian Magazine* on 20 November 1846: "We persist in thinking that a third-rate appetite is far too much bent to in these monthly magazines."[13] But at times he was pleased with both the prints and the printed matter of some periodicals, finding them of a "national character." On 21 August 1847, remarking on the tendency of *Graham's American Monthly* to embellish itself with engravings of royalty and nobility, he asked, "Is there no fitting theme of a more national character?" And he noted that the current *Columbian* had "a spirited engraving of a 'wigwam in the forest.'" He was always pleased with engravings of American natural scenery, American historical events, and American notables. He expressed his complete agreement on 8 January 1847 with the editors of *North America Illustrated* who had suggested that their American prints "may do quite as well for American parlors as Swiss views, or Oriental flummeries."

Though he had accused the *Columbian* of sometimes catering to "third-rate appetite," Whitman applauded it on 20 August 1846 because it "gives us 'semi-occasionally,' a dash of Americanism—an American picture, and a truly American narrative or romance."[14] Who the authors were of these truly American tales Whitman did not say; two of them may have been Mrs Lydia Maria Child, the New England abolitionist poet and writer of moralistic fiction, and Mrs Caroline Matilda Kirkland, sentimentalist of the Michigan frontier. In a review of the *Union Magazine* on 30 June 1847 Whitman said, "At all events we could wish nothing better than the writings of Mrs Kirkland herself, and Mrs Child—writing to our mind among the best, freshest, and most charming specimens of American literature." It was not, of course, only the American geographical and social scene that Whitman wanted displayed in American periodical literature but also American democratic ideals. Displeased by the whiggish, hence depreciatory, inferences in an account of a battle in the Mexican War written by Joel T. Headley in the *American Review*, Whitman declared in the *Eagle* on 26 August 1846 that "democracy is closely identified with a well-developed literature

—and it has always been the highest pride of the best writers to advance the claims of liberal doctrine in government." The *Democratic Review*, he added, had "so noble a scope."

Yet Whitman was not always insistent upon the exposition of American character and ideals in periodicals. His most frequent superlatives were applied to *Littell's Living Age*, a weekly eclectic magazine of Continental and British (and some few American) reprints, published in Boston. Whitman qualified his praise of this journal—which he called "this princely publication," "this royal publication," and a "triton among minnows"— only once, on 12 October 1847, when he confessed it had "just a smattering of an aristocratic tinge." Whitman's essential freedom from literary chauvinism is shown by the fact that though the *Living Age* admittedly had an anti-democratic coloring, he could say on 22 July 1847 that it "affords the noblest reading, of any of its class in our language."

In the scattered comments in the *Eagle* it is possible to glimpse unorganized elements of an emerging theory of national literature: genuinely native writings should deal with American persons and institutions in American settings; and they should be characterized by a spirit of patriotism, a pride in democratic government, and a freedom from excessive admiration of the Old World. That Whitman's concept of an American national literature was not yet clearly formed is evidenced by the relative scarcity of his comments on the subject, by the fact that he implied rather than stated the qualities of such a literature, and by the vague and generalizing nature of his editorial pronouncements on the topic. The qualities he thought necessary to a distinctive national literature were those that other journalists, such as the author of "Nationality in Literature" in the *Democratic Review*, were insisting upon. Whitman supported this reform movement in literature, as it may be called, just as he had supported other reform movements which appealed to him. And perhaps it was his "latent toleration for the people who choose the reactionary course" that preserved him, as it had in other matters, from fanaticism—in this case, literary chauvinism.

Whitman inaugurated a literary department in the *Eagle* (occupying from one to three columns on the first page, which formerly had been entirely taken up by advertisements) and on 1 June 1846 it became a regular feature. The *Eagle* for 30 May 1846, announcing the establishment of the literary miscellany as a daily feature, revealed that on the first of June it would "commence the publication . . . of an Original Novelette, a *Tale of Indian Life*, which we feel warranted in saying the readers of this journal will find of interest."[15] After assuring the ladies and the young that their tastes would not be slighted in the new department, the *Eagle* continued, "Our object is, also, to make the department in question as *original* as possible, in the highest sense —presenting, mostly, sketches, tales, &c., &c., on American subjects, particularly those relating to Long Island, and the neighboring section of the United States." From this it would appear that Whitman planned to give substantial support to the cause of native literature; if so, he failed. He presented (or rather, reprinted) a few tales of Hawthorne, Poe, and Irving,[16] and poems of Longfellow, Holmes, Bryant, Lowell, and Whittier. But these were overwhelmed numerically by the poems, tales, sketches, and didactic essays of the sentimental American moralizers and their anonymous imitators who enjoyed the public favor in the 1840s and later. The volume of "original" American contributions to the literary page was still more curtailed by the frequent selections culled from the literature of Europe. The local Brooklyn contributions—mostly poems, usually unsigned—did nothing to advance the development of a native literature, since they were generally imitative of Mrs Sigourney and Mrs Child.[17]

As in his book reviews, the didactic element was the most important in Whitman's literary section. The motive that impelled Whitman in most of his selections for page one of the *Eagle* was clearly stated on 17 March 1847 in his remarks on a tale then running in the paper—"The Father in the Snow," translated from the German of Wilibald Alexis by Mrs St. Simon and taken from the *Christian Parlor Magazine.*

> Surely no one can read the story now in course of publication on our first page, without deriving an infusion of pure religious sentiment of higher disinterestedness, and more manly courage! The plot is well worked of itself; but the moral reaches far beyond the plot. Parents should read this story to their

children; young men should read it, and ponder on it; it teaches the highest virtue of the soul—the opposite of the weak, discontented, vacillating, uncheerful spirit, which prevails so widely among nearly all classes . . . The whole interest of the tale centres round the character of the Pastor; a sublime character! sublime in its simplicity! It will do everyone good to peruse such a tale.

On a few occasions Whitman succumbed to pure bathos (and critical idiocy), as on 4 August 1846 when he prefaced "Ah, how beautiful is this!— Ed. E." to an unsigned "Ode to a Girl," whose final and perhaps best stanza is

> And the cold sweat pours down, and all of me
> Trembling seize. I paler be
> Than grass, and, scarce removed from death,
> Seem without breath.

(The interested reader may find the original of this travesty in Sappho's poems—"An equal to the gods, he seems to me"—and see why the plagiarist, not the honest borrower, deserves literary lynching.) But much more often the poems on the first page, and the sketches as well, fulfilled the moralistic tone promised by such titles as "To a Dying Infant," "On the Death of a Virtuous Young Girl," "The Child's Grave," "We Miss Thee Mother," "The Prison Convict," and "A Child Praying."[18]

Stories by Hawthorne, poems by Bryant and Longfellow, "Incidents &c. Among the Indians," by a Mr Eeels, first-hand accounts of combat in the Mexican War, and other contemporary writings truer to the American scene and the American spirit fought a losing battle on page one of the *Eagle* with the effusions of the Sigourney-Child school and the American school of graveyard poetry, for which latter "school" Bryant must take partial blame. Whitman was preeminently the pedagogue; and for him to be an effective pedagogue through his paper's literary miscellany, he had no choice but to print plainly didactic works that appealed to the taste of his readers (and to his own taste, to a perceptible degree). He was not yet a reformer of American literature. He was but vaguely conscious, at the most, of the mission that was to absorb his life.

The Stage

IT HAS BEEN SAID that Whitman's "editorials in the *Eagle* on the contemporary stage reveal some of the same forces that motivated his criticisms of poetry and prose: a desire that the drama should exercise a moral function; an impatience with New York critics; and a program for American managers."[19] An important element in this last motivating force was the wish to see, as part of the development of a national literature, the emergence of "original" American dramatists. The stage, like literature, was for Whitman an art form which both entertained and edified; as a critic, he was concerned with its doing both these things well while at the same time expressing the national character.

One of Whitman's many editorials on the theatre asked (12 February 1847), "How Shall the American Stage Be Resuscitated?" His answer was, "English managers, English actors, and English plays, (we say it in no spirit of national antipathy, a feeling of hate) must be allowed to die away among us, as usurpers of our stage." The Park, as Whitman often told his readers, was his favorite New York theatre (remember that there was no theatre in Brooklyn), and as he said on 8 February, "We have excepted the Park theatre in the charge of vulgarity, because the audiences there are always intelligent, and there is a dash of superiority thrown over the performances." Yet it was "but a third-rate imitation of the best London theatres," giving its patrons "the cast off dramas, and the unengaged players of Great Britain." But Whitman had a program whereby the American stage could be revivified: some bold American manager should abolish the English starring system, engage American talent, and give his patrons dramas suited to American sentiments and institutions. Such a revolution in the American theatre (to get back to his editorial of 12 February) would meet with public approval: "With all our servility, to foreign fashions, there is at the heart of the intelligent masses there, a lurking propensity toward what is original, and has a stamped American character of its own."

In Whitman's opinion there were some American actors better than the best of England's dramatic stars. Charlotte Cushman, he said in "About Acting" on 14 August 1846, was without an English (or American) peer;[20] and James Anderson, though not the fulfillment of Whitman's idea "of a really great actor," was better even than Macready.[21] Mr and Mrs Charles Kean (she was the former Ellen Tree) arrived in New York in August 1846 for an engagement at the Park. On 31 August this brief notice appeared in the *Eagle:* "THE THEATRE.—Mr & Mrs Kean commence an engagement at the Park theatre to-night. We have plenty of stock performers better than either of them." From the first, the *Eagle* criticized the Keans' acting ability.[22] The New York press, which had mostly praise for the Keans, sneered at Whitman's comments and in so doing unleashed a barrage from the *Eagle* against the soundness and sincerity of the New York papers. On 2 September Whitman remarked:

> The N. Y. *Gazette* thinks it "funny" and the *News* thinks it "ridiculous" that we look on the Keans as no better than several of our own stock performers. Independent opinions, uninfluenced by the tawdry glitter of foreign fame . . . may, doubtless do, seem ridiculous and funny enough to our city neighbors. Such as we have expressed about the Keans are our *honest* opinions, however; and that's more than a man will get from the New York papers in a month of Sundays.

The drama criticism in the New York papers was valueless—it was nothing but "puffs . . . paid for either in money to the publisher, or treats, suppers, or gifts to the *critics.*"[23] Furthermore, the New York critics imitated the conventionalities of the British critics and praised or damned actors and plays as the British critics praised or damned them. Unfortunately, many of those who attended plays truckled to both the New York critics and British opinion. Whitman was correct in saying his opinions were his own. His comments in the *Eagle* on the plays he saw were fresh, usually valid, and expressive of a genuine appreciation of the stage.

Despite the great dramatic actors of the 1840s, the American stage, particularly so far as the legitimate drama was concerned, was badly attended in that decade. In part this unhappy condition of the theatre was due to a widespread moral prejudice

202

against both the stage and those who acted on it. Though the *Eagle* admitted certain undesirable features about the theatre, it at no time accused actors of anything worse than thoughtlessness of the morrow. On 27 November 1847 Whitman reported the death of Mrs Herring, who for many years had been a member of the Bowery's company, and drawn into reminiscences of "the old Bowery company of fifteen years ago," he noted how many of that group were now old and poor. It was an unfortunate habit of actors, he remarked, to neglect to save; "generous and thoughtless," they spent their money as they earned it.

> As a fact with hardly an exception, it would be found that they have most of the kindly and good-hearted qualities that embellish character. And this must be remembered, while their employment is scouted by the over scrupulous. Let the world treat the faults of these people gently! and have a kind thought, at least, for them, when departed!

As for the New York theatres, Whitman admitted on 8 February 1847, in "Miserable State of the Stage," that certain ones—the Bowery, the Chatham, and the Olympic—were guilty of vulgarity, coarseness, and bad taste "really beyond all toleration."[24] The "miserable burlesques of the histrionic art" which appeared on the boards of these theatres perverted the moral purpose of the stage: to promote philanthropy; to destroy despotism; to "hold up to scorn bigotry, fashionable affectations, avarice, and all unmanly follies"; to warn youth away from wickedness; and to improve relations in domestic life. As Whitman said on 12 February, the presentations of well-regulated theatres such as the Broadway and the Park promoted these moral aims, and the spectator came away from them a better person.

Whitman believed the stage, as an institution, to be a good influence on public morals, and one of the last pieces he wrote in the *Eagle* was a defense of the theatre. "While divines, who will not visit the theatre, and therefore cannot be supposed to know . . . much about it . . . are inveighing against the art which Hannah More loved, and Joanna Baillie wrote for, and Miss Edgeworth defended," he told his readers on 6 January 1848, "while . . . it is considered 'religious,' among a few, to condemn the theatre, it may not be amiss to stop awhile and think whether there be not something in such statements as the following from the *Harbinger*." The *Harbinger* had declared that tired business-men and toil-worn laborers were saved from the vicious "bar-room" and "rum-hole" by finding relaxation in the pit of a theatre. Indeed, said the *Harbinger*, if the theatre were made less expensive and if it were possible for every adult and child in the community to visit the theatre two or three times a week, "it would work an instant and prodigious moral advancement." Whitman, naturally, agreed, citing the plays of Shakespeare as indubitably suited for virtuous relaxation. Many modern dramatists, too, such as Bulwer (whom Whitman here stamped as a genius), provided mental refreshment of a wholesome sort. "There is *virtue in amusement*—let the straightlaced say what they will." Doubtlessly evil got into the theatre just as it did in the streets and in the churches, he admitted, but only "the excessively verdant" imagined there was more evil in the theatre than elsewhere. The stage needed reforming, true enough, but the reform was the sort that would free it from subservience to British conventions and ideas. "Let the virtuous have done with these attempts upon the theatre," demanded Whitman. "Dramatic performances will *always* exist, in every civilized community—and *should* exist."

Music

MISS LOUISE POUND pointed out many years ago that in *Leaves of Grass* Whitman "does not use the verb to write. He says sing, warble, carol, trill, or chant."[25] She attributed this characteristic of Whitman's diction to the influence of singers, especially operatic singers, in the poet's "incubation period," a period including his two years as editor of the *Eagle*. Since Miss Pound's article, numerous studies have been made of the influence of operatic technique upon Whitman's poetics.[26] They have tended to show that there was a substantial amount of truth in Whitman's pronouncement to John Townsend Trowbridge in 1860. " 'But for the opera,' he declared that day on Prospect Hill, 'I could never have written Leaves of Grass.' "[27] Though the opera probably was his chief musical passion, Whitman also enjoyed other kinds of music in varying degrees during his *Eagle* period: band concerts, vocal and instrumental recitals, oratorios, and popular vocal concerts. And, as expected, he was moved from time to time to say something about "national" music.

Judging from the remarks in the *Eagle*, instrumental music had less appeal for its editor than vocal music. The relatively few comments on the former showed a preference for simplicity in both melody and execution, and for the music of a brass band over that of a single instrument. Speaking on 15 April 1847 of William Granger's ubiquitous Brooklyn Brass Band, Whitman declared, "Of all that may be said of *music*—that inspiriting cheerer of the festive scene, and lightener of the cares of life—it is too often forgotten . . . that a *fine brass band* is capable of giving some of the sweetest developments of the divine art." Most of the band music that Whitman heard was played at civic festivals, semi-public halls, and the midnight street serenades so common on Brooklyn's balmier nights; and he often described it as "some of the most delightful music ever listened to." He left a record in the *Eagle* on 7 January 1848 of a formal band concert he attended at the New York Tabernacle given by the "Steyermarkische company—(so named from the Austrian dependency, whence they come)." The elegant musicians of the band had "none of the clap-trap of 'great artists'—no affectation—a youthful leader, who does *not* have his 'grand entrees,' nor flourish his wand with his back to the audience—no discordant tuning of instruments upon the stage." Of all the pieces played that night—and Whitman enjoyed them all—he liked best "The Marseillaise," which sounded "like the united voice of myriads" and filled "every chamber of the air." Though Whitman wrote some appreciative reviews of string and pianoforte recitals, his enjoyment of them was moderate, and he often felt that the musicians who played these instruments were apt to execute pieces too sophisticated for the average American audience. Commenting on a concert given at the Brooklyn Institute, Whitman stated (3 December 1847):

> Indeed it is only through simple, sprightly and unpretentious music that the hearts of a miscellaneous audience can be touched. For this reason the introductory piece by Saroni on

the violoncello and Duggan on the pianoforte, though full of real musical expression, and performed with skill, went off heavily and unsatisfactorily to the audience.

Whitman reported favorably on a Sivori and Herz's violin and piano concert on 14 October 1847;[28] but his enjoyment of the night's music was mixed, for he asked his readers, "Why do concert givers always gratify their own tastes alone, in selecting a programme? Many, no doubt, wished for the soothing influence of some sweet old English song, ever classical, and better than volumes of head aching trills."

Whitman found the simple music that he and the American miscellaneous audience preferred in the songs of such native vocal groups (some of them mixed quartets) as the Hutchinsons, the Cheneys, and the Harmoneons. He was not yet the opera aficionado when he wrote under "Music For the 'Natural Ear' " (3 April 1846):

> After all—after hearing the trills, the agonized squalls, the lackadaisical drawlings, the sharp ear-piercing shrieks, the gurgling death-rattles, the painful leaps from the fearfullest eminences to a depth so profound that we for a while hardly expect the tongue to scramble up again—after sitting in the full blaze of the pit of the Italian opera at Palmo's and nigh "the Borghese," and "the Pico," time and again—after the cracked voice of Templeton, the most consummate of humbugs,[29] the tiger-like piano execution of De Meyer, and all the long train of Italian artificiality—we turn (we are quite ashamed to confess it) with a vivider relish than ever to that kind of music which seems intended for "the natural man"— Whether it be that our palate rejects, in its homeliness, the niceties of spiced cookery, or that the simple wholesome is better in music, as it is in diet—at all events, give us good heart-song before the "fashionable article," any day!

On the night before, continued Whitman, he had attended the concert of the Hutchinson Family—three brothers and their female cousin—whose "true music really surpasses almost any of the vaunted *artificial* performers from abroad." He had been most pleased by their performance of Longfellow's "Excelsior" (a standard on the program of most vocal groups; its musical rendition had been composed and popularized, with Longfellow's approval, by the Hutchinsons), "that strange deep poetry."

It was the kind of music the Hutchinson Family sang that Whitman had in mind when he wrote on 8 September 1847—"A Thought of Ours About Music in the United States"—that "no human power can thoroughly suppress the spirit which lives in national lyrics, and sounds in the favorite melodies sung by high and low." Whitman's most complete statement in the *Eagle* on the subject of national music appeared on 4 December 1846 in an editorial titled "Music That *Is* Music."[30] Here Whitman distinguished between "heart music" and "art music." The latter was the "unreal" sort of melody featured in the concerts of Sivori, De Meyer, and other European artists. The former was what one heard at the concerts of the Hutchinsons and other groups of American vocalists; and it appealed to the American heart because of its "elegant simplicity," its intelligibility, and its "sensible sweetness" as contrasted with "the stale, second hand, foreign method, with its flourishes, its ridiculous sentimentality, its anti-republican spirit, and its sycophantic tainting the young taste of the nation!" Yet two months later the young editor who had turned in relief from "Italian artificiality" to the republican "heart music" of the Hutchinsons was to recommend the Italian opera as a welcome influence on American music.

Whitman's first critical review of an opera appeared in the *Eagle* on 16 January 1847 when he reported on the performance of Donizetti's *Lucia di Lammermoor* by the new Italian company at Palmo's Opera House in New York.[31] Everyone, he said, including the chorus, did well; and the execution of Barili (who played Lucia) was admirable, reminding "the listener of an exquisitely played flute, at once dazzling and soothing." The opening sentences of Whitman's second operatic review (13 February) showed none of the prejudice against the Italian opera he had shown in the preceding year: "More as tending, by comparison and familiarity, to elevate the standard of music in this country— than as anything to bow down to, or servilely imitate—the *Italian opera* deserves a good degree of encouragement among us." Whitman hoped the new company at Palmo's would become a permanent fixture. On the night before he had attended the company's performance of Coppola's *Nina Pazza per Amore*. In his opinion the opera lacked marked "originality or beauty," but it was "written in a light and sparkling style, and one might liken its introduction to the first inhalement of a good glass of champagne." And the performance of Rosina Pico seemed to have chased from Whitman's mind all thoughts of Italian artificiality, for he said her concluding songs were so "exquisite in quality and execution . . . that perhaps even Robie Burns, in his eccentric humor, would not have objected to those sweet and wild 'Italian trills' as concluding strains to 'Old Dundee.' " On 6 March Whitman reviewed the new company's performance in Verdi's *Lombardi*. He found the music somewhat heavy, but he was enthusiastic about the individual performers (including a violin soloist) and advised "all who appreciate the inspiration of true music, to go and hear some of the finest chorus-singing, instrumentation, and arias, ever produced in this part of the country."

In the following months Whitman attended the opera frequently. Companies were appearing at the Broadway, the Park, and Castle Garden, as well as at Palmo's—some of them giving, Whitman noted with approval, English-language versions of the more popular Italian operas. His notices of these performances were always favorable (even when singers were miscast) and usually enthusiastic. The operatic revival in New York in 1847 had worked a sea change on the editor of the *Eagle:* the Whitman who in 1846 had seen the opera as a sequence of agonized squalls was not the Whitman who, on 13 December 1847 at the beginning of a brief announcement of two operatic troupes opening that week at the Park and Broadway theatres, put the exclamation "Good!"[32]

The Ballet

THE EAGLE on 24 December 1847, in a paragraph containing "Pleasant News for the Lovers of the Ballet," remarked that the public liked and patronized musical and ballet performances more than those of the legitimate stage. It should, then, be pleasant news for the readers of the *Eagle* that Signora Ciocca, Signor Morra, and Miss Nallin were to begin an engagement at the Broadway. Perhaps Whitman had seen Signora Ciocca before, since he stated that in many ways she was superior to any dancer, except Fanny Elssler, who had appeared on the American stage. It is apparent from the *Eagle* that Whitman enjoyed musical performances much more than ballet. His remarks on the ballet were rare and usually perfunctory, sometimes expressive more of wonder at the physical stamina of the dancers than at their grace. But he lost his heart to one ballet company—the band of little girls who composed the Viennoise Children.

Whitman first noticed the Viennoise Children (who were appearing at the Park) on 14 December 1846. "The beautiful little creatures" reminded him of "living roses" and "butterflies." "These little Dutch girls," he said, "have the largest sort of red cheeks—forms like big apples—and their black eyes and fat little legs vibrate together, as the band plays those inspiriting German dance-airs! They all look healthy." The number in the program that Whitman liked best suggests, though he seems to deny it, that a degree of sensuality was involved in the appeal the children had for him.

> The dance where half of these engaging creatures are dressed in tight male dresses, is particularly amusing and pleasing. The roguishness of the boy-girls (the two largest good-looking fellows, though, are very sober indeed), and the elasticity of their motions, make a spectacle which the youth of the players only redeems from Sybarite voluptuousness! It is a very tolerable "poetry of motion" however—and the prudish need not be afraid of witnessing it.

The Viennoise Children were not "handsome-faced (which we Americans think more of than the modern, far more than the ancient Europeans)," but they were "well-formed, healthy-featured girls." Whitman wondered where they came from and what their future would be. "O, that some special angel might have them in his harm-defensive care!"

Apparently Whitman went to see the little dancers several times in the week that followed, for on 22 December he said:

"How charming they are! How they grow upon the love, too, every successive evening!" When the children returned to New York in the fall of the next year, Whitman hastened to remind his readers that "those most charming little creatures" were back again at the Park. The strong appeal the Viennoise Children had for the young editor of the *Eagle* probably came, in part at least, from their attractive healthiness. He might fear for their moral future, but he need feel no apprehensions for their health as he had on one occasion for a children's singing group.[33] Whitman had remarked, in reviewing Dr Dixon's *Woman, and her Diseases*, how rare it was to see "a well developed, healthy, *naturally* beautiful woman." On another occasion he had said "how seldom we see a perfectly healthy child, or youth!" Perhaps the little "well-formed, healthy-featured girls" of the Viennoise troupe embodied the wholesome well-being Whitman wanted for American children. Perhaps, too, he saw in them the promise of future perfect mothers.

Architecture

WHITMAN had little to say in the *Eagle* about architecture and probably would have said even less had it not been for the rapid growth of Brooklyn in the late 1840s, which brought with it an increased construction of newsworthy buildings. Most of his architectural opinions were on religious edifices, but business buildings elicited a few comments. His remarks of 20 October 1846 on the new Brooklyn Savings Bank illustrate his basic taste in both sacred and profane architectural design: "The massive, chaste character of the pile, its simplicity,—and the sufficient adornment without flummery, of the windows and door pieces, conduce to make it of such a nature that the eye can always rest upon it with pleasure." Whitman's taste in religious architecture, as briefly noted in an earlier chapter, was prevailingly the same—inclined to the plain and simple. The First Reformed Dutch Church embodied this chaste beauty. "Off south of the new city hall . . . stands one of the best specimens of architecture, one of the best looking churches, in Brooklyn!" Whitman declared on 9 February 1847. "Its clear white walls, its chaste style, the absence in it of all tawdriness and *deception*, have often attracted our notice, while perambulating the demesnes that there adjacent lie." Whitman disliked the over-luxurious ornamentation of Grace Church in New York and objected to the over-decorated tawdriness in the interior of the Broadway Theatre,[34] but he was not so narrow in taste that he could not like a more ornate style than that of the First Reformed Dutch Church.

In the 1840s the American Gothic, as it was later called, began to displace the neoclassical style of architecture, particularly in the North. Its increasing vogue was evidenced in Brooklyn by its influence on church architecture there. On 20 October 1846 Whitman opined that the Church of the Holy Trinity, then under construction, would rival New York's Trinity Church in handsomeness. "The style of the Brooklyn Trinity, is a very rich and florid Gothic," he added. "The sombre color of the stone prevents it, at the same time, from losing that solemn, 'dim religious' cast, which no church should be without, if possible." When Holy Trinity was completed in the following spring, Whitman's approval of its architecture seemed to be more than an expression of civic loyalty. The *Eagle* asserted on 19 April 1847:

> As it appears from the outside [the church] is among the very few fabrics where the eye of taste can behold a most profuse and florid display of ornament, the walls being apparently almost hidden by extraneous additions—and all reduced by the rigidest harmony and architectural truth. The excessive carving, and the innumerable turret-like points, all come in as happy aids to general effect—and that involves what we shall call richness, mellowness, and ripeness.

The sombre walls of Holy Trinity, hidden by florid but ordered ornament, were a complete contrast to the "clear white walls" of the Dutch Reformed Church; but Whitman's taste was broad enough to encompass these dissimilar styles. He was, after all, a young man who took great delight not only in the simple songs of the Hutchinsons but also in the rich but disciplined arias of the Italian opera.

Prints, Paintings, and Sculpture

SHORTLY AFTER he became editor of the *Eagle*, Whitman wrote a piece on "Polishing the 'Common People' " (12 March 1846), in which he suggested ways for "the spreading of a sort of demo-cratical artistic atmosphere, among the inhabitants of our repub-lic." The American people were ahead of the rest of the world in intelligence and education, yet they gave too little encouragement to and had too little appreciation of the fine arts. "Let every fam-ily," he advised, "have some flowers, some choice prints, and some sculpture casts."[35]

The *Eagle's* chief contribution to the fostering of interest in the fine arts was its comments on the engravings in the current periodicals. This contribution was slight, for Whitman's remarks were usually confined to simply stating the subjects of the prints, and he did not think much of most magazine art. "With their ever-lasting frontispieces of round-cheeked and wasp-waisted women, come the monthly magazines again," he said, opening a review of periodicals on 23 September 1847. This was "the old style namby-pamby" which he objected to in the prints of the *Union Magazine* on 28 September. On 14 December, speaking of the January issue of *Godey's Lady's Book*, he praised its good read-ing matter but deplored its "usual sort of commonplace picture," and added, "Magazine pictures, by the by, have long been *the* dishwater of art." But some periodical prints got Whitman's ap-proval since, as seen earlier, pictures dealing with American sub-jects were allied with writings on the same topics in the *Eagle's* minor campaign for a native literature. A few of the engravings that Whitman labelled as neat, pretty fair, or rarely, "capital," were on such non-American subjects as "Anne Boleyn with Arch-bishop Cranmer the Night before Her Execution" and "Christian and Mercy in the Valley of the Shadow of Death." But the major-ity of the prints he approved of had such titles as "The Soldier of Brandywine," "View of the Adirondack Mountains," "Death of the Red Deer," "The Charge of Captain May at the Battle of Resaca de la Palma," "General Taylor," "Dance by the Mandan Women," and "Herds of Bison and Elks."

Whitman's strongest expression of recommendation—"A work of Beauty!"—was reserved not for scenes appealing to national pride but for the colored prints of flowers in *Illustrated Botany*, a monthly he constantly praised. Reviewing the current issue on 20 August 1846, he stated that the study of botany was "well calculated to develope a refinement, and a sense of beauty." And it could do even more.

> To take up the simplest flower—examine it, its leaves, seeds, curious formation and beautiful colors—how well may the intelligent mind be impressed thereby, with the wisdom and vastness of God! For there *is* that in the make of a flower which involves those qualities.

This was a conventional assertion of botanists, but it acquires a degree of interest when one recalls that Whitman later wrote in section 31 of "Song of Myself": "I believe a leaf of grass is no less than the journey-work of the stars."

Whitman had little to say in the *Eagle* about painting, although a few years later he was, with a somewhat authoritative air, to deliver two speeches on art and artists before the Brooklyn Art Union.[36] He naturally was interested in George Catlin's paintings of American Indians (on exhibition at the Louvre, Paris, in 1846-47), and he joined those who were urging the federal government to buy that large collection depicting tribes from Florida to the Yellowstone. "A great deal is said by American writers and orators," Whitman commented on 9 July 1846 in his first article on Catlin, "about the duty and mission of America, *to the future.*" Yet Americans were hesitant to invest money in behalf of that mission, part of which was "to preserve the Memory of the Red Men, the North American 'Indians,' as they are miscalled." In a second article on 22 July he urged the government to act promptly lest "we shall never again have the opportunity of restoring to our country these paintings and memorials, so emphatically American, and of such decided importance to Art and to our national History."[37]

Whitman had access to paintings at the galleries of the National Academy of Design and the American Art-Union in New York, and at the Brooklyn Institute's annual exhibition of paintings. He appears rarely to have visited any of these displays; his references to them largely concerned his wish that works of art might more often be exhibited free of charge (as was the policy of the American Art-Union and the Brooklyn Institute) and also be so cheapened in price that the common folk would be encouraged to refine their taste and character. Almost nothing— except perhaps a pleasure in expansive landscapes—can be determined about Whitman's taste in painting from his remarks on the works he saw. Only Thomas Doughty, co-founder with Thomas Cole of the Hudson River School, and whom he called "the prince of landscapists," was much praised by Whitman. On 18 November 1847, after naming some of the local artists represented in the Brooklyn Institute's exhibition, Whitman said that he saw there "three splendid pictures by the best of American painters"—Doughty. The most beautiful of the three was "A Scene on the Tioga." But it may be that Whitman liked portraits as well as he did landscapes, for the painting that most interested him at this exhibition was one of Frederika Bremer ("understood to have been painted by a Swedish female artist"), the Swedish authoress so popular with Americans and with Whitman.[38] It seemed to him to be a perfect representation of Miss Bremer's "amiable moral and intellectual qualities." At the twenty-second annual exhibition of the National Academy of Design, reported on 14 April 1847, though he was pleased by several paintings (including two large landscapes by Asher B. Durand—"all he does is good"), Whitman seemed most impressed by "our own Frothingham's fine effigy of Rev T. B. Thayer of Brooklyn—a *speaking* portrait."[39]

Perhaps Whitman—who later was to be fond of being photographed—preferred the daguerreotype to the painted portrait. He referred appreciatively to the daguerreotype parlors on Broadway—only once, briefly, to that of Mathew Brady (who was to win fame during the Civil War) and several times to that of John Plumbe Jr at No. 251 over Tenney's Jewelry Store.[40] His comments on the pictures he saw at Plumbe's National Daguerrian Gallery were more enthusiastic than his comments on the paintings shown at the National Academy of Design and the Brooklyn Institute. In a brief paragraph, which was "no 'puff,' either, but a sincere 'narrative of truth,' " on 16 September 1846, Whitman said of Plumbe's daguerreotypes that it was "hardly possible to conceive any higher perfection of art, in the way of transferring the representation of that subtle thing, *human expression*, to the tenacious grip of a picture which is never to fade!" In a longer and more detailed description of Plumbe's gallery earlier on 2 July (in which he speaks of "the well-bred young gentleman in attendance . . . Mr P. himself"), Whitman implied that the daguerreotype was an art form superior to the oil painting. "You will see more *life* there, more variety, more human nature, more artistic beauty (for what created thing can surpass that masterpiece of physical perfection, the human face?) than in any spot we know of." Daguerreotype portraits had a "strange fascination" for him; they were "*realities.*"[41]

Sculpture apparently had much less appeal for Whitman than engravings, oil paintings, and daguerreotypes. Besides some statuary done by Brooklynite Henry Kirke Brown,[42] only one other piece of sculpture was commented on in the *Eagle:* Hiram Powers' celebrated "Greek Slave," which Whitman could not have avoided mentioning. This allegorical representation of Greece in Turkish fetters was an instant sensation when it was first exhibited in the United States in 1847; and the opinion promulgated by a committee of clergymen in Cincinnati that its female nudity was "moral" was accepted by the general public. On 3 September 1847 the *Eagle* carried an advertisement announcing that "POWERS' STATUE of the Greek Slave is now open for exhibition at the *National Academy of Design*, from 9 o'clock A. M. until 10 o'clock P. M. Admittance 25 cts. Season Tickets 50 cts." On September 24 the *Eagle* reported that up to that date Powers' share of the proceeds of the exhibition was two thousand dollars. The popularity of the exhibit was recorded by an ex-mayor of New York in his diary in an entry dated 13 September 1847: "A beautiful piece of statuary, the work of Hiram Powers, the celebrated American sculptor at Rome, is now being exhibited at the National Academy, and attracts crowds of visitors from morning to night. . . . I certainly never saw anything more lovely."[43] Was Whitman among the crowd of visitors to the National Academy's exhibition of the "Greek Slave"? The single comment in the *Eagle*

215

on the statue—aside from the statement on the proceeds from its showing—suggests he was. He wrote on 7 December 1847:

> A BEAUTIFUL SIGHT.—We have scarcely witnessed a more pleasing sight than the visit of the young ladies belonging to the Brooklyn female seminary to the exhibition of Powers' statue of the Greek Slave, in New York. On Saturday, some fifty or seventy-five charming young ladies, between the ages of sixteen and twenty, proceeded in a body to the national academy of design on Broadway, headed by one of the principals, and remained nearly two hours, completely enraptured with the beauties of this celebrated statue. We know of few higher compliments that can be paid to our countryman, Mr Powers, than this.

If he did view Powers' statue on that or any other day, Whitman was strangely silent. Could he not at least have pointed out that the admittedly fine figure of the "Greek Slave" never had been deformed by tight lacing? It may have been that the white marble sculpture failed to move him, esthetically or otherwise, because it was less realistic than oil painting or the daguerreotype and too cold, colorless, and inhuman when compared to such lively beings as the "well-formed, healthy-featured girls" of the Viennoise company. After all, the arts that most delighted the young editor of the *Eagle* were those in which living beings moved, and spoke, and sang—the ballet, the drama, and the opera. And the milieu that pleased him best was the streets of Brooklyn and New York —crowded with humanity.

216

five

APOLOGIA

I RESPECT Walter Whitman, editor of the *Brooklyn Daily Eagle*. The opinions he gave in his newspaper and the style in which he couched them were usually conventional. But he is entitled to respect as a journalist who enjoyed his profession, took it seriously, and devoted it to an earnest purpose. Though Whitman thought the average American newspaper editor was burdened with too many duties—he himself was editor, reporter, reviewer, assisted only by his scissors and pen—he found, as he told his readers, "many pleasures and gratifications in the position of an editor" to compensate for its toils. The general tone of his paragraphs in the *Eagle* conveys his enjoyment in observing and commenting on the varied and stimulating world about him. He wrote with equal relish of national destiny, street lights, philanthropy, ferry boats, the Atlantic dock and basin, cockney journalists, Coney Island, democracy, Broadway, Italian opera, and dirty streets. His contact with his world was broad. He interviewed such personages as P. T. Barnum and the delegates of the Laborers' Benevolent Association; he attended such diverse functions as steamboat christening parties and exhibitions by the blind; and he received copies of new books from publishers and theatre passes from impresarios. To "really feel a desire to talk on many subjects, to *all* the people of Brooklyn," as Whitman declared he felt, was the result of his absorption in his diverse and provocative environment.

217

Whitman's writings in the *Eagle* have been characterized as desultory or impromptu, adjectives which imply a substantial degree of professional unconcern. Some of his pieces certainly were composed hastily: he sometimes was pressed by the paper's deadline or simply was not in the mood. But the body of his *Eagle* articles shows that thought, inquiry, and conviction entered into their composition. I often feel impelled to depreciate these writings because of Whitman's relaxed, sometimes formless, style (but it should be remembered that he believed an editor's articles "should never smack of being uttered on the spur of the moment, like political oratory"), and because of his occasional ingenuousness and superficiality, and because of his conventionality. Yet the sincerity of his opinions on such matters as the Wilmot Proviso, the tariff, capital punishment, bathing, Alderman Fowler, and swill milk can scarcely be denied—those opinions were not perfunctory. Also, Whitman was conscious of the primary responsibility of the newspaper editor to influence his subscribers in the direction of "great principles and truths." As a result, he not only thought that what he said in the *Eagle* was worth saying, but he also made sure that what someone else said was not mistakenly confused with what he said. Communications and extracted articles that appeared in the *Eagle* were not always entirely acceptable to its editor, and so he reminded his readers, "*Our own sentiments are always in the editorial articles proper.*"

The primary responsibility of the newspaper editor, stated specifically, was to school the people. Like many of his contemporaries, Whitman believed that social reform could be advanced by educating the American public, particularly through the newspaper. "People are to be schooled, in opposition perhaps to their long established ways of thought," he proclaimed; and the persistent strain of didacticism in the *Eagle* is evidence of Whitman's professional earnestness. His editorials, reviews, literary extracts, and commentary, it is true, supported the conventional moralities and the more respectable reforms; but Whitman was no mere conformist to the approved points of view. His distrust of the legislation of morals led him to denounce local-option liquor licensing at a time when, as he admitted, the voting public of Brooklyn favored it.

Another reason for respecting Walter Whitman of the *Eagle* is suggested by his advocacy of the Wilmot Proviso, for it proved him to be a man of principle. However, Whitman's faithfulness to principle is better, though not as spectacularly, illustrated by his steadfast adherence in the *Eagle* to what he called an "immutable truth": the best society is that which has the greatest freedom from regulations and restrictions imposed by either legislative bodies or interested groups. This principle formed the basis of his attitude toward the federal and state governments, labor unions, prohibition, tariff, currency, religious sectarianism, abolition, medicine, and the arts. An admirer of Tom Paine and a professed follower of Jefferson, Whitman made excessive legislation and uncritical conformity to precedent his most persistent objects of attack in the *Eagle*. It was his conviction that persuasion and education—not statutes nor dogmas nor appeals to tradition—were the only valid means by which to ameliorate the actions of men in matters other than those concerning the preservation of life, liberty, and property. The individual was not free to injure his neighbor; but he was free to work, worship, think, drink, and write as he pleased. Though his application of this touchstone to the topics he discussed in his paper was not at all unique, it provided Whitman with a critical approach to the social, political, economic, and to a degree, artistic phenomena of the 1840s which was consistent and which imposed a certain unity on the varied commentary in the *Eagle*.

Writing in November 1847 after the Democrats had been defeated in the state elections, Whitman criticized his party for its lack of radicalism and asserted it was inevitable that liberal doctrines would gradually prevail. That to Whitman "liberal doctrines" were those which advocated the lessening of external restrictions on the individual and his activities is evident from what he added: "And it is to this progressive spirit that we look for the ultimate attainment of the perfectest possible form of government—that will be where there is the *least* possible *government*." In the *Eagle* Whitman explicitly condemned the tariff, federal internal improvements, labor unions, temperance and morals legislation, abolition, the enactment of multitudinous statutes by legislators, and the opposition to the sub-treasury as contradictory to that "perfectest possible form of government" espoused by the "sainted Jefferson and Jackson."

By extension of the principle of the maximum practicable *laissez faire* in political, economic, and social affairs, such matters as religion, health, education, literature, and the stage were sometimes judged in the *Eagle* by the same criterion. To Whitman, the intolerance and disputatiousness of religious doctrinaires indicated their wish to impose their beliefs on others. The reluctance of physicians to prescribe treatments not learned in the schools and not hallowed by precedent was a restraint upon the progressive spirit. Whitman blamed the narrow curriculum and the addiction to corporal discipline in the schools upon an unprogressive pedagogic bias that excused its restraint of a child's individuality on the grounds of precedent. His desire for American writings was that they develop their native traits without interference from those who would legislate literary standards upon the model of English literary tradition. Similarly, he objected to the imposition on the American theatre of precedents created by the English theatre.

At first glance, Whitman's eagerness for Congress to enact the Wilmot Proviso seems contradictory to the "immutable truth" that guided his opinion on so many questions. But he had stated that one of the prerequisites for the "perfectest possible form of government" was that "the plague spot of slavery, with all its taint to freemen's principles and prosperity, shall be allowed to spread *no further*." Obviously, slavery was a greater restraint upon the individual than a law which prevented the slaveholder from spreading his peculiar institution to areas still free of it. The Wilmot Proviso was legislation essential to the atrophying of an institution patently and inexcusably at odds with the fundamental axiom of American democracy—"impartial" liberty, as Whitman labelled it. It was clear to Whitman that slavery was an anomaly in any section of the republic, and it would not have been surprising had he supported abolition. That he did not may have been due partly to party loyalty (yet he supported the Wilmot Proviso), or to his reluctance, as he asserted, to see the principle of states' rights tampered with. Another reason may have been his dislike of the immoderate fanaticism which characterized most of those actively connected with the abolition movement. Whitman's eventual espousal of abolition may be attributed to the fact that the Wilmot Proviso made the movement more respectable. At least the proviso, judging by the unique copy of the *Freeman*, led him to align himself for a while with the abolitionists, though he never became a member of any of their societies. If, as he once told Traubel, Whitman was in his early years "very bigoted" in his anti-slavery stand, it must have been while he edited the *Freeman*. His later comments on slavery, as in the *Brooklyn Daily Times* in the late 1850s, were moderate in their condemnation of that institution and somewhat satirical of overly earnest abolitionists.

Writing in the *Eagle* of the necessity for the Democrats to endorse the Wilmot Proviso, Whitman said, "Conservatism . . . must leave the field—and the democracy must unite on its boldest and noblest and most radical doctrines." The Whitman revealed in the *Eagle* was not, however, a radical. Indeed, he seems a conservative compared with such journalists as his Whig contemporary, Greeley of the *Tribune*, though the latter favored a protective tariff and opposed the sub-treasury bill. Unlike Greeley, Whitman did not promote Fourierism and other utopian philosophies, nor did he advocate labor unions or cooperatives.

Whitman was preserved from radicalism by two qualities, one of which was his constitutional antipathy to fanaticism. His dislike of fanatics was evidenced by his remarks in the *Eagle* on the abolitionists—an "angry-voiced and silly set." Whitman showed no signs of fanaticism in the *Eagle* (except perhaps slightly in his pleas for the abolishment of capital punishment, and in that matter his argument was based on more realistic views than those of the abolitionists, and had it been acted upon, would have had no disrupting effect upon society). Though he was ardent in his support of the Wilmot Proviso, he refused to join the extremists who demanded the withdrawal of American troops from Mexico in an effort to force the proviso's passage in Congress. He wanted a distinctively native literature and deplored the effect of European, particularly British, writings upon American literary productions (and democratic virtues); yet his comments upon books, many of them European in origin, almost totally neglected the matter of developing a national literature and were, in regard to foreign works, almost wholly favorable. By conviction Whitman was a free-trader, but he was "not so wild," as he said, to believe that free trade was an automatic and universal panacea; and he was satisfied to settle for the Walker Tariff. Although he regarded peace and universal brotherhood as desirable aims, Whitman did not (as did the members of the American Peace Society and the League of Universal Brotherhood) denounce the Mexican War as unjust, unnecessary, and unholy. He advocated dietary reform, but he did not fall victim to such extreme dietary fads as that preached by Aloysius Graham. For a while he condemned the Italian opera and thought it inferior to the concerts of native vocal groups; but in the end he delighted in the opera and believed it could have a beneficial effect on the development of American music. And although he emphatically deplored the ascendency of the British drama over the American, he wrote with the highest praise of two such dissimilar British playwrights as Shakespeare and Bulwer.

A second quality which saved Whitman from radicalism was his skepticism of perfectionist theories, of utopian theories. A slight hint of this skepticism appeared in his occasional ironic jibes at perfectionists when he noted in the *Eagle* that the police court had had a decline in business. His comments on Robert Owen's trip to the United States in 1846 were positive expressions of his opinion of perfectionist philosophies. Owen's plan for "remodelling the world on an unalloyed basis of purity and perfection" was "utterly chimerical." Since God had ordained evil, it was not likely that Owen could eradicate it. And so it was that Whitman—unlike Greeley, Godwin, and other New York journalists—did not become a Fourierist or some other sort of associationist. Possibly for the same reason, he did not join any societies devoted to reform—not even an anti-hanging society.

Of course, in addition to his antipathy toward fanaticism and his skepticism of perfectionist theories, a third factor which probably preserved Whitman from fanaticism was his fundamental belief that the best government was that which legislated least. True, he wanted to see prison reform, anti-hanging, and the Wilmot Proviso made facts by legislation. But he had said, "You cannot legislate men into virtue!" Prison reform, anti-hanging, and the proviso were objective, even abstract, virtues. Something like temperance was purely subjective—a matter in which every individual was concerned. One chose to drink intoxicants, or one did not. Man, said Whitman, "in his moral and mental capacity . . . is the sovereign of his individual self." The fanatic who sought through prohibitory laws to force his reluctant fellow citizen into temperate habits was demanding that the latter abdicate the sovereignty of "his individual self." It is difficult for a man to become a radical in most things if he believes that men cannot be legislated into virtue. If legislative coercion is ruled out in the matter of reforms that affect citizens in their private capacities, then only persuasion and education remain as modes whereby to effect those reforms. And these sane and temperate modes— gradual in their results and respectful of the individual's moral and mental sovereignty over himself—were those employed by Whitman in his task of educating the subscribers of the *Eagle* to accept desirable reforms.

While he was educating his readers, Whitman was educating himself; the nature of his work made it inevitable. In the opening paragraph of a column headed "Sign Posts of the Times" (28 December 1846), Whitman commented on the unusually large number of new books being issued by American publishers. "Fresh batches are announced every day," he said, "and as it is necessary for all editors, and readers too, who would keep pace with . . . these sign-posts of the times—for such are new books— our good Eagle will proceed to discuss the merits of the latter ones." As a result of his being sent review copies of current publications, Whitman perhaps read more widely, and less selectively, during his two years on the *Eagle* than he otherwise would have done. Not only did this indiscriminate reading introduce Whitman to writers whose philosophies were new to him[1] (and perhaps contribute to that somewhat superficial catholicity of intellectual interests that characterized the later literary man) but it also probably had a chastening effect on his predilection for the overly sentimental. The literary, though not perhaps the didactic, value of such excessively sentimental writers as Mrs Sigourney and Mrs Child must have suffered in comparison with

223

the better authors whom Whitman encountered as he kept pace with the sign posts of the times. For example, the artless and conventional taste that impelled Whitman to write, "O, God above! what a thrill darts through one's heart, (bringing the thing home) at the climax of the following little story!—*Ed. E.*" before a very sentimental little anecdote which appeared in the *Eagle* on 14 August 1846, should have been disciplined by the anti-sentimentality of *Sartor Resartus,* which he reviewed two months later. Indeed, Whitman's response to the four works of Carlyle reviewed in the *Eagle*—a response which began by condemning Carlyle's style and ended by finding it "strangely agreeable"—shows that in one case at least he was educating himself as much as he was educating his readers.[2] And, of course, his attendance at plays, concerts, operas, art exhibitions, and lectures extended the scope of his education still farther.

The education of Walter Whitman was not confined, however, to the field of the arts. His professional duties, particularly those of a reporter, taught him "realities." His experience as a spokesman for his party, as well as an active and fairly prominent member of the local party organization, effectively showed him—as it would seem from the circumstances under which he left the *Eagle*—that loyalty to party is not always consistent with loyalty to principles. The proceedings of the Brooklyn Common Council were graphic illustrations of the incompetence, corruption, and stupidity that were the counterpoint to ability, incorruptibility, and intelligence in that best of all possible governments—the American democracy. The refusal of the drinkers and bartenders of Brooklyn to abide by the license law gave Whitman concrete proof of the validity of his contention that morality could not be legislated. His habit of attending, when he did attend, the services of diverse sects of Christians where he heard conflicting and often intolerant dogmas convinced him of the need of a reform toward a simpler, more tolerant, and more universal doctrine whereby religion could become practical and dynamic. The sordidness that Whitman saw in the police courts and in the slums of Brooklyn and New York, the crimes he reported himself or clipped from exchange papers, the poverty and sickness that haunted the Irish immigrants, the wards of the insane asylum and the halls of the blind school, the brutal treatment of horses, the sickening interior of a swill dairy, the sorrow of bereaved parents—these and other sights the perambulating young editor of the *Eagle* had of the dark side of life prepared him to accept evil in *Leaves of Grass* as the axiomatic antipode of good in the phenomenal world (see, for example, his 1860 poem "I Sit and Look Out"). That he had accepted evil as inescapable was shown by his query in the *Eagle:* "Ah, Mr Owen! when God ordained that evil shall exist, do you think that *you* can banish it altogether?" If one accepts evil as ordained, then one is required, for his own peace of mind, to find an explanation for its ordination. And while there is no hint in the *Eagle* that its editor had arrived at the theory of compensation or polarity, as he did later in the *Leaves* as a rationalization of the existence of evil, it is interesting that Whitman wrote in his little notebook dated 1847,

> I am the poet of sin,
> For I do not believe in sin.[3]

As noted in my Preface, it has been argued that his writings in the *Eagle* make no contribution to "any account of the development of Whitman's genius" because the prosody of *Leaves of Grass* cannot be predicted from those writings. And further, and for the same reason, it has been declared that the similarities in the ideas found in the *Eagle* and in those found in the *Leaves* are of no significance in the study of the antecedents of the latter. A more common and more rational opinion has been that Whitman's criticism of his era in the *Eagle* "is of mediocre literary quality . . . but in his democratic sympathies, his partisan enthusiasms, and his political ambitions we can now see in retrospect the emerging mind and character of the future author of *Leaves of Grass* and *Democratic Vistas.*"[4] Surely the Whitman who in the *Eagle* spoke for the superiority of American democracy over the political systems and creeds of the Old World and for the spread of republican ideals to politically oppressed nations was the same Whitman who in "I Was Looking a Long While" (*Leaves of Grass*), looking "for a clew to the history of the past for myself, and for these chants," found it in "Democracy" and saluted the world in America's name, foreseeing the day when all its nations would come forward to America's side. And the Jeffersonian philosophy of the editor survived in the *laissez faire* doctrine and individualism expressed by the later poet: the "immutable truth" that was an important motif in Whitman's journalistic prose was also an important motif and was still immutable in his *Leaves*. The poet's "great city" in "Song of the Broad-Axe" is a place where the government (to quote the *Eagle*) "is the mere agent, not the principal," and where legislation respects the rights of the individual:

> Where the men and women think lightly of the laws,
> Where the slave ceases, and the master of slaves ceases,
> Where the populace rise at once against the never-ending audacity of elected persons,
> . . . .
> Where outside authority enters always after the precedence of inside authority,
> Where the citizen is always the head and ideal, and President, Mayor, Governor and what not, are agents for pay,
> Where children are taught to be laws to themselves, and to depend on themselves,
> . . . .
> There the great city stands. (Section 5.)

Also in the *Eagle* may be glimpsed the ill-defined half-formed but generative "embryons" of the later poet's theory of American national literature. "Is it uniform with my country?" he asked in the 1855 Preface to *Leaves of Grass;* and Whitman's scattered remarks in the *Eagle* on native literature implied the same fundamental query.

It has been said that Whitman's concern in the *Eagle* over the unfortunate condition of workingwomen, his admiration of Queen Victoria, and his liking for books—such as Frederika Bremer's—with a "maternal point of view" must be considered "as another phase of his emerging mother-religion, later to produce some of his major literary themes and symbols."[5] There were frequent indications in the *Eagle* of Whitman's understanding of and sympathy with motherhood; and what makes this aspect of the young editor's character especially conspicuous is that he almost completely ignored the existence of affectionate

226

ties between father and child. It will be recalled, for example, that Whitman asserted, when describing the sorrow of a father whose small son had been drowned, "But his grief was nothing compared with the mother's"; and that the rest of the account was a tribute to the "immortal beauty" of mother-love. Elsewhere in the *Eagle* Whitman stated that the "crowning glory" of human existence was "motherly love." The mother worship motif in the *Leaves* is commonly explained by citing Whitman's close relationship with his mother and the stern, unaffectionate disposition of his father. Whatever the reason, the psychological groundwork for his later celebration of motherhood seems to have been firmly established by 1846. Fatherhood received scant praise or sympathy in either the *Leaves* or the *Eagle*.

Various facets of the "perfect mother" of the *Leaves* were foreshadowed in the *Eagle* besides that of motherly love. The perfect mother of the *Leaves* is also the physically perfect woman —healthy, well-formed, and free of false delicacy. Whitman's protests in the *Eagle* against tight lacing and his recommendations of Mrs Gove's and Dr Dixon's books on women's diseases and physiology were, after a fashion, anticipatory of his later concept of the perfect woman. The ideal woman of the *Leaves*— though "fierce and athletic"—is man's perfect companion, his equal. Some element of his levelling of the sexes may be seen vaguely in an embryonic state in the *Eagle*. Whitman disliked the idea of native American girls working as servants; he approved of women holding property after marriage; and he defended their right to intellectual equality with men. But Whitman's attitude toward women was largely the conventional one of the sentimental era in which he lived. Women were entitled to intellectual freedom but, Whitman confessed, he liked to see "in all the developments of thought and action, in a woman, an infusion of mildness and of that spirit which 'falleth as the gentle dew from heaven.' " And when he spoke of the nature of woman as being always "beautifully pure, affectionate, and true," even to a brute of a husband, he was simply repeating the sentimental novel's idealized picture of wifely self-abnegation.

When Whitman wrote in the *Eagle* of the things he saw and heard from his editorial window at the foot of Fulton street, or as he sauntered the crowded streets of Brooklyn and New York, or sailed on the Fulton ferry, or rode Messrs Husted and Kendall's omnibusses on excursions, he was not consciously compiling material for the poems he was to write later. Unconsciously, however, the sights and sounds that Whitman recorded in his Brooklyn daily paper were being stored in his memory until they reappeared in *Leaves of Grass*. This unconscious absorption of sensory impressions began, of course, long before the *Eagle* period and continued afterwards; but the files of the *Eagle* for the almost two years of Whitman's editorship provide the fullest and most vivid record available of the raw material from which an essential part of the *Leaves* was later fashioned. Many of the catalogs so typical of the earlier editions of the *Leaves* may be easily duplicated by simply listing not only the references in the *Eagle* to the sights and sounds of Long Island, Brooklyn, and New York, but also the references to the many things Whitman read of in exchange newspapers, periodicals, and review copies of current books. Particular motifs of the *Leaves* sometimes found unconscious, almost prophetic, expression in the *Eagle*. Coney Island especially stimulated Whitman to expressions of this sort. One is at once reminded of passages in the *Leaves* when he reads in the *Eagle*, in the account of a clambake at Coney Island, "The beautiful, pure, sparkling seawater! one yearns to you . . . with affection as grasping as your own waves," or in the record of another excursion to the same place, "There, too, were the white plumes of many a mighty ripple—ere it threw its long shallow scoot high up the shore. . . . How can human eyes gaze on the truest emblem of Eternity, without an awe and thrill?" These lines are far from the poems of the *Leaves*. But the modern reader, with the omniscience given him by his later location in time, can see in them a faint omen of what was to come in 1855.

Little, if any, of the social, political, and economic phenomena of the critical years of the 1840s that Whitman commented upon in the *Brooklyn Daily Eagle* failed to find its place in *Leaves of Grass*, especially in the first three editions. But it is not likely that the young editor was aware (at best, only confusedly) that the things he wrote about in his paper were the raw materials for poems far different from the conventional sentimental verse (sometimes his own) that he complacently printed in his first-page miscellany. Walter Whitman went about his daily work as editor and reporter, enjoying his task of schooling the citizens of Brooklyn (and himself) in conventional language on conventional topics, little suspecting that in a few years he would shock and amuse many of those respectable Brooklynites by suddenly revealing himself to their incredulous eyes as "Walt Whitman, a kosmos"—"he who would assume a place to teach or to be a poet here in the States."

NOTES

Key to abbreviations of frequently cited works

EPF   Thomas L. Brasher, ed., *The Early Poems and the Fiction* (The Collected Writings of Walt Whitman), New York 1963.
GF   Cleveland Rodgers and John Black, eds., *The Gathering of the Forces*, New York 1920, 2 v.
SS   Gay W. Allen, *The Solitary Singer*, New York 1955.
UPP   Emory Holloway, ed., *The Uncollected Poetry and Prose of Walt Whitman*, Garden City, N.Y., 1921, 2 v.
WWC   Horace Traubel, *With Walt Whitman in Camden*, New York, Philadelphia, or Carbondale, Ill., 1906-64, 5 v.
WWS   Florence B. Freedman, *Walt Whitman Looks at the Schools*, New York 1950.

N.B.   References to notes giving full titles of other works cited more than once are in brackets.

Preface

1. UPP, WWS; GF.

2. "Though the actual writing of the poems in the 1855 *Leaves of Grass* certainly came later, Whitman probably started accumulating ideas for the book in the late 1840's before he had either the title or even a general plan in mind. In little notebooks, small enough to carry around in his pocket, he jotted down tentative thoughts, themes, and trial workings of what was to become the 1855 preface and some of the poems in the first edition." (SS: 134.)

In "Walt Whitman's Earliest Known Notebook," *PMLA* 83 (Oct. 1968): 1453-56, Edward F. Grier argues convincingly that Whitman made the entries in this earliest known notebook in 1847. Here, as Grier says, "We can see Whitman's mind at work at a very early stage; we can relate the process of development to events in his external biography . . . and we know that he was composing *Leaves of Grass* at least as early as mid-April 1847." For the contents of this notebook, see UPP 2: 63-76.

3. SS: 80.

4. SS: 81-82.

5. Dealt with earlier in my "Whitman and Universalism," *Walt Whitman Newsletter* 3 (Sept. 1957): 40-42.

6. Clara Barrus, *Whitman and Burroughs, Comrades*, Boston 1931: 362.

7. Ibid.

8. Richard Chase, "Go-Befores and Embryons," in *Leaves of Grass One Hundred Years After*, ed. Milton Hindus, Stanford 1955: 40.

9. Clarence Gohdes, "Democracy in Free Verse," in *The Literature of the American People: An Historical and Critical Survey*, ed. Arthur H. Quinn, New York 1951: 602.

10. His usage was to punctuate, then insert the marks of parentheses willy-nilly, for example, "After this token, (and something more, perhaps,) there is a beautiful pleasure in swift sailing, on a large sheet of water." (*Eagle*, 1 Aug. 1846.)

one

1. A ms. notebook of Whitman has this entry: "About the latter part of February '46, commenced editing the Brooklyn *Eagle*—continued till last of January '48." (UPP 2: 88.) Certainly Whitman was with the *Eagle* by 3 Mar. 1846, for on that date appeared a characteristic editorial directed against a bill to suppress licentiousness recently introduced into the legislature at Albany. The *Eagle* for 2 Mar. was devoted entirely to an account of Marsh's funeral and to testimonials of his exemplary character. As 1 Mar. was Sunday, the paper was not published on that date. It is at least generally agreed that a review of Keats' *Poetical Works* in the *Eagle* for 5 Mar. is Whitman's.

2. Allen Nevins, "The Newspapers of New York State, 1783-1900," in *History of the State of New York*, ed. Alexander C. Flick, New York 1933-37, 9: 292.

3. See below. Other references to the *Eagle* days in Whitman's published prose merely state he was editor of the paper in such and such years, usually wrong by one or two years.

4. Ralph F. Weld, writing of the time when Whitman joined the *Eagle*, says, "The *Eagle* was backed by the regular Democratic organization of the city, a group of practical politicians." (*Brooklyn Village, 1816-1834*, New York 1938: 250.)

5. This ode appeared in the *Eagle* (2 July 1846) in a preview of the program slated for the 4th at Fort Greene; for the text, see EPF: 34-35.

6. "In attempting to trace this legend to its origin the discovery was soon made that the few living persons connected with The Eagle who recalled Walt Whitman in the flesh never knew him as editor of the paper, but as the poet of later days." (GF 1: xx.)

7. GF 1: xxi-iii. Sutton was 90 in 1920; I have often wondered if he was the lad who answered this ad in the *Eagle* (20 Apr. 1846): "WANTED, AT THIS

OFFICE—A boy from 14 to 17 years of age, to learn the Printing business. Apply immediately."

8. The *Eagle* (21 Jan. 1848) suggested the *New York Globe* attend to its own affairs and leave the *Eagle's* alone, and also wanted to know what authority the *Globe* "has for saying that there is any change in the political conduct of this paper? The publisher, in the course of his business arrangements, has found it necessary to dispense with one of its editors . . . If the *Eagle* puts forth false doctrines . . . the *Globe* is at full liberty to expose its errors . . . but in our business affairs we claim the right to act without its impertinent interference."

9. As quoted by Emory Holloway and Vernolian Schwarz, eds., *I Sit and Look Out*, New York 1932: 5. It is a petty matter, but every work I have seen (including my own EPF) on Whitman which has occasion to mention the *Brooklyn Advertiser* spells the paper's name with a "z." Whitman consistently spelled it with an "s," and he was not inclined to this sort of consistent misspelling. In answer to my query, John W. Watson, research assistant at the Long Island Historical Society, confirmed that its masthead reads *Daily Advertiser*.

10. "It [the *Freeman*] is edited and published by Walter Whitman, Esq., who manfully opposes Hunkerism in all its forms." (Quoted from the *Tribune* [1 Nov. 1848] by Holloway and Schwarz [n. 9]: 6.) The *Brooklyn Evening Star* (26 Apr. 1849) said, "The Editor [of the *Freeman*] is an enthusiastic Free Soiler, and flings down his gage of battle for that cause like a fearless champion. Mr Whitman is a vigorous and independent man, and personally we wish him success in his enterprise." (Id.)

11. Nevins [n. 2] unfairly calls Whitman, as *Eagle* editor, "a somewhat inconsistent, hot-headed journalist" simply because he supported with "equal enthusiasm" both the Mexican War and the Wilmot Proviso.

12. Even in his old age, as a rather unfriendly critic has admitted, Whitman, though stubborn and sometimes thoughtless in the fashion of old folk, was always courteous and kind. Mrs Elizabeth Leavitt Keller, Whitman's nurse for two months during his final illness, had this to say: "To Walt Whitman's credit be it said, he never spoke an unkind word to Mrs Davis [his housekeeper from 1884 until his death in 1892]; never was arrogant or overbearing to her; never belittled her or put her down before others; always treated her as an equal . . . but he would have his own way, and she with her yielding nature soon gave in." (*Walt Whitman in Mickle Street*, New York 1921: 32-33.)

13. See William Harlan, *Horace Greeley: Voice of the People*, New York 1950: 66.

14. *Democracy in America*, ed. Phillips Bradley, New York 1948, 2: 56.

15. Weld [n. 4].

16. During June 1846 Whitman from time to time printed brief excerpts from other papers complimenting the *Eagle* on its improved appearance as the result of new type; quite a few complimented its editor as well. Perhaps it is to be expected that Democratic papers should have spoken well of another Democratic paper: Bryant's *Post* described the *Eagle* as "a spirited and well-managed Democratic paper" (6 June); the *New York Morning News* and the *New York Globe* offered "complimentary allusions" to the paper and its editor (6, 9 June); and so it went with other Democratic newspapers in and out of New York State. But Whig journals, too, spoke well of Whitman's pro-

fessional capacity. Greeley's *Tribune* said, "The paper is in every respect—except in politics . . . exceedingly well got up. The Local Department is put together with great industry and cleverness" (2 June); the venerable Alden Spooner, dean of Brooklyn journalists, in his *Evening Star* complimented the *Eagle* on its new type "and a brilliant lot of editorials and original articles to match," and expressed his gratification that Whitman "always had so much good in the midst of" his political heresies (4 June); other Whig papers spoke in the same vein.

17. UPP 1: 115, n. 1.

18. Whitman several times made it clear that his opinions were not passively received from the party. For example, this item appeared in the *Eagle* (30 July 1846): "Our rather impertinent friend and correspondent 'X.' is informed that the Brooklyn *Eagle* is committed to neither of the 'factions' [Hunkers and Barnburners] which raised such a row last winter at Albany. We have a prodigious fancy for keeping the *E.* aloof and clear from all clique and personal influence—and as to the latter part of 'X's' letter, we shall say what we think *right*, without the least alarm or 'hesitation.' "

19. In his "City Intelligence" column (19 June 1846) Whitman quoted the *New York Evening Post* as saying it had got its item on the launching of the sloop of war *Albany* at the Brooklyn Navy Yard from an Albany paper. "What are the Brooklyn papers about?" asked the *Post*. Whitman indignantly replied: "*This* Brooklyn paper, part of it, is 'about' the good city of Brooklyn, every day, actively engaged, at a very considerable outlay of time, work, and money, in getting every possible item of local news—of which we give a couple of columns each day." In fact, the Albany paper's version of the launching had been clipped from the *Eagle* and published as original.

20. Other newspapers employed phonographic reporters. When Louis Agassiz lectured in New York during Oct. and Nov. 1847, his talks were taken down by Dr Houston, secretary to the U.S. Senate and a phonographer, and were reported in full in the *Tribune*. See James P. Wood, ed., *One Hundred Years Ago: American Writing of 1847*, New York 1947: 200.

21. Perhaps Whitman seems inconsistent after having said that an attacked editor was justified in inflicting "the most violent" retaliation. However, he often denounced prize fighting in the *Eagle*—despite the fanciful painting by Eakins, many years later, showing Whitman watching a Philadelphia prize fight with considerable interest. Also, he and Lees never missed a chance to take journalistic jabs at one another.

22. The following appeared in the *Eagle* (30 Apr. 1847): "EDITORS' VISITORS.—Pay as few visits as possible, to editors! Nine-tenths of the matters which people bring to an editor, could just as well be attended to by the publishing department. An editor in business hours, never wants to 'see company.' "

23. SS: 74. Edwin Spooner was the son of Col. Alden Spooner and active editor of the *Star* at this time, though the elder Spooner still contributed editorials from time to time.

24. "Our venerable contemporary of the *Star* calls us a '*pig ringer.*' We don't know what this means; but as we have been tweaking the impertinent noses of the *Advertiser* and *Star* lately, and pretty severely too, perhaps it *is* no more than just to call us a 'pig ringer.' " (*Eagle*, 9 Nov. 1847.)

25. See the *Eagle* (16 Apr. 1847) and again, 2 Sept., when Whitman avowed he was pleased and honored to be called a schoolmaster: "a proper schoolmaster is one who is an honor and a benefit to his race—and many a more famous man don't do half as much good."

26. On 30 June 1847 Whitman remarked: "The Brooklyn *Evening Star*, getting entirely beyond the English language, launches into the county judge case again with volleys of the old Roman tongue! We were never yet able to master the *Star's* attempts in the vernaculiar [this may be a bad pun rather than a typographical error] and shall give it up entirely if it is going into the dead languages."

27. An item in the *Eagle* (30 Dec. 1847), less than a month before his departure from the paper, indicates that Whitman was not personally estranged from the Spooners: "The conductors of the principal whig paper in Brooklyn, being desirous to give character and *eclat* to the new publishing office they have just taken unto themselves in the basement of the Long Island insurance company's building, on the corner of Fulton and Front streets, gave a pleasant little oyster and champaine entertainment to a small party of *very* distinguished persons this morning—the 29th instant. We have not lost our horror of whig *politics*—but there is no denying that the scamps have first rate judgment in *wine*."

28. Whitman's most pronounced breach of good taste in the *Eagle* was this brief item (9 Feb. 1847): "The *Adv*. should have signed the self written letter v. o. m., for sure we are that any decent man who essays its reading will wish to vo'mit." Only a few months earlier (3 Oct. 1846) Whitman had congratulated himself that "our print, passing into so many family *circles* here about, affords from day to day a mass of matter that must make it peculiarly acceptable for the ladies, youth, &c."

29. That the Spooners disliked Lees and his paper as much, apparently, as did Whitman (but it is necessary to remember that readers expected newspaper editors to engage in verbal mayhem and sensible editors obliged their readers) seems indicated by this item in the *Eagle* (23 Nov. 1847): "The Brooklyn *Star* stated on Saturday that 'a *would-be* distinguished editor in this city had been taken to the watch house,' for kicking up a row, etc. Whereupon the *Advertiser* responds in the following manner, to wit: 'We are willing to reply to or pass in silence as our humor takes us, the scurrility of the *Star*, through our columns, but when it comes out and lies wilfully, maliciously, and cowardly, we shall meet it through another source.' So look out for another pugilistic encounter, in the fourth story of no. 35 Fulton street."

30. In a later editorial, "Independent American Literature" (10 Feb. 1847), Whitman explained that the hissing was done by a guest or guests of the association, not by one of its members, and added: "In our former brief notice, certain words were used which we are now convinced did injustice to this really talented band of young men; they are, many of them gentlemen of much literary taste, and true perception."

31. Unanswerable indeed. For several years Whitman had been writing very bad conventional verse, published in sundry newspapers, including the *Eagle*. See EPF.

Despite the sharp interchange between them, Lees spoke well of Whitman in the *Advertiser* when the latter was preparing to edit the *Brooklyn*

Freeman in the fall of 1848, and again in the summer of 1849 when the *Advertiser* anticipated Whitman's "triumphant exultation over the clique which ejected him from the position he once held, because he would not complacently yield to their intolerant dictation." See Joseph J. Rubin, "Whitman: Equal Rights in the Foreground," *Emerson Society Quarterly*, no. 22 (1961): 22. And in 1850 Whitman wrote anonymously for the *Advertiser*, contributing 16 "Paragraph Sketches of Brooklynites." See UPP 1: 234.

32. Despite the strictures of the *New York News* concerning Whitman's use of "grateful" and our own feeling that that use is illogical, I have found in both English and American writings of the 1840s and 1850s—and writings by very respectable writers indeed—such a continual practice of applying "grateful" to what is apparently the wrong noun that I am convinced such practice was idiomatic, not to say colloquial, at the time—perhaps a peculiar twist of the pathetic fallacy.

33. "Walt Whitman and the Dramatic Stage in New York," *Studies in Philology* 50 (July 1953): 538.

34. Strangers to America sometimes spoke of Manhattan as Gomorrah. For example, Ole Munch Raeder, traveling in the United States in 1847-48 for the Norwegian government, wrote: "New York is the Gomorrah of the New World, and I am sure it may well be compared with Paris when it comes to opportunities for the destruction of both body and soul." (Gunnar J. Malmin, tr. and ed., *America in the Forties: The Letters of Ole Munch Raeder*, Minneapolis 1929: 230.)

35. Remember that line in sect. 33 of "Song of Myself" which reads: "Looking in at the shop windows of Broadway the whole forenoon, flatting the flesh of my nose on the thick plate glass."

36. Harriet Martineau, the English writer, had visited the United States some ten years earlier and had found it striking that even mechanics in New York dressed so well.

> One day, in going down Broadway, New York, the carriage in which I was, stopped . . . in consequence of an immense procession on the sidewalk having attracted the attention of all the drivers within sight. The marching gentlemen proceeded on their way, with an easy air of gentility. Banners were interposed at intervals; and on examining these, I could scarcely believe my eyes. They told me that this was a procession of the journeymen mechanics of New York. Surely never were such dandy mechanics seen; with sleek coats, glossy hats, gay watch-guards, and doeskin gloves!
>
> I rejoice to have seen this sight. I had other opportunities of witnessing the prosperity of their employers; so that I could be fairly pleased at theirs. (*Society in America*, London 1837; reprint, New York, AMS Press 1966, 2: 254-55.)

37. Emma Willard's familiar poem, "Rocked in the Cradle of the Deep," first published in 1831, may have suggested—probably in its very popular version set to music by Joseph P. Knight, the English composer—the initial line of Whitman's "Out of the Cradle Endlessly Rocking."

236

38. These remarks about the exposition are an interesting foreshadowing of Whitman's "Song of the Exposition," composed and delivered by invitation 25 years later at the 40th annual fair of the American Institute.

39. In this editorial Whitman discusses the six ferries (as well as I can count) operating from Brooklyn—some with one shabby boat and others with an elegant fleet; two more ferries were projected.

40. H. A. Lees of the *Advertiser* may have acquired by 1847 those "dissipated habits" which led to his "neglect and mismanagement" of his paper in the early 1850s. See Henry R. Stiles, *A History of the City of Brooklyn*, Brooklyn 1867-70, 3: 936.

41. In an autobiographical note now in the Trent collection at Duke University, Whitman recalls the weekly trip his maternal grandfather Major Van Velsor made with a combination stage and market wagon from his farm at West Hills "to the Brooklyn ferry, where he used to put up at Smith & Wood's old tavern . . . near Fulton ferry. . . . I well remember how sick the smell of the lampblack and oil with which the canvass covering of the stage was painted, would make me." (Clarence Gohdes and Rollo G. Silver, eds., *Faint Clews & Indirections: Manuscripts of Walt Whitman and His Family*, Durham, N.C., 1949: 45.) In the opening chapter of Whitman's temperance novel *Franklin Evans*, the hero sets out for New York in just such a Long Island country market wagon. See EPF: 128 ff.

42. Clarke, who died insane and impoverished in Manhattan in 1842, was described by his contemporaries as "the mad poet" of Broadway. Whitman wrote a poetical tribute, "The Death and Burial of McDonald Clarke," which appeared in the *New York Aurora* on 18 Mar. 1842 (reprinted in Joseph J. Rubin and Charles H. Brown, eds., *Walt Whitman of the New York Aurora*, State College, Pa., 1950: 105-8, and in EPF: 25-26).

43. Whitman remarked on this point: "The ferries . . . are now looked upon as one of the advantages. Nothing is more refreshing in a hot day than the pure delicious air that one gets in crossing. The warm and dusty wayfarers of the great Babel . . . often recross several times to prolong the luxury. We have been tempted ourselves repeatedly in this way."

44. On 13 July 1847 the *Eagle* carried an article headed "Pleasant Two Hours' Jaunt.—East Brooklyn Stages," in which Whitman remarked, concerning rural strolls, "An occasional indulgence in this cheap but most rational pleasure, will be more profitable to you than a jaunt to the springs, or a feverish trip to some fashionable country place."

45. The immense popularity of Longfellow's poem "Excelsior" in the 1840s gave a name not only to stagecoaches and omnibusses but also to steamboats and railroad engines and hotels. The reader will learn later that, at least for Whitman, the high point of a performance by a singing group was a rendition of "Excelsior." I believe, and I take the onus on myself, that there was also an Excelsior cigar and an Excelsior beer.

46. UPP 1: 174, n. 1, cites this as Whitman's second and final trip to eastern Long Island while editor of the *Eagle;* apparently Holloway overlooked Whitman's one-day excursion to Greenport on 3 Sept.

47. Three reviews of these phrenological lectures appeared in the *Eagle* during this month (5, 7, 11 Mar.) ridiculing the claims made for the science

of phrenology by Orson Squires Fowler, member with his brother Lorenzo N. Fowler and Samuel Robert Wells in the firm of Fowler & Wells, operator of a New York phrenological parlor, publisher of the *American Phrenological Journal*, and future agent for the first two editions of *Leaves of Grass*. Freedman (WWS: 57-58) quotes two sentences out of context from the last review of the lectures (mistakenly dating the last lecture the 10th) and wrongly uses them as evidence that Whitman at that time approved of the claims made for phrenology. The entire review is ironic in tone, as are the lines quoted by Mrs Freedman. See my "Whitman's Conversion to Phrenology," *Walt Whitman Newsletter* 4 (June 1958): 95-97 (excusing, I hope, my speaking of Orson Squires Wells when it should have been Orson Squires Fowler: many of us born in a certain period can accuse Orson Wells of confusing us). Also see Edward Hungerford's "Walt Whitman and his Chart of Bumps," *American Literature* 2 (Jan. 1931): 350-84, which includes Lorenzo N. Fowler's phrenological analysis of Whitman's character made in July 1849.

48. Ralph F. Weld, *Brooklyn Is America*, New York 1950: 71.

49. Whitman's comments on art exhibits and concerts are in a later chapter.

50. Sir Charles Lyell is best known for *The Principles of Geology* (1830-33) and *The Antiquity of Man* (1863). He made two visits to America, the second in 1846, which are recorded in *Travels in North America* (1845) and *A Second Visit to the United States of North America* (1849).

51. An ode by Whitman was among those sung [see n. 5].

two

1. "Annexation," *United States Magazine and Democratic Review* 17 (July 1845): 5. O'Sullivan denied that the war against Mexico was aimed cold-bloodedly at dismembering that country. See Frederick Merk, *Manifest Destiny and Mission in American History: A Reinterpretation*, New York 1963: 110-11, where O'Sullivan is quoted from the *New York Morning News* (10 July 1846).

O'Sullivan's *Democratic Review* published Whitman's first bit of fiction, "Death in the School-Room," in Aug. 1841 (see EPF), as well as a few other tales. His Whig contemporaries classified Whitman as a member of "Young America," a very general term for young radical Democrats who looked to O'Sullivan, mainly, for leadership.

2. Harry J. Carman and Harold C. Syrett, *A History of the American People*, New York 1952, 1: 530.

3. As quoted by Bernard de Voto, *The Year of Decision, 1846*, Boston 1943: 10.

4. Malmin [n. 34, ch. 1]: 90.

5. Whitman's remarks here clearly refer to the event described in sect. 34 of "Song of Myself": "the tale of the murder in cold blood of four hundred and twelve young men" at Goliad. This reminds me that Milton Hindus—"The Goliad Massacre in 'Song of Myself,'" *Walt Whitman Review* 7 (Dec. 1961): 77

—while correcting the too common and incomprehensible error of thinking the section deals with the fall of the Alamo, makes the strange statement that the "reference is to an obscure . . . episode of the Texas fight for independence." In terms of tragedy and strategical catastrophe, the Goliad massacre far outweighs the fall of the Alamo. "Remember Goliad" should be substituted for "Remember the Alamo."

6. Whitman's old-age memories of Greeley in the various volumes of WWC seem to indicate that he came to know Greeley better during the war years in Washington than earlier: "He was often in Washington—came to see me: would talk freely—try to debate, raise questions, involve me. Many's the chat we've had . . . Greeley was a contribution . . . but he was not a great man. . . . And Greeley was bright—and a Jesuit, too—though not a Jesuit in any worst sense" (5: 295-96).

Though Whitman and Greeley, while the former was still a Democrat in 1846-47, disagreed on many matters, including the tariff and total abolition, they agreed on the need to perpetuate democratic revolutions in Europe. Whitman's leaving the *Eagle* and the Democratic Party in Jan. 1848 removed most of the political disagreement between the two. In 1850 Greeley's *Tribune* printed a poem by Whitman—"Resurgemus" (included in a revised form in the first edition of *Leaves of Grass*)—indignantly concerned with the failure of the 1848 revolutions in Europe, and two more poems directed against the growing sentiment in Congress which was to lead to the Compromise of 1850. See EPF: 36 ff.

7. On 16 Nov. 1846, in an editorial titled "Abetting the Enemy," Whitman said that "these sneaking innuendoes which the *Tribune* is throwing out day after day—its open advocacy of the Mexican cause—its virulent venom of everything appertaining to the American side—comprise a dastardiness, which outrages all the decency that should be observed by the conductor of that print, as an editor of a print, or an American citizen!" Then he accused Greeley of treason.

8. The *American Review* (*Whig* was inserted in its title in 1851, one year before its demise) was founded in 1845 and was edited by Joel T. Headley, best known today for his *Napoleon and his Marshals* and *Washington and his Generals*. Whitman several times attacked Headley in the *Eagle* for his anti-American bias in connection with the Mexican War.

9. On 2 Nov. 1847 the *Eagle* asserted: "We beg to assure the *Advertiser* that our opinions on the subject of 'acquisition of territory,' &c. and in reference to its perfect freedom from slavery, has not changed one iota—and will not change."

10. The first issue of the *Freeman* is the only extant copy of that newspaper; a facsimile is in Ellen F. Frey's *Catalogue of the Whitman Collection in the Duke University Library*, Durham, N.C., 1945.

11. *Eagle* (22 Feb. 1847). Mrs Maury's book was dedicated to James Buchanan, then secretary of state. On 8 Oct. 1846 Whitman had reviewed another favorable book by a foreigner: Friedrich Raumer's *America and the Americans*—"Heaven bless him for it!"

12. Malmin [n. 34, ch. 1]: 83-84.

13. Whitman's classic statement in the *Eagle* on anti-democratic European literature is his "Anti-Democratic Bearing of Scott's Novels" (26 Apr.

1847). Scott's novels, which Whitman read to the end of his life, were "in some respects unsurpassed. . . . But Scott was a Tory and a High Church and State man." *Democratic Vistas* and *Specimen Days and Collect*, products of his later years, reproach both Scott and Shakespeare for their undemocratic view; but he ranks both at the top of "imaginative" geniuses.

14. "Resurgemus" [see n. 6] says this about the revolutions of 1848: "God, 'twas delicious! / That brief, tight, glorious grip / Upon the throats of kings."

15. One other book of this class which allowed Whitman to contrast free institutions with despotic institutions was the radical-liberal John Forster's *Statesmen of the Commonwealth of England*, reviewed 27 July 1846 and again 5 Sept. The comparison of the austere Puritans with the complacent Cavaliers confirmed for Whitman that virtue is the complement of free government, vice that of royal rule.

16. Malmin [n. 34, ch. 1]: 169.

17. Ibid.: 171.

18. Whitman expressed this fundamental idea as early as 1842 when he was editing the *New York Aurora*. See Rubin and Brown [n. 42, ch. 1]: 90.

19. Samuel E. Morison and Henry S. Commager, *The Growth of the American Republic*, New York 1942, 1: 598. Morison and Commager suggest that Wilmot proposed and the northern Democrats supported the proviso as a "mischievous" slap at the southern Democrats for not supporting the fifty-four-forty line in Oregon after the northern Democrats had backed the annexation of Texas in the face of threats of war.

20. The terms "old hunkers" (from the Dutch *Hunkerer*, a selfish person) and "barnburners" (from the mythical Dutch farmer who burned down his barn to get rid of the rats) had been in use in New York State since 1845. The latter were the radicals of the Democratic Party and devout followers of Martin Van Buren. Since Van Buren had opposed the annexation of Texas, they were considered—with only a degree of accuracy—as the anti-slavery faction of the party. See Denis T. Lynch, "Party Struggles, 1828-1850," in *History* [n. 2, ch. 1] 6: 74-76.

21. 9 Sept. 1848 [see n. 10].

22. Talmadge had been a wholesale grocer in New York until 1837 and was to become president of the Broadway Rail Road Company of Brooklyn in 1858. What business he was engaged in from 1840, when he moved to Brooklyn, to 1858, is not clear. But he was an active politician. See Stiles [n. 40, ch. 1] 2: 276-77.

23. "While thus working as a journeyman [in his brother's employ], at twelve shillings per day, he was much surprised in the spring of 1846, at receiving the whig nomination for mayor." (Stiles [n. 40, ch. 1] 2: 277.) Stryker was then 35, ten years younger than Talmadge.

24. The *Eagle* often gave Stryker credit for such charitable acts as nursing a destitute immigrant family, ill with ship's fever, when no one else in Brooklyn would come near them; taking homeless waifs off the streets; and on one occasion, taking home a respectable young lady who had gotten off the Fulton ferry considerably the worse for a toddy she had taken in New York to keep out the cold.

25. This summary of the situation was compiled from several letters to the editor of the *Eagle*.

26. Apparently this was the high point in Fowler's career. I could not identify him after 1847 in any of the histories of Brooklyn available to me.

27. On 2 Feb. Whitman discussed more antics of Fowler under the heading "The Caliban of the Council," claiming his remarks were not motivated by "the political complexion of the alderman alluded to." Indeed, he averred, the Whigs in the council were as disgusted by Fowler's coarse and bullying ways as were the Democrats.

Whitman's jibes at Fowler were returned on occasion. The *Eagle* (14 Jan. 1847) contains this item: "Among divers pretty compliments paid us by a certain Whig Alderman (through the *Advertiser*) appears the remark that we 'look a great deal like Satan,' &c."

28. For example, the *Eagle* reported (23 Nov. 1846): "As it is our office to chronicle all the *very* remarkable things of the age . . . we record that last night, *Sunday* night, the *lamps in Brooklyn* burned till 9 o'clock in the evening. This is still more remarkable, as the preceding evening most of them went out before 8. The lamp-lighting department of Brooklyn is mismanaged, most outrageously!" The street-lighting problem suggested Shakespearian allusions (of which Whitman was tremendously fond) similar to that made on 22 Dec. 1846: "We understand that Simpson of the Park Theatre has engaged six of the Brooklyn street lamps to *darken* the stage in the ghost scene in Richard III, at its next performance."

29. Whitman was indeed a taxpayer, as on 25 May 1847 he had acquired title to the house he and his parents lived in at 71 Prince street, in the seventh ward. See SS: 599.

30. Whitman began using French phrases in his journalistic writings long before he came to the *Eagle* (and the *New Orleans Crescent*), as has been pointed out by Rubin and Brown [n. 42, ch. 1]: 11. The use of French phraseology was characteristic of many metropolitan newspapers of the era, especially in reporting the doings of high society.

31. It was not only against fictitious banks that Whitman warned his readers. On 20 May 1847 he cautioned against doing business with the Mechanics and Farmers Insurance Co., whose president was a Mr Salisbury. There was "*no* such company, and . . . hereabout no sane man would ever think of having 'Mr Salisbury' to insure his property against fire risk . . . Mr S. called upon us the other day; but failed to satisfy us that he was doing a legitimate business."

32. The Brooklyn Savings Bank was established in 1827 "for the benefit of the laborer, the mechanic and domestic servant." (Stiles [n. 40, ch. 1] 3: 823.) The reader may remember that this same savings bank had been savagely attacked in the previous year by Whitman for its slaughter of trees for the sake of one or two more feet for its new edifice.

33. Several factors contributed to the increasing prosperity of the American manufacturers: easier transportation because of extensions of the railway system, a liberal patent policy which encouraged inventions, the population growth, and the rising standard of living.

34. In the matter of taxation in general, Whitman anticipated Henry George's single tax thesis. For example, on 14 Jan. 1847 he said: "As money must be raised for the expenses of government, the question is resolved into that mode of taxation which is the simplest, least liable to litigation, and the fairest to all parties. This is effected by taxation on real property, or *real estate*."

35. By 1845, 1,000,000 Irish had arrived in America; of the survivors of the potato famine, 1,611,000 had arrived by 1860. The Irish who came in the late 1840s "filled the labor gap left by the westward movement, for only 10 per cent became farmers, while the rest, generally too poor to buy land, and too intensely gregarious to endure the isolation of pioneer life, preferred to live in the city." (Harvey Wish, *Society and Thought in Early America*, New York 1950: 314.)

36. 30 Apr. 1846. This welcome was preceded by the pleased observation that the German immigrants included the wealthy and the educated as well as the poor.

37. According to the *Eagle* (15 Apr. 1846), the Nativists were very much of a minority in Brooklyn. Of the 6,920 votes cast in the municipal election of 1846, only 284 were for the Nativist ticket. They were proportionately weak in New York City.

38. The *Eagle* (4 Mar. 1847) remarked: "In the history of the selfish and dark and gloomy things of nations, this act of congress dispatching the U. S. frigates Jamestown and Macedonian at the public expense with food for starving Ireland, appears like a beaming star."

39. A letter from a committee member of the Brooklyn Laborers' Benevolent Society (*Eagle*, 27 Mar.) said the three contractors had also agreed to a ten-hour work day.

40. The Irish had long been squatters in shanties on the company's property and steadfastly balked all efforts to eject them during the strike.

41. On 24 April Whitman accused these New York "rowdies" of inciting the Brooklyn strikers to riot.

42. "Servants," which appeared in the 16 Sept. 1846 *Eagle* and was reprinted in GF (1: 154-56) as an editorial by Whitman, is not his even in part; he makes it quite clear he is paraphrasing, at the very least, a piece from Greeley's *Tribune*. The diction and syntax are not Whitman's, and no deception was intended, since he inserted such comments as "(continues the *Tribune*)."

43. This editorial, "Hints to Apprentices, &c.," was a reprint of one Whitman wrote for the *Brooklyn Star* in 1845. See WWS: 79-80.

44. However, "The Child and the Profligate," a tale by Whitman first published 20 Nov. 1841 in the *New York New World* (revised and reprinted, *Columbian Magazine* [Oct. 1844] and *Eagle* [27-29 Jan. 1847]), deals with a young boy bound as an apprentice to "a rich farmer" on Long Island, and the abuses possible in the apprentice system are made quite clear. For the text, see EPF.

45. Speaking in the late 1880s of this period in his life, Whitman said: "The labor question was not up then as it is now—perhaps that's the reason I did not embrace it. It is getting to be a live question—some day will be the live question—then somebody will have to look out—especially the bodies with big fortunes wrung from the sweat and blood of the poor." (WWC 1: 193.)

three

1. After the Compromise of 1850 the anti-slavery movement tended to usurp the attention of many, perhaps most, American reformers.

2. *The Western World: or, Travels in the United States in 1846-47*, Philadelphia 1849, 2: 237.

3. Alice F. Tyler, *Freedom's Ferment*, Minneapolis 1944: 2-3.

4. WWC 1: 193. On another occasion, irritated by Traubel's socialistic "violence," Whitman declaimed, "Be radical—be radical—be not too damned radical" (1: 223). Traubel also records Whitman's telling him: "But while the conventionals, on their side, are generally too timid, we, the radicals of us, on our side, are often too cocky. . . . Be cocky, be cocky, don't be too damned cocky" (2: 135-36).

5. This so-called World's Convention took place in 1845 and was one of the more-or-less impromptu "congresses" the elderly Owen (he was then 75) delighted in convening for the sake of airing his views. In his eighties he still made excursions from the country to London, calling Congresses of Advanced Minds and Congresses of the Reformers of the World. See G. D. H. Cole, *Robert Owen*, Boston 1925: 230-32.

6. Alfred McClung, *The Daily Newspaper in America*, New York 1937: 608-9.

7. On 27 Oct. 1846 Whitman confessed he had failed to report one burglary: "By one of those mishaps incident to the conduct of a newspaper, we were unfortunately made, in our police report, to represent a highly respectable lady as being the complainant against a person for an act of indelicate assault, instead of one of burglary. We accordingly take pleasure in making the desired correction."

8. Whitman, who defended the stage against those who attacked it on moral grounds, appeared to grant (12 Mar. 1846) that its influence was not always harmless when he reported on a Dennis Macauley, who had stolen a dozen brooms. "The latter boy was arrested in the pit of the Chatham theatre where such characters do most congregate, to enjoy their ill-gained proceeds in admiration of the drama, which is said to 'hold the mirror up to nature.' "

9. The captain of the Brooklyn watch, Jeremiah Higgins, appears to have been remiss at times. On 27 May 1847 the *Eagle* ironically implied that Higgins had been too drunk on the previous evening to perform his duties. On 3 Aug. Whitman printed a letter from a correspondent who said Higgins had been so drunk the evening before that he had to be taken home.

10. The *Eagle* (4 May 1847) reported that Alva Hotchkiss, a jeweler, had been murdered and robbed on his way home from the South ferry. On the next day Whitman was aroused by "the recent murder of Mr Hotchkiss" to the point of condemning the city lights and the city police. Yet the *Eagle* of the same date said Hotchkiss was still alive, though expected to die at any moment (his assailant had used a slingshot). Almost every day the *Eagle* referred to either the "murder" or the "assassination" of Hotchkiss in stories that at the same time reported his progress from a moribund state to the am-

nesiac state he finally reached. I wonder where Whitman's wits were when he wrote in the *Eagle* on 31 May: "We understand that this unfortunate gentleman is in about the same condition that he was after his assassination, and that very little change . . . has as yet taken place."

On 15 Mar. 1847 the *Eagle* reported "a scene of striking horror," quite like a scene "of most thrilling horror" from Eugene Sue's *Mysteries of Paris.* A Mr Rule of South Brooklyn had given a bad check in New York for $20.58. Officer Higgins visited Rule with a warrant for his arrest. Higgins courteously allowed Rule to retire and change his linen, but instead Rule removed his clothes and cut his throat. Higgins stopped him from seriously wounding himself but was assailed by Rule's family, who thought Higgins had done the throat-cutting. Higgins was rescued by some passersby and Rule was conducted to the Tombs in New York. "We are told," said Whitman, "that Rule is a man of more than ordinary education, a native of Ireland, which he left some twenty years since; and was formerly a bookkeeper in the office of the New York Evening Star."

11. This was before W. H. Channing became editor in 1849 and made the periodical into the advocate of almost all existing reform movements.

12. The piece originally appeared in the *New York Aurora* (1 Apr. 1842) under the title "Scenes of Last Night" (see Rubin and Brown [n. 42, ch. 1]: 36-38). The *Eagle's* version was altered a bit to include a few introductory lines relating the holocaust to a possible repetition of it in Brooklyn, the original editorial "we" was replaced by "I," some changes in diction and sentence structure were made, and the irrelevant account of a visit later in the evening to a temperance meeting was omitted.

13. The decency of Engine Co. No. 5 may have improved. The *Eagle* (9 Oct.) reported a "very agreeable reunion of the members of this company . . . at captain Sharpe's hotel" at which there were "toasts, and speeches, and stories, and recitations, and songs from many." A great deal of champagne was drunk in a most peaceful fashion.

14. *The Rise of the Common Man, 1830-1850*, New York 1927: 266. Fish suggests this apparent inconsistency may be explained by three factors: radical reformers considered liquor one of the bonds which had to be removed from the individual to secure genuine personal freedom; the prohibitionists, like many other reformers, were so bemused by the idea of the millennium that they expected their reform to reach fruition in their own lifetime; the prohibition movement was fundamentally a New England movement, and New England believed in "community responsibility."

15. Local option was short-lived; the legislature repealed the act in 1847.

16. Whitman does not seem to have thought very highly of reformed drunkards as temperance lecturers. He remarked in the *Eagle* on 16 June 1846 that he had attended a temperance talk by the Rev. Mr Harvey, a hale veteran of the Revolutionary War despite his 111 years. Harvey looked a vigorous 75, doubtlessly due to his lifelong temperance. "He is worth," said Whitman, "a score of emaciated and feeble lecturers, who have become so from excessive potations, and reformed with blasted constitutions, though he uttered never a word."

17. The novel was first published in 1842 in pamphlet form by Park Benjamin's *New York New World*. When reprinted in the *Eagle* as "Fortunes

244

of a Country-Boy," its sermonizing introduction and conclusion were omitted, as were some interpolated tales. See EPF.

18. Though it is impossible to tell from anything he wrote in the *Eagle*, Whitman may have favored the resettlement of freed Negroes as he did in the *Brooklyn Daily Times* (which he was then editing) in 1858. He noted in the *Times* that the new constitution of Oregon forbade either free or enslaved Negroes to enter that state. "Who believes that the Whites and Blacks can ever amalgamate in America?" he asked. "Or who wishes it to happen? Nature has set an impassable seal against it. Besides, is not America for the Whites? . . . As long as the Blacks remain here how can they become anything like an independent and heroic race?" If they were resettled "in some secure and ample part of the earth," then they could develop into "freemen, capable, self-reliant—mighty." (Holloway and Schwarz [n. 9, ch. 1]: 90.)

19. For example, "The police office was darkened by a large assemblage of the Ethiopian race," said the *Eagle* on 22 Oct. 1846, attracted there by a breach-of-promise suit brought by a forty-five-year-old Negro widow (with twelve children) against a young mulatto who had married another. The proceedings, which went against the defendant, were related in burlesque fashion. Though he usually spoke of Negroes as Negroes or as colored persons, Whitman was capable of using a more invidious term, as when (10 Sept. 1846) he spoke of a minor malefactor as "a crazy nigger . . . Sambo Poney."

20. WWS: 200.

21. This may have been the Rev. M. Giles who, in the winter of 1846, delivered a "noble oration" at the Brooklyn Institute on the sufferings of Ireland. See *Eagle*, 29 Sept. 1847.

22. "A Drive Out of Brooklyn" (18 June 1846), in which Whitman said the previous article on the asylum had been done by another hand.

23. According to the statistics quoted at the beginning of this editorial, the area the asylum was to serve had a population of 800,000, including 600 "deranged persons." Of this 600, some 400 were confined in poor houses and the rest in padlocked rooms in private homes—or were allowed to roam about unsheltered. An asylum for idiots was contemplated in another bill; there were 2,000 idiots in the state, according to one senator.

24. An editorial, "Women Should Possess Their Own" (18 Feb. 1847), explains the rightness of the Wisconsin constitution in this matter: "She who shares in common with man the adversities incident to humanity . . . should, certainly, be made as secure as possible from the miseries entailed by the conduct of thoughtless and improvident men. . . . A being who so deeply interests us as woman, should be carefully protected in the enjoyment of every right which is naturally hers."

25. Whitman did not by any means idealize all the women mentioned in the *Eagle*. The drunken and vagrant women brought before the police judge were described contemptuously, with no allusion to any hidden virtues. Female abortionists were monsters. All Irish servant girls who cried rape were not really raped nor in danger of it. And the new seduction bill passed in Albany tempted unscrupulous women to sue for breach of promise where none existed.

26. I have omitted in this study the topic of education—on which Whitman wrote much in the *Eagle* and often from the attitude of the reformer —because the subject has been exhaustively examined in Mrs Florence Bern-

stein Freedman's WWS. Prof. Freedman reprints almost every one of Whitman's comments on this topic in both the *Brooklyn Evening Star* and the *Eagle*, and precedes them with a summary of his ideas on the subject. Whitman took a broad view of education as contrasted to the prevailing attitude of the time. He believed that the arts as well as gymnastics should be included in school curricula; he favored substantial pay increases for teachers; he believed that learning should be more pleasant for the child to make it more effective; he campaigned for cleaner, brighter, healthier school buildings; and above all, he demanded again and again that flogging be abolished in the schools. His editorials on these and other desirable reforms in education are characterized by an earnestness of tone.

27. On 17 July 1847 the *Eagle* reported, without comment, "Brooklyn contains fifty churches, and not one theatre."

28. Whitman himself was a critic of the Puritans, though not precisely in Chapin's sense. In the *Eagle* of 12 Dec. 1846 he quoted a remark from a New York paper to the effect that the Puritan administration in both Old and New England had been terribly slandered. This was true, Whitman admitted, of the first; but as to the latter, "we have overrated our 'Puritan Fathers.' They were bold and fearless—had a wonderful fortitude, and a staunch determination to enjoy their own opinions;—but they were too harsh and bigoted and fanatical—had too little Christian love—and persecuted others far more than they had ever been persecuted themselves. For it is a mistake to suppose that the 'Pilgrims' fled from *oppression* abroad; they might have had comfort enough, either in England or Holland—but they were too opinionated and domineering in spirit to remain there. Such hardy virtues as they had, were profitable, doubtless, in founding a nation, amid the wilds of the northeast. But we see no reason for this perpetual adulation and sympathy for virtues which they not only had not, but were marked by the very opposites of. . . . The real fact . . . is that if such persons as the early N. E. settlers were to come among us now, they would be drummed out of society by common consent. This we say without wishing to sneer at them at all: the age in which they lived was not a bright one—and they are among its better specimens, even as they were."

29. Whitman condemned pretentious churches on artistic, religious, and democratic grounds. Two editorials—both titled "Splendid Churches" (9, 30 Mar. 1846)—were concerned with the new and "showy" Grace Church in New York, where the "comfortable pews, the exquisite arrangements . . . lift man into a complacent kind of self-satisfaction with himself and his own doings." The church services were more of a spectacle than an Elssler benefit at the Park Theatre, with haughty aristocrats occupying their expensive pews. "We don't see how it is possible for people to *worship God* there."

30. The nearest Whitman came to being uncomplimentary was on 8 June 1846 when he described Rev. Hodge of the First Baptist Church as having "little talent as an orator," but added he appeared to be the sort of speaker that one could grow to like because of his distinct enunciation and the "plain terse sentences" in which his ideas were delivered.

31. Thomas B. Thayer, pastor of the First Universalist Society in Brooklyn since 1845, was popular among certain of the Brooklynites, judging from the large number of marriages he performed as listed in the vital statistics

section of the *Eagle*. He certainly was popular with Whitman, who praised and printed a number of his philosophic-poetic essays and poems, and often referred to him in the *Eagle* as his friend. He gave Thayer's sermons many puffs in his paper (one—"The doctrine of endless punishment, with its accompaniments, leads to infidelity"—was quite suited to outrage the Presbyterians). Once the *Eagle* devoted one and a third columns to reporting one of his sermons; Thayer, like Whitman, was an anti-hanging man.

32. On 24 Oct. 1846 Whitman said of F. A. Farley, pastor of the Second Unitarian Church: "We like his unimpassioned, but smooth and mild, sort of eloquence—the easy and graceful reading, and the absence of all commonplace, which mark both his discourses and their delivery. His discourses are frequently remarkable for their deep views, and yet easily comprehended ones." The Unitarians (dating in Brooklyn from 1833) and the Universalists were united in tribulation. In 1841 when the Universalists tried to rent a hall for a year, there was "much opposition . . . among the orthodox denominations in the city, and further use of the hall was denied them by its owner on the ground that 'Brooklyn was bad enough without having Universalism preached in it.'" However, the Unitarians offered them the use of a small building, which they accepted. The Universalists finally got their own edifice in 1843. (Stiles [n. 40, ch. 1] 3: 779, 809-10.)

33. Rubin and Brown [n. 42, ch. 1]: 8, see also: 58-82.

34. From time to time Whitman reprinted from exchange papers articles lauding the progressive spirit of Pius IX. Typical is one titled "The enlightened statesman-Pope" from the *Washington Union*, reprinted in the *Eagle* on 18 Nov. 1847, which called him "the great reformer of the age."

35. Years later he told Traubel: "I have not been without friends even among the Catholics. I have had friends in the priesthood . . . So far as concerns the Catholic church . . . I have seen a little of its pageantry and read with deep interest of the royal, gorgeous, superb displays in its cathedrals, especially those down in Rome—in St Peter's. It is grand . . . Yet it has one defect: it lacks simplicity—it has deferred too much to certain sensational elements in its history and environment." (WWC 1: 142-43.)

36. In an earlier piece (17 June 1846) Whitman had given an additional reason for Brooklyn's good health: it had, as yet, no "impure spots" like the Five Points slum section of New York. But Brooklyn was not a complete paradise. Malaria was prevalent in some of its suburbs as well as in other parts of Long Island. Whitman mentioned malaria only once—on 23 Sept. 1847. His attention had been called to the disease because, due to wet weather, it had been more common than usual since Aug., even in those parts of the island where it was endemic. Cases had occurred "even in the very heart of Brooklyn." Ship fever, brought by Irish immigrants, assumed epidemic proportions in some wards of Brooklyn throughout 1847 and into 1848. Whitman had little to say of it other than to accuse the public officials of dereliction of duty in placing those ill with the fever in the county almshouse where the infection spread to the unlucky poor.

Rabid dogs became a problem every summer in Brooklyn, as they did in most American cities. A city ordinance required that dogs be muzzled but, as Whitman remarked on 9 July 1847, "the streets are thronged with dogs, which with utter contumaciousness entirely refuse to provide themselves with

247

muzzles." The common council offered a bounty of one dollar for every set of dog ears turned in to them. Whitman, who at no time showed any liking for canines, suggested that "an ingenious person with a small quantity of prussic acid might do an extensive business upon a small capital." Apparently few people had the stomach for this sort of business, and Whitman lamented from time to time that few dogs were slain, blaming the aldermen of course.

37. These three essentials to health were urged again and again in the *Eagle*. Moderation in eating was a desideratum indeed for a generation made dyspeptic by starchy, greasy foods (of the innumerable patent medicine ads appearing in the newspapers of the 1840s, the majority promoted potions for the cure of dyspepsia). Diet reformers had arisen—notably Sylvester Graham with his boiled vegetables and graham bread. Hydropathy was to some extent popularizing bathing and the drinking of water. Though Whitman thought baths like Gray's best, he sometimes reminded his readers that only a basin of water and a large towel were necessary for "a thorough ablution." In a time of medical fads, Whitman's objections to medicines were based, as will be seen, on a distrust not only of drugs but of doctors and druggists as well.

38. Whitman seems to have been favorably disposed toward hydropathy. His review (21 Oct. 1846) of James Gully's *Water Cure in Chronic Diseases* was brief but expressive: "The publishers of this work deserve the good will of the whole community." On reviewing the anonymous *Water Cure in America* (10 Jan. 1848) he noted that books on hydropathy were marked by "the confident tone in which both patients and physicians speak of the means of remedy." He liked "the *openness* of those means; every thing being done fairly and above board."

39. Thomas L. Nichols, *Forty Years of American Life*, London 1864, 1: 368. Nichols, a Grahamite, hydropathist, and sanitary reformer who got a medical degree from Columbia in 1855 and died in England in 1901, was noted as an advocate for dietary reform. A writer and editor as well as reformer, he lived in New York from 1840 until 1855 and may have known Whitman. He speaks of "an original American style of poetry invented by Walt Whitman, a New York poetical loafer, not destitute of genius, and patronized by Emerson" (1: 299).

40. Ibid.: 363-64.

41. During the 1830s and 1840s "a variety of new schools of medicine, each with extravagant claims . . . . preached a hygienic millennium while they attacked the orthodox medical profession. The common people listened—and believed. Out-and-out commercial quacks with their elixirs, syrups, and magical pills succeeded even better in winning disciples." (Merle Curti, *The Growth of American Thought*, New York 1943: 339.)

42. Throughout Whitman's stay on the *Eagle*, items appeared from time to time with such headings as "The Last Druggist's Blunder," "Another Shocking Result From Druggist's Carelessness," and "More Druggist's Carelessness." The stories related instances in which blundering apothecaries had given their customers poisons instead of the relatively harmless preparation called for by their physicians. Whitman himself seems to have been the victim of a bungling druggist. On 17 Aug. 1847 the *Eagle* remarked, "Ever since we came very near being poisoned, and a family of seven or eight with us, by the carelessness of a druggist in Myrtle avenue, who sent us a prodigious dose of

oxalic acid instead of tartaric acid (which was wanted to put in some batter cakes), we have known how to sympathize with those who are the victims of such inexcusable conduct." Mrs Freedman, who reprinted this item in WWS, suggests, perhaps whimsically, that this "narrow escape from poisoning" may have had something to do with Whitman's transformation, which began in the late 1840s, into the embryonic poet of the *Leaves.* See WWS: 10.

43. Whitman possibly would have included psychosomatics in "the whole bearing of things." Reviewing Dr George Moore's *The Use of the Body in Relation to the Mind* on 20 Dec. 1846, he remarked, "Few persons realize how intimate the relation of mental causes and processes toward the body, and its well or ill being." Whitman's interrelation between the mind and the bodily functions may have dated from his reading of Dr J. G. Spurzheim's *Phrenology,* which he enthusiastically reviewed on 16 Nov. 1846; though on 27 Mar. he had quoted a Dr Metcalfe as saying that a tranquil mind contributed to health and longevity. For an account of his attitude toward phrenology during his *Eagle* days, see my "Whitman's Conversion" [n. 47, ch. 1].

44. For a while Whitman ranked with the medically conservative when he derided the claims made for ether (or letheon) in some brief comments in the *Eagle.* But on 5 May 1847 he reported a lady of his acquaintance had had eight or ten teeth pulled while under ether, and no pain had been felt or ill effects suffered. On 30 June he briefly admitted his previous error and said ether was all that was claimed for it. He was completely convinced of its efficacy after watching a child's dislocated thumb put back in place (as he reported on 14 Oct.) without any of the usual severe pain of such an operation, due to the use of ether.

four

1. *Western World* [ch. 3, n. 2].

2. C. C. Felton, "Simms's Stories and Reviews," *North American Review* 63 (Oct. 1846): 377.

3. "Nationality in Literature," *Democratic Review* 20 (Mar.1847): 265-67.

4. For the influence of the *Democratic Review* on Whitman, see John Stafford, *The Literary Criticism of "Young America,"* Berkeley 1952: 126.

5. To Whitman the literary criticism in the New York papers was specious. He said in the *Eagle* (25 Sept. 1846): "There is a great deal of small potato criticism in the newspapers of New York. . . . How often have we seen a new book, well written and quite original, passed by with silence, or damned with faint praise; while tinsel and vapid nonsense has been puffed by the efforts of friends into public notice!.....They want in N. York some periodical of more comprehensive and critical ability than any that as yet exists in this country. Much is said about the profusion of cheap literature, and its injurious effect on popular taste.—But there is really no harm in books being cheap, if they are *good.* A high-toned critical authority would do much to root out trashy literature." Whitman's remarks were inadvertently ironic, for about

nine years later he ran into "high-toned critical authority" and *Leaves of Grass* was put into Harvard College's "hell box."

6. The *Eagle* said, however, under "Young Ladies Beware" (18 Dec. 1846): "An alarm of fire occurred last night before about 10 o'clock, which proceeded from the house No. 72 Concord street. The fire had communicated from the lamp to a bed upon which a young lady had been cozily reading Bulwer's last 'poisonous' emanation, and fallen asleep; an engine company having arrived in time to prevent anything more than the destruction of the bed. If this is not a warning to 'novel readers' we won't guess again."

7. Two of Ainsworth's novels were reviewed: *The Tower of London* (19 May 1846) and *The Miser's Daughter* (27 Sept. 1847). Both are described as full of incident and interest. There is no suggestion in either review of the criticism of Ainsworth found in " 'Home' Literature" (11 July 1846).

8. On 8 Apr. 1847, reviewing Jared Sparks' *Library of American Biography*, Whitman said, "Every youth in this country should be familiar with . . . the great and good men who ushered into life rational liberty and planted the landmarks of political rights." Earlier, he had remarked (23 Nov. 1846), "It must be considered among the good things of this literary age, that a great portion of its books (and not the least in merit, some of them) are the works intended for *youth*." He suggested to his adult readers "that the providing to boys and girls of *a liberal quantity of good reading matter*, is among the first duties which parents and friends of youth should perform." His 94 reviews of "youth" publications carried the general refrain that books should inculcate in the child those moral and intellectual virtues which are desirable in the grown person.

9. Of *Typee* Whitman said, "As a book to hold in one's hand and pore dreamily over of a summer day, it is unsurpassed." He liked *Omoo* because of its "richly good natured style" and because it was thorough "entertainment." Probably Whitman read nothing else by Melville, since in commenting to Traubel in 1889 on Edmund C. Stedman's *Library of American Literature* and on its engraved portraits of authors (Whitman's was included), he said of Melville, "I know little about him but they make much of him here." (WWC 5: 446.) So far as I know, this remark, along with the reviews of *Typee* and *Omoo*, is all Whitman ever said about Melville.

10. On 22 Nov. 1847 Whitman said of Daniel Thompson's *Locke Amsden*, "It is equal in every respect . . . to works that are much vaunted, being written by foreign authors."

11. Whitman was also a conformist in the writing of verse. His pre-*Leaves* poems published in the period from 1838 to 1850 were, to speak as kindly as possible, the conventional poems published in profusion in newspapers, magazines, and gift books. I hate to admit it, but I am sure Lydia Sigourney (five of whose poems Whitman reprinted in the *Eagle*) wrote much more polished and slightly less maudlin verse than he did during these early years. See EPF.

12. Whitman came close to expressing such a sentiment once when he printed Street's "Gray Forest Eagle" (9 July 1847). "A Magnificent Poem, by a Young American," he proclaimed in bold type—then added prefatorily: "We have often read with pleasure the descriptive poems of that son of nature, in her western guise, Alfred B. Street. . . . The vein of Mr Street's poetry

is a rich and original one—and we can only wish he would delve into it oftener." Whitman shared the common taste here, for Street's nature poems were greatly admired by American poetry lovers.

13. In a review of but not in reference to the *Christian Parlor Magazine*, Whitman expressed "impatience at the flippancy of the 'popular' monthly magazines—with their fashion plates, and their sentimental love stories" (8 Mar. 1847).

14. Whitman was pleased by "a very handsome mezzotint of the Charge of Capt. May, at the battle of Resaca de la Palma. . . . Moreover, we like the print, because it does not descend to the poor wit . . . of making the Mexicans perfect scarecrows, or frightened into agues."

15. Actually titled "The Half-Breed: A Tale of the Western Frontier. By a Brooklynite," who was Whitman. It appeared originally as "Arrow-Tip" in the Mar. 1845 issue of *The Aristidean* (ed. Thomas Dunn English). Whitman reprinted in the *Eagle* several more of his conventional and poorly written tales. See EPF.

16. Hawthorne, "Old Esther Dudley" (28-29 July 1846), "The Shaker Bridal" (8 Oct.); Poe, "A Tale of the Ragged Mountains" (9-10 Oct.); Irving, "The Broken Heart" (11 Oct. 1847), "Pelayo and the Merchant's Daughter" (26 Oct.).

17. T. B. Thayer, the Brooklyn (later Boston) Universalist minister, was a star performer of the Brooklyn literati; in introducing his short "poetical" essay "Autumn" (11 Nov. 1846), Whitman spoke of him as "one of our tastiest Brooklyn writers—a frequent (but not half frequent enough) correspondent of our own."

18. A rather non-genteel poem appeared in the *Eagle* on 28 Aug. 1847 at the bottom of the usual Saturday column of "Sunday Readings." I would like to think Whitman wrote it, but it could have been composed by someone in the *Eagle's* business office. At least Whitman approved of it enough to print it.

ADVERTISEMENT

Lost, yesterday, in Fulton street,
　Suppos'd by a fair Brooklyn daughter,
Something whereof both ends did meet
　In compassing her trunk-supporter.

(I don't know but a wealthy heiress she may be,
And this a precious fixture of her *leg*-I-see.)
Now any lady who has lost a knitted garter,
Can have't by to the Eagle office *sending arter*.

19. J. J. Rubin, "Whitman as a Drama Critic," *Quarterly Journal of Speech* 28 (Feb. 1942): 45. This article summarizes the dispute the *Eagle* had in the late summer and early fall of 1846 with several New York newspapers over the relative merits of American and British actors and plays, and over the uncritical (to Whitman) drama reviews in the New York papers.

20. Whitman particularly liked Miss Cushman's ability to completely identify herself with the character she portrayed—such as "her appalling Nancy Sykes."

21. "Theatricals" (22 Dec. 1846). In this editorial Whitman ranked Anderson above even Edwin Forrest, easily the most popular American actor. He mentioned that Forrest was to open an engagement at the Park on 25 Dec. and was to be followed by Anderson. "Would it not be a happy thought to join the two in the same play? Both these actors are great favorites of ours. Forrest exemplifies a sort of massive freshness—a freedom from the cant of playing—has a kind of thoroughness in all he says and does—which it is quite beautiful to see." Still, Anderson "is our preference, for his smoothness, his buoyancy, and his fluent ease and grace upon the stage. . . . Mr A. is 'great' as far as he adheres to Nature, the true and only copy for both dramatist and player." Above all, Anderson had "good taste" in his acting technique, which Whitman may have begun to doubt that Forrest had sufficient of. Whitman attended Forrest's opening night on 25 Dec. in *The Gladiator* (Forrest's perennial vehicle written by his friend Robert Montgomery Bird) and admitted the actor's "herculean proportions" were as impressive as ever but felt his over-all performance was only "passing well."

22. For example, in "Plays and Players" (3 Sept.) Whitman said the Keans, like too many, were examples on stage of "the almost unmitigated falseness to nature, which the drama presents." But on 19 Nov., having seen the Keans in Shakespeare's *King John*, he spoke of Mrs Kean's portrayal of Queen Constance as "*perfection* in acting." "Of Mr Kean's portrayal of King John," he continued, "we must confess, though we are no admirer of Mr Kean, that he, in King John, left little to be asked for more, by the reasonable spectator."

23. Later, Whitman found proof of this system of theatre criticism when the *New York Herald* printed a "long cut and dried puff . . . of the Keans' acting in a play *which accidentally didn't come off!*" (7 Oct.)

24. For an account of the burlesques, acrobatic acts, and spectacles put on at the Bowery, Chatham, and Olympic, see Meade Minnigerode, *The Fabulous Forties, 1840-1850*, New York 1924: 147 ff.

25. "Walt Whitman and the Italian Opera," *American Mercury* 6 (Sept. 1925): 62.

26. The best is Robert D. Faner's *Walt Whitman & Opera*, Philadelphia 1951.

27. "Reminiscences of Walt Whitman," *Atlantic Monthly* 89 (Feb. 1902): 166.

28. The day before, under "The New Violinist," Whitman had reported on Camillo Sivori's concert on the evening of the 12th at the New York Tabernacle. He was "a true artist," and Whitman scorned "to join in the ready cry of 'humbug' at such a man as Sivori—merely because he speaks broken English, and has ascended in his profession to that 'height of the great argument,' for which the vulgar taste has no appreciation!"

29. Whitman's nationalism was not so narrow that it kept him from praising English singers who deserved praise. On 5 Aug. 1847 he was enthused by the pure soprano voice of Mme Ann Bishop (Ann Riviere), "an Englishwoman, considerably Italianized." But he disparaged tenor John Templeton whenever he mentioned him. On 19 June 1846, Whitman reported he had been sent tickets for Templeton's concert that night in Brooklyn and said he had nothing but contempt for Templeton's claims as a " 'first rate' vocalist, or

to the position of a gentleman." (Templeton was 44 and finally retired six years later; the *Dictionary of National Biography* says his "weakness was an occasional tendency to sing flat.") Whitman was surprised that the public could swallow "superannuated third-rate artists from the Old World" simply because they were puffed by newspapers. "Templeton's voice," he asserted, "is inferior to many a man's singing in our Brooklyn church choirs. . . . When he returns to England, no doubt, he will spirt his vulgar venom at our country, like all his tribe before him." Whitman attended the concert, as he reported next day, and saw no signs of disapproval in the small audience; in fact, there was "considerable vociferous applause." His sole comment was that Templeton committed a "cool piece of impudence" in his rendition of "The Star-Spangled Banner" by omitting the third verse, which asperges the bravery of the British. For the next two or three months Whitman delighted in noting that Templeton's New England tour was a financial failure, and he often reverted to Templeton's omission of the third stanza of the national anthem.

30. The sentiments of this piece had been expressed earlier by Whitman —"Art-Singing and Heart-Singing"—in Poe's *Broadway Journal* (29 Nov. 1845). See UPP 1: 104-6.

31. Faner ([n. 26]: 7) says Whitman's first critical review of an opera appeared in the *Eagle* on 23 Mar. 1847. Actually, three operatic reviews appeared before that date.

32. Whitman occasionally heard a type of singing more related to operatic arias than to the popular songs of the Hutchinsons—the oratorio; several that he attended were mentioned in the *Eagle*, but only two got extended comment. "Too elaborately scientific for the popular ear" was his estimate of Mendelssohn's *Elijah* (9 Nov. 1847). Probably the oratorio *per se* did not appeal to Whitman, for he expressed pleasure in the performances of several of the singers. Too, for several months he had been enjoying operas that had their share of scientific elaborateness.

A less heavy oratorio was Felicien David's *Desert*, which Whitman heard twice in Apr. 1846. On 7 Apr. he said that rarely had his "inward sense" been so gratified "with the tinglings of beauty"; on 16 Apr. he described *The Desert* as having "something divine about it, wildly and indescribably beautiful." The oratorio was repeated several times in the next months in both New York and Brooklyn, and Whitman continued to praise it.

33. Whitman described the Apollonean Children (7 Jan. 1847) as "among the most talented musicians of the age," but he feared they did not get enough outdoor exercise. The one girl in the group made him irresistibly think of a prominent element in sentimental literature and mortality statistics —the high death rate among children. "As the B. E. has gazed in the fine face, the large prematurely angelic and full eyes of the girl—the sweet, fair haired one! it has trembled to think—on what it thought."

34. On 26 Nov. 1847 Whitman remarked that this theatre was architecturally perfect in its interior except for one thing. "We allude to the tawdry figures (some kind of 'cross' knights, we are told) which stand on one foot against the front of the second tier, and are bound round the shoulders in colored stuff, and hold out the chandeliers! They hugely mar the prettiness of the rest of the house, and we advise their being forthwith taken out and buried decently."

35. The American Art-Union in New York, founded 1839, was encouraging the middle-class American family to appreciate prints, paintings, and sculptures, and was making them more cheaply available. Whitman referred only once in the *Eagle* to the Art-Union—"Matters Which Were Seen and Done In An Afternoon Ramble" (19 Nov. 1846)—when he spoke briefly of "giving a passing glance in the rooms of the Art Union (a perpetual free exhibition of Paintings, Broadway, near Pearl st., which we advise our Brooklyn folk to visit often: it will cost them nothing, and there are always good things there)." For an account of the influence of the American Art-Union on American interest in art in the period before the Civil War, see Carl Bode, *The Anatomy of American Popular Culture, 1840-1861*, Berkeley 1959: 60 ff.

36. *New York Evening Post* (1 Feb., 21 Mar. 1851); texts reprinted, UPP 1: 236-38, 241-47.

37. Though for years it debated the matter of purchasing Catlin's Indian Gallery, Congress did nothing. Eventually his paintings were given to the Smithsonian Institution (whose opening Whitman noted with pleasure in 1846) in 1879 by the heirs of Joseph Harrison of Philadelphia, who had saved Catlin from debtors prison in London in 1852 and had shipped the collection for storage in Philadelphia as collateral for a large loan. On the wall of Whitman's bedroom in the late Camden years was a large print of Catlin's Osceola, the Seminole chief. As he told Traubel, "I don't remember where we were when he gave me that picture . . . whether it was in New York or Washington, but it was before the War, maybe as many as forty years ago." Catlin "was an interesting old codger." (WWC 2: 348, 354.)

38. Miss Bremer first visited America in 1849, but her novels (inculcating the virtues of charity, love, and peace) were extremely popular in America by the early 1840's. Rather amusingly, Whitman found one innocuous flaw in Miss Bremer's fiction—"in one or two of her novels there is a little infusion of transcendentalism; but we can easily pardon it, for it can do no great harm" (18 Aug. 1846).

39. On 15 Nov. Whitman reported that Frothingham's painting of Thayer had been excellently engraved and was on sale at T. D. Smith's bookstore. He objected to an alteration, the addition of spectacles. "The subject . . . does wear spectacles, at times, it is true, but the picture was more artistical and simply beautiful without them. The mental expression of our friend's face is copied faithfully in both painting and engraving."

40. Plumbe was much better known in the 1840s than Brady. Plumbe gave up his profession of railroad construction engineer to become a daguerreotypist and in 1846 had a chain of fourteen daguerrean galleries—from Boston to Petersburgh, Va., and Baltimore to Dubuque, Iowa—with headquarters on Broadway in New York. Plumbe took bankruptcy in 1847 (which Whitman did not mention), and after a stay in Dubuque, went to California in 1849 with the gold rush. He returned to Dubuque, "where he died in 1857 by his own hand, during a fit of despondency," at the age of 46. See Robert Taft, *Photography and the American Scene: A Social History, 1839-1889*, New York 1964: 49-52.

41. Many years later Whitman told Traubel: "Of all the portraits of me made by artists I like Eakins' best: it is not perfect but it comes nearest being me. I find I often like the photographs better than the oils—they are perhaps

mechanical, but they are honest. The artists add and deduct: the artists fool with nature . . . to make it fit their preconceived notion of what it should be. We need a [J.F.] Millet in portraiture—a man who sees the spirit but does not make too much of it—one who sees the flesh but does not make a man all flesh—all of him body." (WWC 1: 131.)

42. Whitman reported on two bas reliefs and an Adonis by Brown, which he saw at the American Art-Union (19 Nov. 1846); his comments were brief and insignificant. On 30 July 1847 he mentioned Greenough in one sentence as "busily engaged on a group which is intended to adorn the steps of the capitol in the great city of 'magnificent distances.' "

43. Allen Nevins, ed., *The Diary of Philip Hone, 1828-1851*, New York 1927, 2: 218-19.

five

1. Since some of his *Eagle* book reviews were first printed in GF and UPP, it has become increasingly commonplace for scholars to stress the importance of Whitman's reviews of works by Carlyle, Sand, and Goethe as evidence that those writers may (or must) have had some influence upon the development of the ideas eventually expressed in *Leaves of Grass*.

2. Whitman reviewed *Heroes and Hero Worship* and *Sartor Resartus* on 17 Oct. 1846, *The French Revolution* and *Past and Present, and Chartism* on 23 Nov. 1846. He remarked of the last that, despite Carlyle's "weird, wild way" and his puzzling chapter heads, "there lies rich ore under that vague surface."

3. UPP 2: 71.

4. Gay W. Allen, *Walt Whitman Handbook*, Chicago 1946: 327.

5. SS: 80-81.

INDEX

Brooklyn Female Seminary, 216
Brooklyn Flint Glass Co., 44
Brooklyn Freeman, 20, 92, 107,
164–65, 221, 233, 236, 239
Brooklyn Institute, 13, 77–79, 151,
164, 170, 205, 213–14, 245
Brooklyn Is America, 238
Brooklyn Laborers' Benevolent
Society, 129–33, 242
Brooklyn Navy Yard, 67, 234
Brooklyn Savings Bank, 62, 122,
210, 241
Brooklyn Village, 232
Brown, Charles H., 237
Brown, Henry Kirke, 215, 255
Bryant, William Cullen, 14, 18–19,
36, 195–96, 199, 200
Buchanan, James, 239
Bulwer-Lytton, Edward, 190, 192–
93, 203, 250
Burns, Robert, 208
Burroughs, John, 232
"By Blue Ontario's Shore," 25
Byron, George Gordon, 190

Calhoun, John C., 93–94
"Caloya," 194
Carlyle, Thomas, 99, 192, 224, 255
Carman, Harry J., 238
Castle Garden, 208
Catlin, George, 213, 254
Catlin's Indian Gallery, 254
Channing, William Ellery, 176, 179
Channing, William H., 244
Chapin, Alonzo B., 174
Chase, Richard, 232
Chatham Theatre, 65, 203, 243,
252
Cheney Family, 206
Child, Lydia Maria, 197, 199, 200
"Child and the Profligate, The,"
242
"Child Praying, A," 200
"Child's Grave, The," 200
Christian Parlor Magazine, 199,
250
Church of the Holy Trinity, 211
Church of the Pilgrims, 77

Ciocca, Signora, 209
Clarke, James B., 62
Clarke, McDonald, 58
Clay, Henry, 123, 125
Clinton, De Witt, 70
Cole, G. D. H., 243
Cole, Thomas, 214
Columbian Magazine, 197, 242
Commager, Henry S., 240
Compromise of 1850, 239, 243
Coney Island, 72 and *passim*
Constitutional History of England,
99
Cook, Eliza, 160
Cooper, George H., 27
Coppola, 208
Curti, Merle, 248
Cushman, Charlotte, 201–02, 251

Daily Newspaper in America, The,
243
David, Felicien, 253
Davis, Mary Oakes, 233
Day, Benjamin, 140
"Death and Burial of McDonald
Clarke," 237
"Death in the School-Room," 238
De Bow's Commercial Review, 157
De Kock, Paul, 190
De Meyer, 206–07
Democracy in America, 95
"Democracy in Free Verse," 232
Democratic Review, 85, 90, 189,
198, 238, 249
Democratic Vistas, 225, 240
Desert, The, 253
De Voto, Bernard, 238
Diary in America, 95
Diary of Philip Hone, 255
Dickens, Charles, 51, 95–96, 114,
153
Dix, Dorothea, 169–70
Dixon, Edward H., 186, 210, 227
*Domestic Manners of the Ameri-
cans,* 95
Donizetti, Gaetano, 207
Doughty, Thomas, 214
Duggan (?), 206

Index

259

Index

Index

263

Thomas L. Brasher is professor of English, Southwest Texas State University, San Marcos. His studies of Whitman have appeared widely, especially in the *Walt Whitman Review* or *Newsletter,* over the past decade or so. He also edited *The Early Poems and the Fiction* (1963) for New York University's series, The Collected Writings of Walt Whitman. Dr. Brasher has received degrees from Hardin-Simmons University and Louisiana State University.

Charles H. Elam edited the manuscript. Donald Ross designed the book and jacket. The typeface is Times Roman, designed by Stanley Morison. The paper is Warren's Olde Style Antique. The cover is Interlaken Arco Vellum over binder's board. Manufactured in the United States of America.